# Somewhere & Nowhere

Emily Buehler

Two Blue Books
Hillsborough, North Carolina

SOMEWHERE AND NOWHERE

by Emily Buehler

Published by:
Two Blue Books
PO Box 1285
Hillsborough, NC 27278 USA
emily@twobluebooks.com
www.twobluebooks.com

ISBN: 978-0-9778068-2-9

Library of Congress Control Number: 2016915598

Printed in the United States of America

*This book is dedicated to everyone who gave us somewhere to sleep,
who refilled our water bottles (or bought us beer),
who made us dinner or paid for our pie.
To everyone who shared a kind word in the middle of a hot and endless day.*

*And especially, to Mary.*

# Contents

The land is the appointed remedy for whatever is false and fantastic in our culture. The continent we inhabit is to be physic and food for our mind, as well as our body. The land, with its tranquilizing, sanative influences, is to repair the errors of a scholastic and traditional education, and bring us to just relations with men and things.

—Ralph Waldo Emerson, "The Young American," *Nature, Addresses, and Lectures,* 1849

In the wilderness, you have to deal with things head-on because there are few distractions. The problems that you face keep resurfacing and you realize that you are the only one who has the power to change or improve yourself.

—Virginia Heffeman, "Simple Lives," *Glamour,* 1998

And all plans, safeguards, policing, and coercion are fruitless. We find after years of struggle that we do not take a trip; a trip takes us . . . Only when this is recognized . . . do the frustrations fall away.

—John Steinbeck, *Travels with Charley,* 1962[1]

# Prologue

I SAW THE ROCKY MOUNTAINS ON the third of July. At first I thought they were a low bank of clouds, hovering over a blue haze at the horizon. Unsure, I watched as I pedaled, hoping they'd resolve into clouds or mountains.

The sun beat on my back. I moved slowly, pulling my hundred-pound bike up a hill until I crested it and rolled gratefully down the other side. The forms at the horizon disappeared behind a distant butte, then emerged unchanged.

The road started up a taller hill, and I shifted to my lowest gear and settled in for the climb. It was two months since Mary and I had left from the beach in Cape May, New Jersey. Before that I'd been in North Carolina, working in a bread bakery. What was everyone in the bakery doing right now? I checked my watch—almost noon. The bakery shift finished at noon.

*But I'm in Wyoming,* I remembered. It was two hours earlier here. The bakers would already be done.

I'd gone to Chapel Hill, North Carolina, to attend graduate school in chemistry. I'd liked chemistry, but it hadn't been all I wanted to do. I'd had this idea that life would *really* start when I finished school. But then, as the end had neared, I'd caught myself thinking, "I'll get a job for a few years, and *then* life will start."

But I hadn't wanted to wait any longer. After graduation, I left science.

I took a job in the bakery at the local food co-op. On my first day, I arrived before dawn and joined the activity as the others taught me to shape boules and baguettes. I took my "lunch break" at eight AM, sitting on a bench under an oak tree and eating a French roll warm from the oven. "I can't believe they're going to pay me to do this!" I thought. After four years of struggling with depression through college, followed by five years of intermittent misery in graduate school, the bakery was heavenly. I would be happy from now on.

But three months later, my happiness had eroded back to its usual level. Every day, something upset me. If my roommate was in a bad mood, I wondered what I'd done wrong. I pined over a coworker, who flirted with me but dated someone else. I couldn't talk myself out of feeling sad. I'd been this way ever since college, when my parents had stopped being around in the evenings to provide distraction.

"Maybe this is just how I am," I thought. "Maybe I'm just depressed." But I couldn't accept it. There had to be something better: a happiness that would last.

I'd started riding a bike to save money and to exercise, back when I first moved to Chapel Hill. A guy in my program also biked to school, and he described a cross-country trip he'd done. "I'd like to do that," I found myself saying. But I was not athletic—a slow runner, too passive for sports, picked second-to-last for teams in grade school only because I had more friends than Deanna Abernathy. I'd never done anything remotely like a bike trip. I'd never even been camping.

"Why don't you start with North Carolina?" my schoolmate said. So I planned a four-day trip with two friends. Setting off was easy for me, bolstered by my friends' confidence. On the road, our only concerns were staying on our route and finding restrooms and campsites. The clutter of life disappeared. I became irritated only when I grew hungry, but the irritation evaporated as soon as I ate. My thoughts and emotions felt clearer. I knew I'd gain something on a longer trip.

The summer after I graduated, two friends rode cross-country. They invited me, but I didn't want to be a "third wheel," and besides, they rode faster than I did. But seeing their trip made mine seem possible. I already biked every day; I even sold my car. I didn't stop to think about what might go wrong, or how scary a trip would be. I just kept asserting to myself that I would do it, and did not leave any room for fear.

I talked with Mary, a friend at the co-op where I baked, about biking cross-country. She was younger than I was, but I biked more regularly, so I thought our speeds would match. And she worked behind the bakery counter, interacting with customers; being comfortable talking to people would help when traveling. I didn't expect that she'd share my goal of finding happiness. But she planned to hike the Appalachian Trail, and the physical challenge of a cross-country bike trip might appeal to her.

"Maybe we could do the bike trip next year," she said. But then her hiking partner backed out, and she suggested we bike instead.

I'd already saved thousands of dollars; I'd always been saving for something, and this was it. I arranged a leave-of-absence from the bakery starting in May. I sent away for state maps and brochures, picking places I'd like to see, and daydreamed endlessly about what the trip would be like. But Mary, who'd been living in the apartment next door, moved away. That winter, we kept in touch about our jobs and crushes but didn't talk much about the trip.

My parents didn't want me to go. All winter, every time we talked on the phone, my dad brought up terrible things that might happen: flat tires, tornados, rapists. "If you change your mind," my mom said as spring arrived, "we won't think any less of you."

April came and I packed my things for storage. With the trip only a month away, it became more scary than exciting, but I wouldn't back out. My panniers arrived and sat in a corner, as if I could slow down this last month by ignoring them. Finally, I forced myself to attach them, loaded them with random books, and biked thirty miles out into the country and back. Friends talked of their own travels and how jealous they were of my trip. I just felt mildly sick whenever I thought of it.

The last day of April came. Mary arrived in town. "I can't believe it's here," I said as I wheeled my bike out to her car. She grinned, and I grinned back. But my insides careened from dread to nervousness to an unstable excitement. We loaded my gear into her car and left.

On the eight-hour drive to Mary's sister's house in New Jersey, a panorama of worries played through my mind. Would we find places to sleep? Would I have to knock on strangers' doors and ask to camp on their lawns? And what about the Rocky Mountains? After seven years of biking every day, I knew I could make it across the country, but everyone mentioned the Rockies. Was I being naive—were the Rockies impassable by bike?

What would happen after we reached the Pacific? I'd taken six months off work, but Mary had only four. Would another friend join me to bike the West Coast? Would I keep biking alone? Would I meet someone on the beach, and we'd fall in love and bike together into the sunset?

"Don't worry," I told myself. By the end of the trip, surely I'd be more confident, after being forced outside my comfort zone to ask for water or for permission to camp. And the trip would be fun, just as the four-day trip across North Carolina had been.

Over all my reasoning hung a hope that out there—living outside on the road under a big, open sky—life would be clearer, and the chaos of moods I experienced would finally settle.

My daydreams coalesced into one scene: me standing on the beach at the Pacific Ocean. By that moment, by the time I reached that place, I would finally know how to be happy. Inspiring music swelled in my imagination as the camera panned around me standing on the smooth sand. I faced the water as the sun sank down the western sky, my hand on the handlebar of my bike. Waves rolled in to tumble at my feet.

THE HILL BEGAN TO FLATTEN, and my mind returned to the heat of Wyoming in July. Mary's bike leaned on a chain-link fence at a gravel turnout. As I ascended, Mary appeared over the ridge with her water bottle, pushed it into its holder on her bike, and dug in her panniers for her camera. After two months on the road together, the familiar sight of her buzz-short hair and small frame could trigger relief or annoyance, but right now I felt nothing.

I chugged toward her, and she looked up. "This is two thousand miles!"

I managed a smile. She'd added up our miles last night—just in time. I rolled to a stop and paused, catching my breath and balance before lifting a sore leg over the bike and wheeling it to lean by Mary's. Looking through the chain link, I saw the white forms at the horizon clearly, resolved into snowy peaks. The Rocky Mountains. They stretched north and south as far as I could see, forming a barrier to the West.

In two days, we'd be biking up them.

# PART 1:
# The Beginning,
# in Which We Battle
# Hills, Rain, Cold, Wind . . .
# and More

## Cape May, New Jersey, or the first day

A BURST OF SALTY AIR HIT me as I tugged open the minivan door. The beach began a few feet away, at the edge of the parking lot. An expanse of empty sand spread between me and the ocean, where small waves rolled under a blue sky. "I guess May 2nd is too cold for tourists," I thought. My insides turned, the familiar feeling of dread, and I tried to push it aside. At least it was sunny.

Around me, Mary and her family bustled out of the van. We'd spent last night at her sister Laura's house, an hour away, and the whole family had come to see us off. They weren't the only ones; as we set off down the sidewalk, I marked the Victorian bed-and-breakfasts until familiar figures appeared on one porch: my parents.

We'd picked Cape May for our departure so our families could come. But also, on its website, Cape May looked quaint, and I wanted the trip to be scenic. I'd pictured my parents in a Victorian just like the one they were now exiting, along with their friends Nan and Frieda. Mom hugged me when we reached them, and everyone else shook hands. Then we continued on to breakfast.

"So the Lenni-Lenape Indians!" Nan began in his usual abstract manner.

"The who?"

"Lenni-Lenape, lived in Cape May. Named after a sea captain, Cornelius Mey, spelled M-E-Y." Thank goodness for Nan; his rambling conversation would keep my nerves at bay. I let him talk on, nodding and trying to focus.

Mary chatted with everyone and, once we reached the restaurant, ordered a stack of pancakes, which she smeared with peanut butter and doused with syrup before digging in. I forced down some eggs and toast, trying to remove the weight settled in my chest by ignoring it. Was I the only nervous one? Maybe setting off on a trip wasn't frightening to Mary; she'd lived in Thailand for a semester, and traveled around Asia. If we'd been alone, I would have asked how she felt, and she probably would have reassured me. We'd had lots of heart-to-heart talks. But with our families there, I kept quiet.

After breakfast, we returned to the van and unloaded. Leaving our bags, we rolled our bikes onto the sand. Our entourage followed with cameras clicking and a video camera rolling. After a few yards, I hefted my bike onto my hip to avoid sand in the tires. I had a twenty-pound mountain bike; I'd swapped the nubby tires for slick ones.

Mom hurried over. "Let me help." As she took some of the weight, the center of gravity shifted away from me, which made carrying the bike awkward, but I didn't want to hurt her feelings by telling her to stop. As soon as the sand became packed, we lowered the bike to the ground.

Cameras snapped as Mary and I neared the water and circled around to face west. We backed our rear tires to the surf line. A wave crashed, and we smiled at the cameras as the water swirled around our tires. Another crashed. "Hurry up," I thought, "before a big one soaks our shoes!"

At last the cameras abated, and we headed back. "I got it okay," I said when Mom came to help carry my bike. She continued to walk by my side.

Back at the van, Laura slid open the door and passed out our bags. We each had two panniers that hung on a rack over the rear tire. We bungeed our sleeping gear on top, making the bikes camel-like. I hadn't practiced riding with the smaller front panniers, which I now attached.

As loading wound down, departure grew imminent, and the sick feeling I'd been ignoring reared up in my chest. Mom wiped a tear as it rolled down from her sunglasses. A lump rose in my throat, but I swallowed it.

Mary began hugging her family, and I turned to mine. Dad held aside the video camera to make room for a hug. "You can still change your mind."

"Okay." I wished he'd said something encouraging. Mom slipped me a note before hugging me. What if it expressed worry, or anger about the trip? I tucked it away for later.

"Remember to call," she said.

"Or email." We'd said every other day. "I'll try, but we might not be able to find a phone." I didn't want them worrying extra if I didn't call. Mary's family hadn't placed any obligations on her.

Laura hugged me, and then there was no one else. "Should I get on my bike and go?" I wondered. It seemed like the only way to start. I wheeled my bike a few steps, and the crowd drew back. Mary wheeled hers around, too, so we both faced the exit. Dad resumed filming. I threw a leg over my loaded bike, which wobbled. I'd have to adjust to it being this heavy. After a weak smile at my parents, I faced ahead and pushed off.

My bike wobbled again as my legs strained against the pedals. I steered left, and the handlebar swerved, pulled by the added weight of the front panniers. I teetered back to my course, steering carefully and pushing hard to build speed. "Don't let me fall over," I prayed, thinking of the video camera at my back. Was Mary following? I couldn't risk looking.

The bump at the end of the parking lot drew near, simultaneous with a right turn into the road. There were no cars. I focused on keeping upright and moving as I went over the bump and made a wide turn into the street.

I wanted to look back at the spectators, to give a final wave before I disappeared behind buildings. But I didn't think I could do it without falling over. Would my parents think that I didn't wave because I didn't care? The buildings closed in, and the crowd of cameras disappeared.

I took in the street, quiet now that buildings blocked the crashes of the ocean. Now I could hear Mary behind me. "Thank you, Universe," I thought, "for the absence of traffic!" I settled on my seat and relaxed my grip on the handlebar. The sick feeling was going. Puffy clouds stood in the blue sky, and the clear breeze blew cool air across me. It was perfect weather for our first day.

Was the group in the parking lot dispersing?

I'd memorized the route out of Cape May and also tucked directions behind the window on my handlebar bag. We neared the first turn. I risked a glance back. "Right turn, up ahead."

I turned, and a half-minute later, Mary panted up beside me. "Well, here we are!" she said, and we both smiled. The downtown had given way to small houses with lawns. We rolled past one after another. The trip had begun! After months of anticipation, it was happening. Right now. I couldn't stop grinning.

A stop sign neared. I braked, and my heavy bike leaned left. My foot hit the pavement, and I held tight to my handlebar and forced my bike upright. Next to me, Mary stopped, her foot jerking in her clipless pedal, which attached her shoe to her bike. The shoe wouldn't come loose, and unable to lower her foot, she fell sideways. Her panniers hit the pavement with a thunk.

I began to laugh but stopped myself. "Are you okay?"

"Yeah." She wiggled out from the bike, her feet still attached. I hadn't meant to laugh. I'd just been so scared of falling; then it happened to Mary, and it wasn't a disaster.

Mary yanked a foot out of its pedal and extracted herself. She stood, examining a bruise on her knee, and then heaved her bike upright.

Two women marched up the sidewalk, arms swinging in a power walk. "How far have you come?" one asked as they slowed, eyes wide.

"One block!" We laughed.

They smiled as they passed. "Good luck!"

For thirty minutes the roads stayed peaceful. Then we turned onto Route 47, a four-lane lined with businesses. "It's just New Jersey," I reassured myself as cars whizzed past. "It won't be like this all summer." My thoughts flitted from the busy road to my bakery job to my family. (Were Mom and Dad back on Interstate 95? Or had they stayed in Cape May for the day?) My left knee twanged. I had knee exercises to do each morning to strengthen the muscle that caused the discomfort, but its appearance made me feel rickety.

In spite of the scenery, my spirits stayed up. "The trip has started," I kept reminding myself. "We're actually doing it." I was twenty-some years old, and at last I'd made something happen in my life.

"Let's take a rest stop!" Mary called. I scanned the roadside. Would these businesses let us use the restroom? But then a cinderblock building appeared with signs reading "Men" and "Women": public restrooms.

After that first restroom, we stopped at gas stations. Each time, I felt compelled to buy something. This posed two problems. Snacks were pricey, and I didn't want to eat the junk sold in gas stations: colorful cubes of gum, blaze-orange corn chips, cinnamon rolls with artificial icing stuck to cellophane wrappers. But I felt uncomfortable using the restroom for free.

At our fourth rest stop, I settled on honey-roasted peanuts. Outside, Mary sat on the curb and munched on almonds from a baggie she'd packed at home. She hadn't felt obliged to buy something. I wished I hadn't. I pulled out the map and joined her.

Our destination, Parvin State Park, beckoned as a green block amid the clustering roads of New Jersey, fifty miles from Cape May. We hadn't calculated how far we had to go each day; we didn't even have a set end date, although Mary had a new job as a field organizer with an activist group that started in four months. I'd made a safe estimate (three thousand miles in three months was about thirty-three miles a day) and felt sure we'd travel faster than that.

But the fifty miles to Parvin that had seemed an easy ride were taking longer than expected. Was it because of our heavy bikes? I couldn't wait to arrive at the park, to set up camp in the quiet woods.

Mary traced a road on the map. "Bobbie's house is a mile from the gate, Laura said." Laura had suggested we camp with her college friend Bobbie and Bobbie's husband, Brett, who lived near Parvin State Park.

"Would you rather go there?"

"It just might be easier, for our first night. Cooking in a kitchen, and having a real bathroom."

I didn't want to camp in a yard with people nearby. But I didn't want to deny Mary the house. There'd be more parks, later in the trip. Maybe I could bike over to Parvin just to see it.

"Okay. You have their number?"

Mary nodded and looked at the office building across the lot. "Let's go see if we can use a phone."

We wheeled our bikes over, leaned them on the building, and entered a deserted lobby. A brown phone hung on the wall. "What time is it?" Mary asked as we crossed the room. She couldn't find her watch and had been asking the time all day.

"Just about four."

I crossed my fingers as she picked up the receiver. A dial tone hummed into the air. The phone—like the public restroom earlier—had come along when we needed it. We got directions to Bobbie's and headed on.

The roads grew busier. My head buzzed with the echoes of the passing cars. The wind buffeted me, my legs began to tire, and the bike seemed heavier and slower. Since Cape May, I'd taken only one picture. I'd thought I'd take lots, but I kept passing interesting sights because it would take more physical effort to stop. But I'd have plenty of time for pictures in the days to come.

An hour later we neared the turn to Parvin State Park and Bobbie's. By now, all the adrenaline of the morning send-off had dispersed. My legs didn't hurt, but my shoulders were stiff from hunching all day, my elbows unexpectedly hurt, and I had to shake out numb hands.

We turned, and the road at last grew quiet. Buildings gave way to farms and fields. My legs circled endlessly. So much for riding an "easy fifty miles" on the first day! We passed a sign for the park, and my heart sank because I no longer had the energy to bike an extra mile to see it.

We turned onto Bobbie's road. The first house stood three stories tall, with leaded glass in the front door and spiral-cut bushes lining the front walk. The second had a portico like a miniature Greek temple. Did Bobbie and Brett live in a palace like these? It would be fun to tell friends about our first campsite, at a mansion.

We reached Bobbie's driveway and bumped down the gravel. A hum grew into the roar of a lawnmower. Over the bushes, I glimpsed a manicured yard:

too-short grass, one trimmed shrub, a perfectly stacked woodpile, a cheap tool shed plonked in the middle of the space. The noise grew louder, and a small, prefabricated house came into view, and then a man on a lawnmower. He looked up. As we stopped, he cut the engine, slid off his seat, and swaggered over. I thought of a seedy bar.

"He's a friend of Laura," I reminded myself. *Well, his wife is.* Mary smiled as he reached us and held out his hand to shake.

"I'm Brett," he said loudly. We introduced ourselves. "Bobbie's not home yet. So . . . you're riding across the country?" His eyebrows went up. "You know there's the Rocky Mountains out there, don't you?" His voice rang in the silence left by the mower.

I tried to grin, as if he'd made a joke. After a pause, he snorted. "You can pitch your tent over on the side," he said, pointing, and returned to his mowing.

Mary and I wheeled our bikes toward the woods that bordered the yard and leaned them on a tree. We unsnapped the bungee cords and took off our sleeping bags and pads. Mary also had the tent; I had the stove and gas. We'd pitched the tent at Laura's house, to practice, and now, as we fumbled to fit the poles into the right grommets, I was glad we'd done it once. Just as we finished, a car crunched down the drive. A bark drew my gaze to an enclosure behind the house; two dogs pranced inside.

The car stopped, and a dark-haired woman got out. She walked over, smiling and looking over our tent and bikes. "Hi, I'm Bobbie," she said. "This is so exciting! How was the first day?"

"It was okay," Mary said. Bobbie turned to me.

"It was farther than I thought . . . our bikes are so heavy, we went slower."

"Well, come inside when you're ready."

Bobbie walked to the cage, where the dogs leapt about, tails frantic. When she opened the door, the dogs bounded out, turning to jump on her but torn with the desire to run. The dogs dashed away, past our tent, then looped back to jump on Bobbie again. I unrolled my pad and laid it on the floor of the tent. Bobbie petted the dogs, then sent them back into the cage and went inside. Another cage stood under the trees with two cats inside, one pacing like a tiger in the zoo. It made me feel sad.

As the sun dropped, I set up the camp stove on a patch of dirt. We'd practiced lighting the stove at Laura's, where after several tries it had produced a roaring flame. Tonight I got a normal flame on the first try. "Do you want to use the stove first?" I asked Mary.

"Nah, I'm going to use the kitchen. It just seems easier." She rummaged through her supplies. Bobbie's stove *would* be easier, but I wanted to jump right in and cook like we'd cook all summer. Plus, Brett had gone inside, and it was peaceful in the yard.

I had Boil-in-Bag rice for easy camp-stove cooking, but I had some ordinary rice to use up first. I put my pot of water over the flame and dropped in the rice. As the water heated, something poked my neck. I reached up, and my necklace came loose in my hand. Pieces fell to the ground. I'd tied the necklace on two years earlier, stringing metal bike hardware onto a cord. I gathered the pieces, feeling sad. The remaining cord poked me again.

"Hey Mary? My necklace broke—can you cut the rest off?" I picked up my pocketknife and searched for the scissors. "It seems like kind of a bad omen."

Mary considered. "Maybe when you put it on, it was about doing the bike trip. And now here you are doing it, and you don't need the necklace anymore." She was so positive; I wished I could feel it. She snipped off the remaining necklace and handed it to me. Then she went inside.

The water was boiling, so I got a spoon to stir the rice. It had already stuck to the pot. I scraped it off the bottom, then turned the gas down. The stove flickered out. A lump formed in my throat.

I removed the pot to relight the stove, but now the stove was hot and the fuel evaporated as it left its bottle. I'd have to let the whole thing cool. I took a deep breath, trying to swallow my disheartenment, and waited a minute, then two. I relit the stove and returned the pot. Gooey water swirled over a block of rice. I added more water because most had boiled off. Should I keep stirring, or keep the pot covered?

After twenty minutes of alternate stirring and adding more water, I gave up. When I dished out the burnt, undercooked rice, the hard spot in my throat swelled. I picked up my packet of instant gravy. Tears pricked at my eyes while I mixed the powder with water and, sure I'd destroy it if I tried to heat it, poured the lumpy sauce straight onto the rice. I crunched through the disappointing meal.

By now the sun had set and darkness neared, and I still had to wash the dishes, repack the stove, brush my teeth, and find my sleeping clothes. I gave in and took the dishes inside. In the bright kitchen, Mary and Bobbie sat talking. They both smiled. I gave a brief wave and went to the sink.

After dishes, I used the bathroom, and when I flushed, I watched with apprehension as the toilet clogged and the water began to rise. "Don't overflow, don't overflow, don't overflow," I prayed. The water stopped rising and swirled in the bowl; I needed a plunger. I went out to the kitchen to ask Bobbie. To my embarrassment, instead of getting me a plunger, Bobbie sent Brett to look at the toilet.

I escaped into the twilight. I'd hoped to be meditating in Parvin State

Park, writing in my journal as the sun set, enjoying the peace of nature and life outdoors. Instead, I was stuck with loud Brett, the caged animals, my broken necklace, burned rice, and now the humiliation of stopping up the toilet! And I hated the traffic we'd had all day. My elbows hurt, my hands hurt, and my knees felt unhealthy. I was terrible at cooking on the camp stove. My bike was awkward and heavy. I felt the same desperate loneliness I'd felt as a sixth grader when none of my friends had made it into the all-state orchestra, and I'd gone to the two-day festival with seventh and eighth graders who didn't talk to me. I'd eaten all my meals alone.

Mary bustled around near the tent. "She had a nice dinner," I imagined, "enjoying Bobbie's company, while I fail at everything." I tried to stop the tears as I dug out my pajamas. Mary looked over.

"You can start crying if you want to," she said. When I smiled, my tears overflowed.

# We enter Pennsylvania

A T TWO O'CLOCK THE NEXT afternoon, I spied pale blue tips over the trees—the towers of the suspension bridge across the Delaware River. According to our map, our road was not an interstate, meaning bikes were allowed. But the tiny stretch that crossed the river was a double line; did the road suddenly become an interstate at the bridge? Would they allow us to continue? There was no other way across.

We'd had a scenic morning across western New Jersey, with open farmland and boarded up, white-painted farm stands. At the only stand open for business, I'd bought a bunch of asparagus for a dollar seventy-five. After lunch in Swedesboro, we'd checked our email at the library, and I'd emailed my parents with our location. That morning, I'd opened Mom's note. She'd written out the old Irish blessing—"May the road rise to meet you, May the wind be always at your back," et cetera—and enclosed a clipping from *Country Living* magazine about pursuing your dreams. I chose to interpret this as Mom accepting the bike trip, in spite of concern for my safety.

Now the road widened to a four-lane, like an interstate. We rounded a bend and a toll plaza barred our way. Overhead, large green signs announced the

Commodore Barry Bridge, which rose behind the tollbooths. A guard station sat at the right.

I slowed to wait for Mary. I had to shout over the traffic noise. "Should we stop and ask permission?" She didn't answer. "They'll see us anyway, since we have to stop at the toll."

"Okay."

We rolled up to the station. Two police cars waited nearby.

Inside, two men slumped on office chairs. A row of monitors showed the toll plaza from different angles. "Hi," I said. "We're on bikes and were wondering if we're allowed to cross the bridge."

"No," one of the men said, not quite glancing over.

Could he escort us with one of the police cars? He continued to stare at the monitors. I turned to Mary.

"We'll have to call Laura," she said, sighing. "She'll come take us across." It felt silly after our grand send-off the day before, as if we'd biked for a day and a half only to end up back in Laura's van. Plus Laura's house was an hour away. But at least we were close to Laura; were there other rivers without bike access? I hadn't planned for this at all. Surely they let bikes cross the Mississippi, right?

"Is there a phone we can use?" I asked.

The officer jerked his head toward the door without looking. "Pay phone's outside."

After the call, Mary and I took the panniers off our bikes and sat on a patch of grass alongside the toll plaza. It was another sunny day with fresh gusts of wind. Cars pulled into the tollbooths, stopped, pulled out. Mary dug out our M&M cookies, and we devoured them. Laura had offered to replenish our supply.

Mary tuned my solar-powered radio to NPR, and I half listened. Guitar music poured out. The reporter talked of a famous classical guitarist. I'd never heard of classical guitar. That story ended with another blurb of music. Then a new voice came on: a historic pine tree in New England had fallen in a thunderstorm the previous night. The story caught my attention—we'd seen that tree! On a family trip when I was in middle school.

The report continued, describing cables that had been holding up the white pine. The huge tree had existed before colonial America and had survived logging for ship masts when Europeans came to the land. A lump rose in my throat as the reporter described people in tears looking at the fallen tree. Its demise at the start of my trip made it into a symbol of my childhood. It had been leaning for years, ready to fall, held up by cables attached by people who weren't ready to lose it.

Were the cables my own?

A familiar van turned into the lot, and Mary snapped off the radio. A few minutes later, Laura had paid the toll, ferried us across the river, given us more cookies, and left us in a seamy parking lot. Rundown warehouses lined the roads. "Mom never would have dropped us here," I thought. Thankfully, Mom wasn't there to see it.

Mary and I reloaded our bikes and set off, past car garages and auto parts stores. Traffic flew by inches from my shoulder, but a tall curb lined the road so I couldn't move away. At last we turned onto a smaller road, headed into Pennsylvania.

The holdup at the bridge had wasted the afternoon, and now the sun was sinking. We passed a town park filled with people playing ball. "Please be somewhere to sleep," I thought, "somewhere that is clearly the right place." But there was nothing. The sun neared the treetops. *What will we do if we don't find somewhere?*

Ahead, Mary moved slowly up a curving hill. I chugged along after her, fighting as gravity pulled back on my overloaded bike. Across the road, a driveway sloped up the embankment, then turned and disappeared. It made a perfect triangle with the roadway. Trees lined it, and grasses hung over from the hillside behind. On the hill stood gravestones.

I pushed harder on my pedals. "Mary!" She pulled into a driveway and stopped, then turned to watch me approach. "What about that?" I pointed. "Looks like a cemetery."

She raised her eyebrows and slowly nodded. We rode back to the driveway and made the sharp turn. As we pedaled up the slope, the noise from the road began to fade.

The gravel and the hill became too much to pedal against, and I wobbled to a stop. Leaves stirred above in the quiet breeze. I dismounted and began to push. Late sunlight poured through the headstones and grasses and beamed onto the roadway where I crunched upward. Then church bells began to strike. Six o'clock. The bells welcomed me.

At the top of the hill, the driveway turned left. It passed a small white church with a red tin roof and ended at a cluster of houses. The graveyard spread out opposite the church. A slow-moving car rumbled up the hill, passed us, and parked at a house. What if the driver came to bother us in the night? I wouldn't think about it.

The church was Episcopal, so the pastor lived next door, but when we knocked, no one answered. But we were meant to sleep here. I just felt it.

"We could go over the hill, behind those bushes," I said, pointing, "so we wouldn't be obvious."

"They might kick us out," Mary said. Usually, I worried about this, but I wasn't worried now.

"Let's just wait and see. We haven't seen anywhere else, and it's getting late." Mary nodded.

She walked to the side door of the church and tried the knob. It opened. Sleeping in the graveyard was one thing, but trespassing inside? But Mary entered so I followed. We descended a few steps to a hallway. My knees ached with each step down. At the end of the hallway was a restroom. My knees creaked even worse when I sat.

Back outside, we pushed our bikes across the graveyard toward the evergreens. Each time we spotted a flat area, we arrived to find it sloped as much as everywhere else. Finally, we gave up and pitched the tent.

Mary got out a can of chili beans. I'd imagined we'd share meals, but Mary liked spicy food and I didn't, plus I wasn't sure she wanted to share: I was certainly hungry enough to eat a whole can of beans. "Do you want to cook first?" I said.

"Sure."

"Should we go to church in the morning?" I'd had this idea to visit different churches all summer. I liked the Methodist church I attended in Chapel Hill, but I wasn't convinced Methodism was right for me. Maybe another religion would resonate.

"Yeah, sure. The early service is at eight," Mary said. Mary's family was Catholic, but I wasn't sure how she felt about it.

As it grew dark, we secured the camp stove against a headstone and brushed our teeth, spitting toothpaste into the bushes. I had time for only a brief note in my journal before the light faded. "The trip doesn't feel the way I imagined it would," I wrote. I'd expected to have loads of free time and had planned to continue a "silent prayer" practice I had started that spring. I'd thought that once I was on the trip, I'd have time to sit in silence every day, for an hour. I imagined a feeling of peace descending, once I sat regularly. But so far, I hadn't had time, and I felt jumpy. I crawled into the tent.

The previous night, we'd slept with our heads at opposite ends, but in the sloping cemetery, we both put our heads uphill. My sleeping bag slid down as I squirmed into it.

I lay on my back and let out a deep breath. We were sleeping in a graveyard! It wasn't scary like I would have thought. I imagined the letters I'd write about it until I drifted off.

Throughout the night, I woke periodically to find my feet bent up against the end of the tent. Each time I hitched myself back up the hill. Then I woke with birds singing and light filtering in. After stretching my stiff muscles, I checked my watch: six. I wanted to use the church bathroom before anyone was around.

Chilly air and wet grass met me outside the tent, but the clear sky promised another sunny day. After visiting the church, I found Mary up as well, boiling water for breakfast. I performed my knee exercises, crab-walking across the cemetery, and took a photo of the tent with the gravestones around it. "Do you want Malt-O-Meal?" Mary called.

I wanted to share breakfast. As neighbors, Mary and I had often crossed the yard to sit on each other's porch, to eat and talk. But I had Cream of Rice for breakfast because I wanted to eat less wheat, and Malt-O-Meal was made of wheat.

"No, you go ahead." She poured off some of the water for tea and stirred in her cereal. I got out the map and sat by her, trying to plan a route among the confusion of roads.

By eight o'clock we'd reloaded our bikes and wheeled them to the church. A few cars had parked, and when we entered, several older ladies looked up. I smiled, not wanting to disturb the pre-service hush, and followed Mary to an empty pew. The door opened again, and a lady tottered up the aisle. "Those must be your bikes!" she whispered loudly as she passed. I smiled and nodded.

The woman in front of us turned. "Are you the campers?" We nodded. "Where are you headed?" A woman across the aisle leaned over to listen. I glanced at the priest sitting up front, and the silent congregation.

"Amish country next," I whispered. The two women nodded.

"You want to go north to Route 30, that'll take you straight to Lancaster—"

"Oh, not on bikes!" the one across the aisle interrupted. "They'd rather take 82 across, that's a better road for bikes."

The priest stood and cleared his throat, and I smiled at the women as they drew back to their seats.

I'd never been to an Episcopal church, but the program looked similar to a Methodist program. Maybe Episcopalian would be right for—

"What would Jesus do?!" the priest boomed. I cringed. This was just what I disliked about church: overused words that meant nothing. But then the priest continued. "Those words have become a slogan, and slogans rapidly lose meaning." He began to speak about an Episcopalian activist, describing his civil rights work and his antiwar position. I began to relax—it was a history lesson.

After the service, several women surrounded Mary and me. They asked questions about our trip and suggested routes to Lancaster. "I'm Darlene," rasped a short woman, and I felt her take my hand. She slipped me a five-dollar bill. "For a drink." She winked, and I grinned back.

"I wish I could have gone on a trip like that!" someone said. Everyone nodded. "You're going to see the whole country! Imagine that. The farthest we ever got was New York City."

At last we said goodbyes. My watch read nine-forty-five; I liked the idea of visiting churches across the country but hated to get such a late start.

Headed to Lancaster, the road climbed one hill after another. I passed a sign, "Lancaster 23." Thirty minutes later, my heart fell when I passed, "Lancaster 20."

Just as I got a rhythm going, we stopped to use a restroom, and a Spandex-clad man pedaled up on a road bike. He beamed at us, asking about our trip. As lunchtime neared, we'd barely progressed.

At noon, we turned in at the Brandywine Battlefield. Peaceful green hills spanned the historic site in sharp contrast with the violence that had occurred there in the Revolutionary War. I tried to imagine it as I crunched through my remaining asparagus spears. (They tasted just as good raw, and it was easier.) "I wish we could sleep here," I said.

"I know, but we haven't gone very far."

"It's probably not allowed anyway, since it's a historic site."

"Let's not stop again for an hour."

"Okay." Hopefully if we kept biking, we'd cover some distance.

But thirty minutes later, I saw a natural food store in a strip mall. I hadn't expected to find many of these. Mary glanced back. "Want to stop?"

I nodded. "Oh, well," I thought. After this we wouldn't stop again.

Inside, I got a bunch of kale and an apple. A heavyset man in glasses waited at the register. "Where are you from?" he asked as I put down my produce.

"North Carolina, but we started biking in Cape May, New Jersey."

"Wow! Where do you camp?" He slid the apple onto the scale.

"Last night we slept in a church cemetery." He added the kale, and $2.79 popped up. I dug in my wallet for change. "Tonight we're not sure yet." I laid the money on the counter.

He pushed the money back. "I'm Joe. My wife and I live over in Cochranville, about fifteen miles. You can camp in our yard."

"Thanks!" I looked around for Mary. Joe seemed safe, but I wanted her input. A customer got in line behind me, but Joe ignored him as he reached for a scrap of paper and began to draw a map to his house. Mary appeared. "We can camp at his house."

"Oh, thanks!" she said. We took Joe's map and thanked him again.

Suddenly, the day was fun. Our slow pace didn't matter. If we'd been faster, or stuck to our decision not to stop, we'd have missed meeting Joe. His map led through a town called Kennett Square, where Latino music blared at a Cinco de Mayo festival on the streets. If we hadn't met Joe, we'd have missed it!

We locked our bikes to a tree and entered the crowd. A vendor made us huge, gloopy quesadillas with cheese, beans, salsa, and cilantro and charged us only two-fifty, not the three-fifty that the meat ones cost. With paper plates sagging with quesadillas, Mary and I sat on a curb. We watched a mariachi band as we ate. We had a place to sleep! I radiated happiness. Mary looked at me. "If everyday is this much fun," she said, "I don't care *how* far we get!"

After eating cotton candy, we continued following Joe's off-the-map directions. Yellow flowers waved alongside green fields, like Hobbiton in *Lord of the Rings*. The hills rolled like a roller coaster, steep but short and fun. Bunches of dandelions crowded the narrow road. At last we arrived at Joe's, a cottage tucked into a dip in the road, surrounded by ramshackle gardens.

An hour later, I sat writing in my journal by our tent as the sun set. Mary had gone inside with our hosts, who'd invited us in for showers and dinner. I was glad she liked talking to people, because it allowed me to sit outside alone.

So far, the bike trip was louder than I had anticipated; I'd imagined biking along quiet roads without a thought in my head. Also, I hadn't had time to write in my journal. And I barely managed my knee exercises each morning, much less the silent prayer I had envisioned. I couldn't stop reorganizing my bags, even with my minimal belongings. Today had been fun, with the church ladies, Joe, and Kennett Square. I wanted to have fun. But I also wanted solitude; peacefulness seemed like the way to happiness. What could I do to make life peaceful?

## Eastern Pennsylvania, in which it starts to rain

THE ROAD REMAINED PEACEFUL ALL day. Mary and I stopped only once, at a gas station where we sat on the curb to eat snacks as clouds moved into the sky. A woman hobbled over from the house across the street to meet us, and asked if we'd send her a postcard. Her name was Dolores. Mary wrote down her address.

"Make sure you see the view from Grasshopper Level!" Dolores said as she turned to go.

"What time is it?" Mary hadn't found her watch and feared she'd left it at home.

"Twelve-thirty. Should we stop in Strasburg?"

"I don't know—let's just wait and see when we get there." The words were our new motto: *let's just wait and see.* Things could be totally different by Strasburg—maybe we wouldn't even *reach* Strasburg! Maybe we'd meet another Joe, who'd invite us to stay at his house. I fought against my impulse to make a plan and tried to be open.

As clouds built in the sky, I fell behind Mary. Although I sometimes started in front, she rode faster than I did. She'd wait in Strasburg, I told myself. Still, I found myself passing scenery without stopping for photos. I imagined that

Mary would be annoyed if she had to wait long, and my imaginings made me anxious to catch up.

The air began to speckle with rain. I stopped to put up my hood, under my helmet.

The road flattened at the top of a hill, and a panoramic view spread below. I stopped in the quiet drizzle. This had to be Dolores's "Grasshopper Level"— I'd need six photos to fit it. A pattern of green and brown rectangles filled the valley. Barns with silos, tractors, horses, and houses dotted the landscape, while a railroad train moved across the middle of the scene—not a sleek silver Amtrak, but a black engine billowing smoke, pulling an assortment of cars. The view called to mind the 1855 painting *The Lackawanna Valley* by American artist George Inness. I'd spotted Lackawanna on our map to the north and thought, "It's probably ugly by now," but this valley looked just like the painting, as if Grasshopper Level ran past a special window that looked back in time.

The drizzle increased as I neared Strasburg. I pedaled into downtown, where the wet street reflected the traffic lights and the headlights of slow-moving cars. Through the rain, I scanned the eighteenth century brick storefronts and railroad-themed decor. I didn't see fast food restaurants or chain pharmacies. Mary's bike leaned under an awning outside a coffee shop. Strasburg was the epitome of the small town I hoped to find across America.

I leaned my bike near Mary's and went in. My coat dripped on the floor while I wiped my glasses. As I got my bearings, I spotted a coat rack. Was it safe to leave my gear? No one would take it, I told myself. I'd been leaving my bike unlocked, too. I liked the idea of trusting, but it was hard to feel it one hundred percent.

Free of my dripping gear, I got a mocha with whipped cream and found Mary in the back room, in an upholstered wingback chair. I sat by her and pulled out the map. We were five miles south of Amish country.

"Maybe we should stay in a campground," I said. "Amish country is touristy, so they might not allow camping just anywhere. And it might be easier in the rain." I also wondered if the Amish might spurn women bikers camping behind their churches.

"Okay." We picked a campground called Lucy's.

Knowing where I'd sleep, I relaxed. "Look at me!" I thought, "in my posh wingback chair with my fancy coffee drink!" Even with the rain, the bike trip kept turning up good things. I opened my journal and began to write.

Once, the door jingled, and an excited man walked straight to the back room. "Are those your bikes?" he asked. "My wife and I go touring!" He proceeded to tell us about the trips they'd been on. Before leaving, he gave me his card and said, "In case anything goes wrong in the next fifty miles."

An hour later, after emails at the library, Mary and I set off to Lucy's. The map showed several covered bridges, but in the cold afternoon, going off route seemed like a lot to ask. I wanted to see one. But I didn't want to ask Mary to do it, convinced she wouldn't like the idea. She hadn't said this; I just imagined her saying no, or worse, agreeing to go and then resenting me. Maybe I'd bike back to see them, after we set up camp.

The cold drizzle settled into a steady rain, soaking into my fingers and the gray scenery. At last we reached Lucy's Campground: RVs with noisy motors filled a treeless lot. The wooden screen door of the office slammed shut behind us as we entered. A sign on the wall read, "All sites $26." Twenty-six dollars?! For an ugly patch of gravel surrounded by RVs?

"We're just on bikes," Mary said to Lucy. "Is there anywhere cheaper?"

"You could try Rolling Meadow." She gave us directions—five more miles.

We returned to the dreary day. Rolling Meadow was to the northeast—the wrong direction for our overall journey—but I couldn't think of a different option. The rain rushed down, and the wind picked up. Even with the murky sheets of rain, I noticed the adorable farmhouses on rolling fields, but my fingers had stiffened and I couldn't enjoy the scenery. A horse trotted past pulling an Amish buggy; a minute later, a truck bellowed by.

As another hour passed, I gave up on the idea of exploring. When we finally arrived at Rolling Meadow Campground, my mood plummeted. "Twenty-four dollars!" Mary said as I read the sign. We'd biked all that way to save two dollars!

"What do you want to do?" I asked.

"Let's just stay," she said, shaking her head.

As we pushed our bikes to our spot, I felt guilty—I'd suggested we stay at a campground. I hadn't realized a tourist area would mean high prices. Mary was quiet. I stayed quiet, too, in case saying anything would make her feel worse. She looked at me. "What time is it?"

I checked my watch. "Six-thirty."

Maybe other factors were affecting Mary, not just my bad decision about camping. I had better rain gear; she was probably colder and wetter than I was. And I'd biked almost every day for years, but Mary hadn't. Maybe the long day of biking was harder on her.

We leaned our bikes on the ends of our picnic table and unloaded. Gravel covered a long, rectangular parking spot for an RV. We pitched the tent on the patch of balding grass on the side, struggling to drive the tent stakes into the hard-packed ground. Each campsite had one thick tree trunk, the branches high overhead. A view spread out to the right of the office, but a giant RV blocked it.

"The day was a success," I told myself, "in spite of the dismal ending." We'd seen Grasshopper Level and had fun in Strasburg.

"We only went twenty-five miles today." Mary interrupted my thoughts. "And we just wasted five miles going northeast."

"I know." Maybe I should've thought to call and ask the price, or to look for options on our westward route. But I'd been tired. And Mary was probably tired, too.

Cold and damp, Mary and I decided to take hot showers before dinner. We wouldn't have had showers if we'd camped by a church. And we walked into town instead of biking. Biking would have used the same sore muscles, and our tires would have spewed rainwater onto us, but walking relaxed me and kept us dry. We kept our hands warm in our coat pockets.

Darkness crept in. We found all the shops closed in the deserted town except the sub shop. Not needing to make a decision was perfect.

I SAT AT THE PICNIC table in the clear morning air and assessed my sore spots. My wrists hurt. The pain extended up my forearms almost to the elbow. I gingerly twisted an arm to the left, then the right. The twisting created a new pain that somehow felt pleasant. My hands had gone numb a few times yesterday; padded bike gloves hadn't helped. My shoulders, neck, and back weren't bad, just stiff and mildly sore, but my seat ached. I didn't like padded bike shorts, tight and sticky, but I had a padded, women's-style bike seat.

How were my knees holding up? They didn't hurt until I sat. I'd brace my arms against a nearby object to lower myself onto a seat. I'd noticed my old pain, which I hoped to fight off with my morning exercises. But I'd also noticed pain at new places on my knees. When I felt a twinge, I'd massage the spot while riding, until the pain left.

A figure approaching pulled me back to the present. A young man in an Amish hat and clothes walked on the elevated roadway alongside the campground. He didn't have a beard; was he going to work in a field somewhere? As he passed, he called down hello. Mary looked up from the map, and we waved. My imagination swept me away into a daydream of marrying a cute, beardless Amish guy and living in an old-fashioned home . . . but realities kept intruding. Maybe I wouldn't be able to listen to CDs of loud Chapel Hill bands, or wear shorts. Maybe I wouldn't be allowed to bike! And probably he'd grow a beard when he got older. But I was glad he'd said hello.

Mary looked up from the map again. "I'd like to cover more miles today," she said. I nodded. I'd wanted to explore Amish country, but after my unsuccessful plan of yesterday—the expensive campground, the extra miles in the wrong direction, the new campground that cost as much—I didn't want to make any demands. I wouldn't enjoy exploring alone, I told myself; I'd just be anxious to catch up. I could always come back someday.

"What time is it?" Mary asked. I wished she'd stop asking me.

"Almost nine." She stood and stretched, then folded the map.

The air felt fresh, washed by the rain, and hopeful. But soon we rode toward Lancaster along a busy route lined with strip malls. We biked right through Lancaster and continued west toward the Susquehanna River.

An endless procession of thoughts ran through my head. I wondered about Cory, my most recent crush. I hadn't had many boyfriends, just a few short-lived ones in college that had each left me depressed for months. Since college, for seven years, I had not so much as been on a date. Instead I developed obsessive crushes that I kept hidden. Cory had been the latest; we'd become friends and would hang out almost every day. But then, out of the blue, he'd said he didn't want to see me at all. I'd hoped I'd stop thinking about him when I left on the trip. The idea of biking cross-country filled me with such space and openness that I imagined my thoughts dissolving into the air, leaving my head empty and peaceful—but now, I plodded along, assaulted by thoughts of Cory.

My head will empty eventually, I consoled myself. The trip had only just started. I'd make time for silent prayer, and adjust to life on the road, and things would eventually calm down. I had many miles to go.

LATE THAT AFTERNOON, MARY AND I neared Seven Valleys, Pennsylvania. We'd made good progress, covering twenty-five miles in the morning and then another twenty-five through the town of York and onto the Heritage Rail Trail. After the busy streets, the peace of the trail had calmed me. But the roads we'd crossed were unmarked, so we'd lost our place on the map. We'd followed a sign to a campground, only to find another expensive place for RVs. We'd tried to continue on the roads but had realized we were lost, so we'd returned to the trail. Seven Valleys was on the trail, so we couldn't miss it.

"Will there be a church?" I wondered. "Or a schoolyard where we can camp?" We could ask to camp in someone's yard, but I hated the thought of knocking on a door to ask.

We arrived at a small park with a metal sculpture of a gigantic, yellow and green bike. With its porta-potty and picnic shelter, the park felt homey. "It's too bad we can't camp here," I thought, assuming it wasn't allowed. Leaving the trail, we rolled downhill into town and found a bar but no churches. And then the town ended! Mary and I pulled up on a sidewalk.

"The park's our only option," she said.

"But is camping allowed?" I got out the map, hoping it could help. "The trail heads southeast after Seven Valleys, so we're back on the road . . . and

Jefferson is just as small." Jefferson was another five miles. It might not even have a park.

"Let's just go up there and see," Mary said. "Maybe they won't kick us out."

We biked back uphill to the park, wheeled our bikes under the picnic shelter, and got out the cooking gear. "We could simply be travelers stopped to make dinner," I thought. As we sat, joggers and dog walkers passed on the trail, and no one bothered us. We decided to stay.

After eating, we pitched the tent under the park's two trees, leaving our bikes under the shelter. The day had become cloudy. As darkness came, traffic on the trail slowed, and I crawled into the tent. In spite of my tiredness, I lay awake, listening to each noise. Was someone creeping around outside the tent? Were they going to yell at us for camping there?

But the night passed, and the next morning, it struck me as silly that I'd worried about whether or not to sleep in the park—the park that had come along, on the trail, right when we needed somewhere to camp. Our detour to the RV campground and getting lost now seemed like good fortune that had led us to the park, as if we'd been herded toward Seven Valleys.

I'd been looking for the "right" place to sleep each night, as if not finding it would leave us stranded. But now I thought, "Wherever we are at the end of the day, we'll be *somewhere,* and we can sleep there. It might not be comfortable and safe, but it will still be *somewhere.*"

## Central Pennsylvania, in which the weather and our moods become even worse

THE HILLS WERE GETTING LONGER, and it couldn't seem to stop raining. As we pedaled up today's mountain, fog rolled in to fill the valley that spread behind us. Soon only scattered treetops stood above the white haze. In the distance, the tops of hills rose above the fog, forming hazy dark shadows; close to the road, dark evergreens stood out, palpably near in the quiet gloom. I climbed, listening to my breathing, one pedal stroke after another. The uphill work wasn't hard first thing in the morning.

A raindrop plinked on my arm. "Great!" I thought. "We finally got our things dried out, and now it's going to rain on them again." I couldn't accept life as an endless series of getting rained on and drying out; I hung on to the dry moments.

We'd spent last night behind a church in Fort Loudon, Pennsylvania, and awoken when the sky got light. (I thought I'd brought an alarm clock, but I couldn't find it in my bags.) It was now May 9th: we'd survived a week on the road and covered 275 miles.

The night before that, we'd set up camp in a drizzle at a state park. There'd been nowhere to escape the rain except a damp concrete restroom with no hot water; I'd tried to warm myself under the hot-air hand dryer. The rain had continued all night, so we'd packed up in it, too. At least *last* night, the sky had cleared before bedtime. We'd spread our things on the grass to dry. But now they were getting wet all over again.

We climbed for almost an hour, the road twisting out of sight each time I rounded a bend. The raindrops continued to plink and plunk until they fell steadily. During yesterday's rainstorm, as we'd climbed a similar hill, I'd donned my raincoat only to start sweating inside. Today, I took off my hoody before putting on the coat. And yesterday, splashing had soaked the bottoms of our panniers, wetting our belongings. Today, our things were inside garbage bags that lined our panniers.

At last a blue highway sign came into sight: "Tuscarora Summit, Cove Mountains, Elevation 2123 ft." Beyond it, the road curved sharply and disappeared. A rough building with dark windows stood at the tip-top behind an empty gravel parking area: The Mountain House.

Mary pulled her bike onto the narrow concrete porch of The Mountain House just as the rain grew heavier. I quickly followed, thrilled that we'd reached the top and shelter just in time. Sheets of rain fell off the roof, creating gray walls around the rectangle of porch. After leaning her bike, Mary sat on the concrete and leaned against the building's stone wall. Silently, she got out her almonds.

It was ten AM. Did The Mountain House open for lunch? Did I want it to? The desolate restaurant sheltered us, but it also looked menacing, with its tiny windows, and all the beer signs.

Sometimes the trip seemed blessed, with people offering places to stay, like Joe or the librarian in Fort Loudon last night. But other times, like now, people or places seemed menacing. Was the perception accurate, the result of intuition, or was it phony, varying with my mood?

What caused my mood to change? I'd been in such a bad mood at lunch two days ago. I'd been daydreaming all morning, which was hard not to do during the long stretches of biking. Daydreams could make me happy, bursting with whatever wonderful story I created. But sometimes, daydreams made me unhappy, worrying about situations I'd fabricated. Had that happened two days ago?

Now, fog rolled across the mountaintop as the rain came harder; thunder drummed in the distance. We had shelter, but the weather didn't seem likely to improve. We'd have to leave sometime. My fingers fumbled to unzip my handlebar bag and pull out the Pennsylvania map. I'd left it folded to our current section—it took us a few days to cross one fold. I found Fort Loudon and followed the road west. A town called McConnellsburg sat just beyond this pass.

I hated riding in thunderstorms. And I was cold, even in my waterproof gear.[2] Mary had only a light wind breaker; she must be cold, too. I sat next to Mary and held up the map, trying to keep it off our wet clothes. "There's a town four miles ahead. We could find somewhere to eat and warm up, and maybe the weather will clear." She glanced at the map and agreed. So after another minute, we pulled ourselves up and prepared to go back out into the rain.

The road dropped steeply. Mary coasted into the fog and disappeared. I couldn't bring myself to coast without brakes; I kept imagining my front wheel popping off, my body flying over the handlebar as the front fork dug into the pavement. So I coasted with the brakes half on. How long would it take to wear out my brake pads?

As the road leveled, a branch of lightning struck down from the clouds ahead, where the road climbed again into foggy hills. I had a *Lord of the Rings* moment as I scanned the hills, imagining dwarf mines hidden beneath them and a month-long journey to cross them. I got the feelings I always got from mountains: remote, vast, empty, sad. I turned from the lonely hills and rolled down the exit ramp, where a sign pointed left to McConnellsburg.

When I reached the town's one intersection, Mary's fluorescent rain covers caught my eye. She stood in front of a house across the street, talking to six or seven older ladies who sat on the porch, safe from the rain. I pedaled over, smiling hello. She was telling them about our trip.

One of the women, a big woman in front, spoke out. "You go down to Johnny's Motel and tell 'em Nana Joan sent you," she said. "I take care of the transients 'round here, and I guess you count." I wasn't sure about that, but I didn't argue. I knew we *could* pay for the room, and Nana Joan's money could help someone else. But we *wouldn't* pay for a room; we'd sleep outside.

"Things just keep happening to us," Mary said as we walked to Johnny's.

We checked into the brick motel. Our room came with dinner and breakfast at Johnny's Diner next door. "I wonder if all the rooms come with dinner," Mary said, "Or if we're getting the 'Nana Joan Special.'"

We pulled our bikes under the overhang that ran the length of the building and unloaded our things. Our plastic-lined panniers hadn't leaked, but everything still felt damp.

Mary had the first shower. When the water came on, strange moaning noises began in the wall. I laid out my books and maps under the bedside lamp to dry. When Mary emerged, she crawled straight into bed.

"Wait until you hear the noises the shower makes," I said, grinning.

"Maybe this is the room they reserve for the transients."

In the middle of the night, a massive lightning storm rocked against the windows. I lay awake thinking of our bikes; we were being sheltered, we and our bikes. I was glad we'd leaned them against the wall. I'd almost leaned mine on the exposed roof post, so that I could lock it.

In the morning, I got up and began packing, but Mary stayed in bed with her head beneath the covers. Rain still fell. I didn't particularly want to leave, but we couldn't stay in the motel another night; getting on our bikes and going was our only option. But how could I get Mary to go? Was she merely procrastinating, or too depressed to move? As nine o'clock neared, I sat on the edge of my bed and thought out a helpless little prayer for guidance.

A convenience store stood across the road. "I'll go get us some baggies," I told Mary, putting on my raincoat. We'd discussed using small plastic bags to try to keep our feet dry.

In the store, I found a box of half size trash bags. I took a pack of peanut butter cups for Mary, but then I saw the gum ball machine and changed my mind. Peanut butter cups were my favorite, but Mary liked red and yellow, and I suspected a gum ball would excite her.

Back in the motel room, I gave Mary the bright red gum ball. She sat up and put it in her mouth. A minute later, she got up and began to dress. We both put garbage bags over our dry socks and pulled our shoes over them.

The road west from McConnellsburg climbed up and then down, one hill after another. Why did the hills have to keep coming? With yesterday's big climb, I'd reached the top. I kept expecting it to last, just as I expected to stay dry, even when it began to rain again.

But today the rain tapered off, and in spite of the clouds and chill, the air felt drier. I reminded myself to look at the view of forested hills. After about ten miles, the road began to climb without stopping. I imagined I'd round each bend to see the top—marked with a blue highway sign—but instead rounded it to see another loop of road winding upward. Even when I saw no trees beyond the curve, only sky, the road kept climbing. And it was steeper.

At last the blue sign appeared: "Sideling Hill Summit, Blue Ridge Mountains, Elevation 2195."

"Thank God," I thought. I pulled into the turnout and stretched. Then, crunching on raw green beans and honey-roasted peanuts, I sat on the gravel to wait for Mary. The clouds were clearing; a fresh breeze blew. Across the road were bright yellow warning signs. They warned trucks of the long, steep downhill—I'd just come up three and one-half miles at eight percent grade!

A man in a pickup truck pulled in and called out his window, "She's on her way—almost here!" I smiled and waved, and he waved and pulled out.

After Mary arrived, we rolled together down the other side. At the bottom sat Fat Jimmy's Outfitters. Just last night, I'd called a bike mechanic friend in

Chapel Hill, who'd recommended I carry a spare tire, and here was a place to buy it. The salesman twisted and zip-tied my new tire into a neat circle, and I looped a bungee cord through it, adding it to the pile on the rack of my bike. I also bought a canvas bag to hold my sleeping pad; I'd been using a garbage bag, but it might rip. Mary bought warm socks.

After that, we aimed for a town called Bedford, where we planned to sleep. For a while the road stayed flat. But then the hills resumed. "They're not getting any easier!" I thought. Instead of accepting them, my mood sank with each new hill.

By the end of the day, everything Mary said sounded snippy. "Don't take it personally," I told myself, knowing that the long day affected both our moods. But I had no willpower. Instead, I shut down every time she spoke, and grumbled against her in my head.

More clouds had moved in and the wind now whipped across us. In Bedford, we saw a Catholic church. It was Saturday night again—a week ago we'd been setting up our tent in the cemetery—and we'd arrived just in time for mass, so we parked and went in. Since Mary's family was Catholic, the church felt welcoming. I was glad just to sit and rest.

After the service, Mary and I met the priest at the door. He shook our hands. "We're on a bike trip," Mary said, "and wondered if we could sleep in the church." In the church? I'd have asked to camp outside.

The priest hesitated. Dark clouds swirled in the sky, and wind gusted in the door. "I can't let you sleep in the church, but you could sleep in the garage at the rectory," the priest said. So after the church emptied, we followed him home. He showed us a side door to the garage where we could enter.

The garage smelled like gasoline, but it was dry and protected from the wind. Shelves lined the walls, filled with cans of paint and plastic jugs of cleaner. Bags of potting soil, buckets, planters, a wheelbarrow, and a lawnmower all sat on the dirty floor, and a cluster of yard tools stood against the wall, but there was plenty of space in the middle.

We spread the tent's tarp on the cement, then unrolled our pads and sleeping bags. Even with the pads, our beds looked hard. But dry.

We cooked dinner out of the wind by the side of the garage, and then left our things and walked to town. Partly this was to find a bathroom, and partly we wanted to treat ourselves to a night out. We'd dutifully saved Darlene's five dollars for the past week and now went to a bar to spend it on "a drink" as ordered. I felt guilty for drinking when we were staying at a church, but Mary pointed out that Catholics don't have a problem with alcohol the way some religions do.

I pictured Mary and myself entering a rustic Old West scene, or a bar where men in turn-of-the-century suits toasted before going home to dinner. Instead, the place was like any other bar I'd been in, with dark rooms and gloomy customers. We sat at the counter and ordered beers. I remained tense even though no one approached us.

I hadn't been missing home, but suddenly I did. It was as if, once we left our bikes in the garage, we returned to the ordinary world, and thoughts from that world crept in. What was going on in Chapel Hill? My friend Bill's band had a show that night. Who'd be there? Did they miss me?

*Why did Cory suddenly stop hanging out with me—what had I done wrong?* Had I done anything wrong? I automatically thought I had, but reasoning showed that maybe I hadn't.

I'd hoped to eliminate these irrational responses, like "I did something wrong" or "He's mad at me." I'd thought the trip might help, and I'd thought I was improving.

Now that I'd left my bike and returned to "the real world," though, I realized I hadn't gotten better at anything. I'd simply filled some of the brain space with new worries: "Where will we sleep?" and "Will they mind if we use their restroom?" Now, at the bar, I didn't have to think about where to sleep, and old worries returned.

Had I always been like this? I'd experienced depression since my teens, but now I noticed the thoughts running rampant in my head, worries and self-doubts and interpretations of other people's actions. Had these thoughts always been there?

"Are you gonna have another one?" Mary asked.

"Nah, it'll put me to sleep. You?"

"No, I don't want to spend the money." Unlike me, Mary had a strict budget for the trip. Did she think I wasted money? My imagination leapt ahead, imagining the things Mary might think. *Maybe she thinks I'm wasteful because I bought that eleven dollar storage bag at the outdoor store. She keeps her pad in a garbage bag.* Then my thoughts defended my actions against accusations Mary hadn't made: *I want to take care of the pad so it'll last! I'm saving money in the long run.*

I'd been so excited to have a "night out," and it hadn't been any fun. I started to see a pattern of feeling fine in the morning but terrible by the end of the day, when I was tired. And biking made me more tired than usual; maybe it made my moods more extreme. I resented Mary if she took the bigger piece of a chocolate bar or used the camp stove first without asking. I didn't want to be like that.

Depressed, I accompanied Mary back to the garage. "At least we have the garage," I thought. A garage was a unique spot to add to our growing list of sleeping sites: backyard, cemetery, campground, town park, state park, churchyard, motel, and now garage—the funniest place by far. If only I'd known how much funnier it was going to get.

BY LATE MORNING, WE'D LEFT behind the interstate and mess of roads that crossed our route at Bedford. We followed a river, the flat road passing under a leafy ceiling. Then we left the riverside for yellow flowering fields, and the wind blew across us. The sun peeked in and out of billowy clouds. Out in the open, the wind slowed me more than a hill! I tried singing to pass the time; "Blowin' in the Wind" seemed appropriate, but I didn't know the words.

"How, are the times, of a man, um-de-ahhh . . . before he's asleep on the sand?" I sang. "How many laaa, da-da, white dog ale, before it's for contraband?!" When I reached the chorus, I belted it out.

The road left the river for good and began to climb. I caught up with Mary. "I've been singing 'Blowin' in the Wind'!" I called out.

"Ha!" She laughed. "So was I!"

After lunch in West End, where we cooked pasta under an oak tree in the cemetery because the "town" was nothing but houses, the wind only increased. The road rolled over one hill after another, with sloping fields on all sides under a blue sky and white clouds. We weren't climbing mountain passes, but these hills were worse, with the wind buffeting us across the open space. At least it wasn't raining.

The hills culminated with a long climb. I pushed and pushed, waiting to see some sign of the top; this hill had to be steeper than the others. Ten minutes passed, then twenty. The hill went on forever. The wind kept gusting at my side.

At last I saw the back of a large sign in the other direction—the downhill warning sign for trucks. As I struggled past the sign, I looked backward: "Trucks Test Brakes, 14% Grade, 1 ½ miles." Fourteen percent! Mary waited at the top. We coasted into the next town.

## Ohiopyle, in which things begin to clear up . . . for now

IN TEN DAYS WE'D HAD rain, thunder and lightning, cold, fog, strong wind in our faces, and long, steep hills. But we'd never had them all at once, only warm, rainy thunderstorms, or sunny, windy days with hills. The morning we got on the Allegheny Highlands Trail, my wet fingers clutched my handlebar, stiff with cold, but it quickly became apparent that the trail, winding alongside the Casselman River, was perfectly flat. Crushed gravel slushed under our tires as we pedaled, and rain pattered down through the leafy canopy.

Until now, power lines and parking lots had marred the view. But here, trees, rocks, and the wide, rushing river filled every scene. On our left rose a forested hillside. The sounds of the road had disappeared—the rush of cars, the howl of a semi hitting its brakes as it bore down on us. Instead, a peaceful pitter-patter filled the air, and my breathing, and the louder patter of collected rain dripping when the wind stirred the trees. At times the crunch-crunch-crunch of my tires rose above the soft noises; at other times the river grew louder, when it cascaded over rocks.

In spite of the peaceful scenery, I counted down the mile markers, looking forward to being warm and dry. We had thirty-six miles to cover to Ohiopyle State Park. "Look at the scenery!" I reminded myself again, scanning the river.

But before I realized it, I was watching the ground roll under my tire, waiting for the next mile marker. I didn't stop for pictures; it would've been hard to work the zipper on my bag with my frigid hands. The constant drizzle would've soaked the camera by the time I snapped the picture.

The cold worsened as the day progressed. My gloves had proven not to be waterproof as advertised, merely thick enough to keep off rain for several hours. By midday, the rain had soaked through, creating giant sponges that I couldn't wring out. Water had penetrated the plastic bags around my socks, so my pedaling feet swished along like they were in a fish tank. I couldn't stop wishing we were at Ohiopyle.

The trail crossed the river and abutted a road near a town called Rockwood. We could see only one building. Mary had decided to buy better rain gear, and as the building passed, we realized it was a discount clothing store! Two days before, I'd decided I needed a spare tire and Fat Jimmy's Outfitters had appeared, and now Mary needed rain gear and we found this. We turned off the trail and biked over.

A bell dinged as we entered, dripping. I tried to shake myself out near the door. A woman walked out of a back room. "Come on in!" she said. "You must be freezing! Would you like some tea?"

Mary and I nodded and smiled. "Do you have rain gear?" Mary asked. The clerk pointed toward a rack.

I left my coat by the door and wandered along the nearest rack, thumbing through outdated sweaters and nylon slacks like my grandma used to wear. Mary returned with a full yellow rain suit—the rubber kind—for twenty dollars.

The clerk talked incessantly while we had tea. I wanted to feel grateful for the welcome and the hot tea, but instead I sat on edge, irritated with her unending conversation. Why was I irritated? Was I just tired from biking? I'd thought I was a kind and patient person, but it didn't seem like it now. Mary socialized while I guiltily sipped my tea—Mary deserved the tea, keeping up the conversation the way she did.

After thirty minutes, Mary suited up in her new gear, and we headed out. The rain had momentarily abated, so we stopped for a picture at the trailhead. Mary balanced her camera on a concrete post and turned it to face me on the trail. She pushed the timer and ran to join me. Then we stood like two rubber ducks, smiling under our helmets and waiting for the camera to click. Mary fumbled to fit her camera back into its case, and then we set off down the trail. Only twenty-eight miles to go.

We left the trail again for a late lunch in the town of Confluence. As we emerged from the forest and rode up a hill into the town, gusts of wind hit my side. I focused on keeping my balance as I crossed the town square, but when I rounded the corner and met the wind head on, it was too hard to ride. The trail, down by the river, had been protecting us from this terrible wind!

Gray rain filled the deserted square, slanting sideways or churning chaotically in the evil wind. "Are there more tornados?" I wondered as I pushed my bike alongside Mary. We'd heard a news report yesterday of tornados. The sky looked greenish. We must've looked insane.

Only one building in Confluence had lights on and cars out front: Luigi's Place, which we found down a narrow side street. We parked against its wall and entered.

A trio of people looked up from the bar. Unsmiling, they eyed us from their seats, cigarettes slowly burning in their hands. A puddle began forming around me.

I wiped my feet on the doormat, emphasizing the motions to show that I was trying not to dirty their floor. It didn't look all that clean to begin with. The woman leaning on the bar snapped her gum, watching as I struggled to wiggle out of my sopping coat. Finally, one of the seated staff slid off her barstool and begrudgingly carried her mass across the ten feet to where we stood. She reached up to take two menus off a shelf, let out a small sigh, and in a monotone, addressed a spot slightly over my head: "Two for lunch?"

"Maybe this isn't a restaurant at all," I thought, joking with myself. "Maybe it's a cover for a drug smuggling ring, and all the locals know it and avoid the place, and we're ignorant strangers who've wandered inside." Mary must've answered "Yes" because the woman turned and waddled to a doorway opposite the bar. At least we wouldn't have to eat near the sour-looking, smoke-churning staff.

Dank air filled the dimly lit dining room. Dark wood paneled the walls, adding to the gloom. An ill assortment of artwork hung over the sticky vinyl booths: faded Klimt lovers kissing, an 80s poster of a black-haired woman with triangular purple earrings, a wolf howling over a dull Grand Canyon.

I scanned the menu for vegetarian options: spaghetti. When a waitress brought a breadbasket, I grabbed a roll, unable to wait. My teeth tore into stale bread. The thin waitress, not one of the trio from the front room, returned with two sweating glasses of water, deposited them on the edge of the table, and scurried off. I chugged a mouthful, only to spit back my second mouthful as the horrific, chemical taste of the first hit me. The waitress returned a third time and asked in a shaky voice, "Are you ready to order?"

An hour later, we returned to the blessed wind and rain.

As the name suggested, three rivers met in Confluence: the Casselman, which we'd been following; the smaller Laurel River; and the Youghiogheny (pronounced Yock-uh-gain-ee), which seventy miles later would join the

Monongahela, flowing into Pittsburgh. These final ten miles of the trail along the Youghiogheny River were part of Ohiopyle State Park.

All day we'd had cascades and scenery with a limited palette of greens, browns, and white. Now, towering, thin trees lined the trail so that we biked down a dramatic cathedral aisle. The dark trunks passed in rhythm, the random greenness of the leaves filling the spaces between like stained glass windows.

With the heavy clouds, it felt like twilight. We were soaked, our hands stiff, teeth chattering. It seemed we'd never reach the town. Then the trail widened, and the crunching gravel gave way with a small bump to smooth-rolling concrete. "Is this really it?" I wondered. A building came into view: an old train station. Our bike path lay where the train tracks once had been, and we played the part of the train, pulling into the station.

Warm lights glowed in the station windows as I coasted to a stop. An open door beckoned.

The presence of people lingered in the empty station. Two rolling wooden desk chairs waited in the middle of the hardwood floor, pulled up to a checkerboard resting on a barrel. A pile of checkers sat on top. The ticket window stood open, with a light on in the back room, as if the clerk had stepped away to check a bag. But no one came to the window after we'd clattered inside. I pulled off my hood to enjoy the dry space. I felt magic in the air, like entering the station might transport us back in time; when we exited, we'd find the train tracks running past instead of a bike trail, and a train puffing toward us out of a gloomy night.

Signs in the station welcomed visitors to the park, and a rack of brochures stood by the ticket window. It must've been a slow day—early in the season, with terrible weather—but the visitor center had stayed open . . . like they'd known we were coming. I wanted to get our sleeping bags and lay them on the floor in the glowing warmth of the station. The feeling of magic in the small building made me think we could; no one else seemed to exist in the world.

But someone would kick us out. Some disgruntled park ranger or rule-abiding caretaker would come to close up eventually. Then it would be dark out, as well as wet and cold, and we'd again be looking for somewhere to sleep.

I unfolded a brochure with a map, trying to find the campground. The mesh of lines and dashes swam before my eyes.

"There's a hostel," Mary said from across the room.

"Should we check it out?" I asked.

"Sure." I tucked the map into my pocket and put my hood back up.

We wheeled our bikes down a ramp to the street. Away from the lights of the station, our eyes adjusted to the gloom. It was not yet twilight, but nearing the end of the day. The grid of the town lay in the corner made by the bike path and the river, which rushed at the far side of a green lawn. All the trees budded green. In spite of the wet, deserted streets, I liked Ohiopyle—an outpost with everything one needed: a park by the river, a post office, and a boxy, white church of no particular denomination because it's the only church in town and anyone who wants to attend church has to go to it. I felt sure there'd be a coffee shop here, making Ohiopyle the perfect town.

We came to the hostel: closed for the winter. In the drizzle, I pulled out the map. The swerving brown road lines and dashes of trails still confused me. My brain seemed to be shutting down for the night. "I think we're here," I said, pointing. "And I see the campground, but I don't see which road goes there."

"We could ask at that convenience store," Mary said.

"There was also that motel. We could just see how much it is—it's on the way." I did want to budget, but setting up camp in the rain would be miserable.

We walked back through the town. We reached the motel, with its long arms bordering a square parking lot, and found the office. It cost 140 dollars a night.

"We just can't afford that," Mary said.

The owner suggested we try the convenience store. It had rooms for rent upstairs. We trudged over and inquired—they were sixty dollars.

My tired brain struggled to assess our options: expensive room, wet campground that we hadn't yet found. I looked at Mary. She didn't ask the clerk about the campground, she just nodded. We paid and followed him up a narrow flight of stairs and down a creaky hall to a small room with bare walls. Two double beds were wedged in under a too-high window with a lace curtain. The blue bedspreads resembled oversize bath towels. The only other furniture was a wobbly plastic bar for hanging clothes.

Mary and I carried our gear up the stairs, one load at a time. We hung as much wet clothing as we could on the bar and spread the rest on top of our tent's tarp on the floor. It wouldn't dry overnight, but at least it could start.

"I miss the old days," Mary said, and I knew what she meant. We'd had such good camping for our first week. It seemed like ages ago. Now we kept getting stuck inside. And today we had to deal with wet, sandy gear.

There was nothing to do but shower and go to bed. Alone in the shower, I found myself lingering as the stress left me. I'd never recognized it before, but the shower was an opportunity for alone time. Maybe that's why I'd dawdled in the bathroom as a child: since I'd shared a room with my sister, my only alone time had come in the bathroom. "What are you doing in there?!" Mom would holler. "It's been twenty minutes and I haven't heard the water running!" I'd been talking to myself in the mirror. I'd been wrapping the flowery cotton shower curtain around myself to make it look like a sexy strapless dress. Then

I would stand in the shower in a daze, my thoughts wandering far away without any interruption except the distant sounds my mother would periodically make, which I'd learned to respond to automatically, to keep her from coming to check on me.

Sand swirled in the bottom of the stall as I turned the water off. I stepped in the clear pools to keep my feet clean. Back in our room, the sand coating our gear had started to dry, falling off in chunks. I nudged a bag farther onto the tarp, but a clump of sand dropped onto the inn's rug. I hoped the rain was cleaning the sand off our bikes outside.

Mary lay on her bed. If she felt as weary as I did, she might want to talk, but I just wanted to be silent. Did she sense that and keep quiet for my sake? I knew I should say something nice, in case she needed to talk, but couldn't think what. I wished I could just buy her another gum ball.

"I'm sorry I'm in a terrible mood," I said at last. She made a small noise but didn't move.

I lay down to sleep, lying straight on my back. "I'm empty of kindness," I thought, looking at the ceiling. When I closed my eyes, I felt each grain of sand that had escaped the shower and now roamed my sheets.

THE MORNING DAWNED GRAY BUT no longer rainy. When Mary returned from the bathroom, I pointed to the map. "So Fallingwater's up here." We'd planned to go out of our way to visit the house designed by Frank Lloyd Wright. But something about Ohiopyle drew me in. "I kind of want to stay another night. By the time we get organized, it'll be lunchtime, and we didn't really see the town. We could find the campground, so it won't cost so much."

"We could bike up to Fallingwater for the afternoon," Mary said. I let her suggestion hang in the air. I just wanted to find the campground and stop moving.

To reach the campground, located on something called "Kentuck Knob" on the map, we'd take the bike trail another mile, then turn off onto a hiking trail through the woods. This seemed more scenic than the road.

The Youghiogheny River made an oxbow in Ohiopyle, so that the trail crossed it twice in quick succession. The first bridge came right after the visitor center where we'd stopped the night before. In the middle of the long expanse, I stared in awe at the swollen river rushing below us. Pickle green water churned with white waves and rocky cascades. In the park that lined the town, water rushed over the grass, disrespecting the rocky boundaries of the normal river. A few small trees stood out in the flood, but no large ones.

The view from the second bridge was even more awesome. The land had dropped significantly, so that now the river moved far below us, coursing along between forested hills. Our wooden trestle ran straight as a laser beam, the unnerving length and perspective like an optical illusion, where you might start walking across and never reach the other side. Way down at the far end, the trees opened like the entrance to a tunnel.

Mary and I reached the woods and then the trailhead to the campground. I'd imagined biking up it, but there wasn't a chance: it ascended steeply into the trees, blanketed with last season's leaves, which hid rocks and roots. We soon panted with the effort of pushing our bikes, taking careful steps to avoid twisting an ankle on the unpredictable ground. The steepness only increased as we progressed, until I found myself halted. I summoned my strength, adjusted my footing, and then pushed, rushing uphill. If I could just gain a little momentum before gravity kicked in . . . the effort moved me two feet. Mary was doing something similar. I tried again.

At last we abandoned my bike and concentrated on Mary's, one of us on each side. We struggled to move it, a few feet at a time. After twenty minutes, we reached the top and rolled the bike into a deserted campground. We parked it at a site and trudged back down to retrieve mine.

We'd spent most of the morning packing and moving, but finally I sat still while Mary rode to find the campground office. I had the whole afternoon. At last I had time for silent prayer!

"I will meditate right now," I thought, noticing the silence and peacefulness around me. "In the quiet forest, it should be easy."

I closed my eyes, shifted my seat, looked around once more, then shut my eyes again. A minute ticked past. *How long will Mary be gone?* I tried not to think of it, to focus on sitting. Another minute passed. Two minutes. *Mary must be on her way back.* I opened my eyes. I was alone. I checked my watch: it had only been one minute.

I tried again. A minute passed. *Why is this so hard?* I found myself leaning toward my bags for a snack. I hadn't meant to. I sat back, sat up straight. But then Mary did return. She began setting up camp. *What does she think of me, sitting here?* It was impossible. I opened my eyes and got up.

The clouds had cleared, and pale sunlight shone through the leaves as the damp earth began to dry. We set up the camp stove, and I made pasta for lunch, followed by hot chocolate for dessert. Everything felt cleaner; outside the convenience store, I'd lubed my bike chain to work out the grit from yesterday's trail, and more hot showers awaited us.

I hadn't succeeded in meditating, but at least we were stopped for the day, staying at the nice campsite. Wind stirred the treetops. The river rushed in the distance, and occasionally a train whistle sounded. Mary turned the radio on, and as I got out my journal, the song "Valerie" by Steve Winwood came

through the static, like 1990 reaching out through the years via our solar-powered radio.

I wrote about our adventures the day before on the cold, rainy trail. I'd
failed to capture so many events over the past week, when I hadn't had time
to write, so I captured them now: Johnny's Motel, Sideling Hill, Fat Jimmy's,
Bedford, the Catholic church, our night at the bar, a red barn full of chickens,
lunch in West End—

"I'm going to town," Mary said. I looked up in the middle of my eleventh
page, hesitating.

"I'll go, too." I wanted to see Ohiopyle while I had the chance.

We lurched down the woodland trail to the paved one, then crossed the
bridges toward the visitor center. Below, the town lay like a child's play set, with
its grid of roads, its single church and smattering of buildings. We descended
and traversed the park. The river rushed over the grass at the edge.

"What time is it?" Mary asked. I checked my watch: ten o'clock?

"I think my watch stopped." Now we had no watch between us.

We started up a street. Paint peeled on many of the houses. Boards were
nailed on at imperfect angles, like a camp cabin built by teenagers. "For Rent"
signs hung in windows. We found the House Cafe and scanned the menu by the
door. Salads cost twelve ninety-five! It didn't make sense; no one was here, and
the town was rundown, but salad cost almost thirteen dollars?

There was something afoot that I didn't understand. It felt *alive* here, in
spite of the deserted streets.

We kept walking until we'd seen every street; the other restaurants, the coffee shop, and an out-of-place, chain-store Dairy Queen were all closed.

We passed another nailed-together house with a "Rooms for Rent" sign. It
made me think of somewhere . . . the rafting camp in the Carolina mountains
where I used to visit a raft guide friend. That was the secret: Ohiopyle was
a rafting community. The housing would fill in the summer with raft guides,
while the expensive restaurant would cater to tourists. We'd arrived before the
season began, with the river too swollen to raft, and the weather too cold.

Darkness crept near as we turned toward home. The visitor center once
again glowed in welcome, waiting for someone new to enter town. Would anyone arrive tonight, out of the trees? Mary and I crossed the lower bridge. The
river should calm down for the night, I thought, when stores closed and lights
went out and the wind died. But the river never rested. We stopped on the second bridge and faced upriver. Over the trees, colors like abalone shone in the
western sky.

## Western Pennsylvania, in which I begin to question the efficacy of worrying

I BEGAN TO NOTICE THAT, UNLIKE in modern subdivisions with meaningless names (e.g., Rustling Pines with no pine trees in sight), town and road names could mean something. I now dreaded roads with names like "High Ridge Road" and "Windy Mountain Pass." An especially bad sign was a name referring to a weather tower.

That afternoon, we climbed a pass to the town of Summit, where the Summit Hotel nestled into the hillside facing west. Afternoon sun lit its Mission-style towers. A curvy, red roofline came to a point over the grand front door.

We pulled into the parking lot to catch our breath, and Mary went in to use the restroom. I stood by our bikes, wanting to see inside but worried that someone might notice I wasn't a guest and ask me to leave. "Who cares?" I told myself. "If they do, you'll just leave." But I took a picture of the hotel instead.

We coasted down the pass into the buildings of Uniontown, rundown factories with broken brick doorways and boarded windows. Was it safe here? The factories gave way to houses with tired-looking people on the stoops, drinking out of brown paper bags, like a museum display of poor, downtrodden Americans. They watched us ride by.

A Catholic church appeared, perched on a hill behind a chain-link fence. An open gate led to a lot filled with cars. "No Trespassing" signs hung on the chain link. Could we go in? Mary did so I followed.

At the door, two men sat at a table with a moneybox. Inside, a crowd buzzed in a large room.

"We were wondering if we could camp on the lawn," Mary said.

The men exchanged glances. "We'd better get Father Thomas," one said. "He's passing out chips." He disappeared into the hall. A minute later, he returned with a man my age, small and thin with spectacles. I'd been expecting an old man; how did someone so young lead a congregation? Did he really know all his beliefs already?

Mary explained our trip, and Father Thomas nodded. "Why don't you go stay at Mount Saint Macrina. It's the church's monastery, it's a few miles west. I think you'd be more comfortable."

"I'm going to meet nuns!" I thought. I imagined one of them my age, and how I'd ask what her life was like . . . was it filled with silent prayer?

I also wondered if Father Thomas thought we'd be safer at the convent.

Father Thomas described the entrance, opposite the Uniontown Mall. We thanked him and left, wondering if his directions were any good, but soon the mall parking lot spread out on our left, and we saw the monastery's sign.

The chaos of the road faded as we biked up a winding, twilit drive. To the east, atop the forested mountain, the white dot of the Summit Hotel shone in the sunset. The drive curved around a bend and a mansion loomed before us.

A middle-aged woman answered our knock. She wasn't dressed like a stereotypical nun, just wearing a plain dress, with short hair and a cross hanging from her neck.

"Father Thomas sent us," I said immediately. At the mention of his name, her questioning look faded. "We stopped at the church, to see if we could camp, and he thought we'd be more comfortable camping here."

"Oh, we can put you in the dormitory!" she said and invited us in. "I'm Sister Carol. Would you like something to eat?"

"We're okay, we've got food," Mary replied. After we explained our trip, Sister Carol retrieved a key and led us outside to a brick building with dark wood trim that made me think of a summer camp. Inside, dozens of metal beds with thin mattresses stood in four long rows.

"Why don't you join us for breakfast?" Sister Carol said. Then she continued, sounding worried. "We eat early, though, and then go in to prayers."

"What time?" I wanted to meet the other sisters.

"Eight-thirty." We agreed to go for breakfast if we awoke in time.

We left our things at the monastery and walked down the driveway to the mall. Like in Bedford, it felt weird to "go out," away from our bikes, and even weirder to go to a mall, the antithesis of our minimalist bike trip travel. Once inside, the cool cleanness of it all subsumed me—the fragrances, the clothes, the food smells. In my usual life, I considered this atmosphere false and devoid of humanity; malls represented sprawl, they encouraged people to drive instead of walking, and they ruined the small businesses located in cute town centers. Yet now the mall appealed—why?

I liked feeling anonymous; no one knew we were out-of-towners on a bike trip. And I felt that I deserved to buy something indulgent. Walking past the shops, I struggled to stay focused on my goal: a watch battery. As I'd antici-pated, the mall had a Radio Shack with batteries; the sameness of malls came in handy. Maybe mall-goers appreciated malls the way I had appreciated the Louvre in Paris: after an unpleasant day of being unable to communicate in French, I'd escaped to the Louvre, knowing it would be similar to other art museums and therefore easy to navigate.

WE GOT UP IN TIME for breakfast. Excited as we walked to the mansion, I imag-ined a long table of women in traditional habits, some of them my age. I want-ed to ask about being a nun; was it possible to live a monastic life without being Catholic? The idea of escaping the world and living in solitude and prayer had always fascinated me. As a teenager, I'd read an article about a weekend getaway where you stayed with monks and took a vow of silence. I hadn't had the free-dom to do it then, and afterward I'd forgotten.

But it turned out only three sisters of the Order of Sisters of St. Basil the Great currently lived at the monastery: Carol, Barbara Jean, and the elderly, quiet Thomasina. They wore normal clothes, although Thomasina had a veil on her head. They'd set the table like an Easter display at a chain store pharmacy: purple place mats on a yellow tablecloth, with silk daffodils in a vase in the middle. It was touching that they'd decorated for us . . . or did they decorate the table every morning?

Carol had microwaved frozen pancakes with tiny pinkish-purple blueber-ries and opened a bag of cinnamon raisin toast. The sisters asked about our trip, telling us they'd included us in their early prayers, and after we ate, Carol gave us a tour of the building, a mansion built by a coal baron that the church had bought when he went broke. The church used the mansion grounds for retreats; I liked to think of kids playing ball on the lawns and happy families sleeping in the dormitory beds. It contrasted with the dying feel of the town: the closed factories, the expired coal. Even the mall was closing, the sisters told us.

I called my parents from the phone in the kitchen, using my phone card. "We're at a convent," I said, grinning. "We had breakfast with the nuns."

"Oh, my!" Mom said. "Be sure you thank them. Are you paying for this call?"

Then we took pictures with the sisters and promised to send postcards. We had a long day ahead: Mary and I aimed to reach the oddly named Ryerson Station State Park on the western border of the state, more than fifty miles away. We'd been in Pennsylvania for two weeks. We were eager to reach the border, as if we'd make faster progress once we escaped the state. The nuns told us they would continue to pray for us and sent us off with bananas and cookies.

I HADN'T SEEN MARY ALL morning. Usually she passed me, but today I'd been flying down Route 40, high on the nuns' sugary raisin toast. But five minutes after I stopped to eat my banana, a state trooper's car approached and slowed. The handlebar of a bike poked up in the back seat. What had happened? Was she hurt? I scrambled up.

The car pulled over, and Mary hopped out. "What happened?"

"My bag cover caught in the derailleur. It got all bent, the chain won't move." The cover had caught just after she'd pushed off, when her speed was slow. If she'd been coasting downhill, she could've wrecked. The troopers had seen her sitting by her bike. ("They asked if I had a flat tire," Mary told me later, "and I wanted to say, 'If I had a flat tire, I'd fix it, not start crying!'")

The trooper in the driver's seat hung up a phone and got out. "The nearest shop's in Connellsville. But I talked to Otto's, and he has a derailleur he can put on." Connellsville was thirty-five miles back the way we'd come, but Otto's was just half a mile back.

"Sounds good," Mary said.

The trooper looked at me. "We can come back for you . . . ?"

"Oh, I'll ride! So it's just back that way?" He nodded, and they left.

I rode after them and soon saw a gravel driveway with a large, peeling white sign that read, "OTTO'S AUTO'S AND MORE" in puffy black letters. Words floated around the title: "ATV's, Automobiles, Chain saws." The bottom of the sign read, "OTTO'S 'AUTO' AND 'BIKE' REPAIR" with the words "auto" and "bike" enclosed in quotes as if they were code for some other service. Under that, the sign advertised "brake pads & tires," "garage sale," and "new & used washers." Behind the sign, a row of hot tubs filled a dirt turnout.

I bumped up the gravel drive into trees, waving when the troopers passed on their way out. The drive opened into a pebbly lot strewn with busted-looking automobiles, with a garage at the far side. I kept riding until I spotted a cluster of appliances near the building: white washing machines and ovens mingled with the odd olive-green refrigerator. I leaned my bike on a huge, chocolate-brown fridge and approached Mary, who came out a side door of the garage. A burly man was talking to her.

"I think I can get that dee-ray-ler on, but I have to run some errands for Reggie first."

Mary thanked him, and he got in a truck and left. Two younger mechanics sat in the rolled-up door of the garage, but neither looked at us. Mary and I returned to the lot and sat. Would the man return? Could he fix Mary's bike?

"Reggie must be the owner," Mary said.

"Maybe he inherited the business from Otto."

"Look, there he is." A beefy man strode into the garage. One of the young mechanics moved to lean over an open hood. The other, tall and lanky, continued to sit immobile in an office chair. He appeared to be playing video games.

"That's Reggie's little brother," I said.

Fifteen minutes slowly passed. "The officers didn't want to leave me here," Mary said. She ate a cookie from the nuns.

"I'm glad they're praying for us," I thought. "I hope it works."

My nerves squirmed inside each time I wondered what would happen. Hoping to calm them, I dug out my journal. "May 15, 2 PM," I wrote. "Oddly, after being prayed for by nuns, we're now sitting in a field of automobiles, waiting for the guy who thought he could rig up a derailleur to fit on Mary's bike." I stopped writing. I couldn't focus with the anxiety in my chest.

After thirty minutes, the man hadn't returned. *What if he doesn't? What if night comes and we're still here?*

"Maybe Reggie would drive us to that bike shop in Connellsville," I said. "We'd have to redo thirty-five miles, but at least we'd be sure of getting your bike fixed."

"We might as well ask." My nerves jangled as we stood and spotted Reggie, now strutting through the rusting autos. He kept moving as we approached, so we had to trot after him. There was a wolf tattooed on the back of his calf, and it bulged in and out as he walked, as if it were panting.

"Excuse me, we wondered if you might give us a ride to Connellsville?" Mary said. "The state troopers said there's a bike shop there." My face burned.

Reggie grunted with a shake of his head. He kept moving without looking at us. "Got deliveries to make."

We let him go. "He could've at least looked at us," I mumbled when he was out of earshot. We returned to our seats. I found myself resenting Reggie, even though I knew we'd asked for a lot.

Reggie continued to walk through the vehicles until a flashy car pulled up. A woman in short shorts, a halter top, and sunglasses got out and sidled over to him. She pressed herself against his leg and ran her hands over his chest as he grinned down at her. Then they walked to his truck, his hand on her bottom, and drove down the drive.

The sudden development distracted me from my worries. "Deliveries, eh?" I said to Mary. She grinned.

But as another fifteen minutes ticked past, my worries returned. Should we keep waiting? What else could we do? *Where is he? We've been sitting here forever.* Another minute dragged by.

Then a truck barreled down the drive, and I recognized the driver as the man who'd said he'd help. My heart leapt. As we wheeled Mary's bike toward the shop, he came to meet us.

"Well, let's take a look at that dee-ray-ler," he said, clamping her bike into a stand. The new derailleur didn't fit, so he drilled out a hole to make it work and fiddled with the gear cables until the bike could shift. Mary could only use three gears, but the bike was fixed.

My worry evaporated. "Thank you so much!" Mary said.

"I didn't know what we'd do if you couldn't fix it." I didn't say that I'd feared he wouldn't come back at all. As we laughed, the two young mechanics came over. I wished we'd met them sooner. In my anxious state, I'd imaged them unfriendly, but they were nice.

The man charged Mary ten dollars, and we returned to the road.

We had forty-four miles left to Ryerson Station State Park. The ride must have taken hours, but all I remember is flying over the road late in the day as clouds moved in. We'd climbed yet another hill, but this time the road had continued along the ridgetop. To the south, dark clouds gathered as the wind began to whip at my hair. I pedaled harder. Could we beat the storm to Ryerson Station and pitch our tent before it rained?

A green sign flashed past: "Wind Ridge." Then a row of houses flew by, facing south, and I registered that people sat on their porches to watch the storm. "Wind Ridge is special," flickered in my head, "like Ohiopyle and Strasburg!" I wanted a picture, but the wind gusted and I kept biking. After the houses, the road dropped.

I flew down the hill. Just in time, I spotted our turn and squeezed my brakes. Screeching, I slowed and turned. I followed Mary into trees. Thunder rumbled as we rolled into the park past a small lake. We pulled up at a kiosk. Ryerson Station referred to a small hydroelectric plant! A posted map showed the campground—up a steep, gravel driveway. The ranger station was closed.

"Let's just pitch our tent here," I said. A lawn spread out along the lake. We didn't waste time deliberating. Soon the tent was pitched, but the wind faded and with it, the threat of rain.

We hurried through our evening routines as darkness fell. Instead of taking turns with the stove, we shared pasta with fresh zucchini, mushrooms, and garlic. At last we could slow down. "I can't believe we made it!" I said between bites.

"I know."

I thought about the nuns' prayers. Mary could've been hurt, if the bag had caught as she rushed downhill. And what were the chances of a repair shop being half a mile from where I'd stopped?

Now that things had worked out, I wished I had not ruined the afternoon by worrying. But how? It was so hard. The worried thoughts came constantly, and when I grew tired, it got worse. Was there a better method than trying to fight each thought as it came? Could meditation (or "sitting still," as I was starting to think of it, because full-on meditation was far too hard) help? If I sat still regularly, would my brain be calmer?

Anyway, I felt thankful that Reggie *hadn't* given us a ride—we'd have been back where we'd started the day. Instead, we camped just a few miles from the border.

## West Virginia into Ohio, in which I resolve to stop worrying

JUST OVER THE WEST VIRGINIA border, our map ran out. I wasn't worried. The thrill of reaching the border still tingled in my brain.

Mary and I coasted along a ridgetop, enjoying the murky blue-gray clouds and windy day and the fact that we stayed at the top of a hill, with a downhill in our future. We needed to go to Wheeling, West Virginia, to a shop where Mary could get a proper derailleur. I figured when our road ended, we'd just try to keep heading north.

But a store stood at the end of the road. "Do you have maps?" I asked the clerk, a plump woman in a tee shirt with a row of birdhouses on it.

"Well, I can't let you take it," she said, turning slowly to pull a map from the piles of stuff behind the counter. "I've just got this one." She unfolded it and spread it on the counter. "I'm Dolores. Where you headed?"

"Wheeling," I said, spotting it on the map and tracing a road that led there.

"That road's going to be hilly," Dolores said. She traced a different line. "You could take the Knoxville Road to Moundsville. It follows the creek, it's nice and flat." From Moundsville, we'd follow the Ohio River north to

Wheeling. It seemed like a good plan, although I had doubts about roads described by non-bikers as "nice and flat."

Mary and I chatted with Dolores and ate snacks (which Dolores wouldn't let us pay for). Then we set off for the Knoxville Road. The first road we reached was unmarked and dropped steeply.

"Do you think this is it?" I said.

"I don't know." There was no one to ask.

"Should we try?" If we were wrong, we'd have to climb back up that hill; but what if this was the turn, and we kept going? "Let's try it," I said.

I let go and coasted off the ridge, breezing down until the road leveled out and followed a creek, as Dolores had said. The road was twisty but flat, and the miles passed easily. As lunchtime neared, the road deposited us in the center of Moundsville.

We split up for lunch because Mary wanted pizza and I wanted to see the local diner. I slid onto a seat at the counter, hoping the waitresses might talk to me. I'd always thought I needed quiet time to recharge, but the past two weeks, I'd noticed that sometimes talking had the same effect.

At the library after lunch, we asked the librarian for a map. They had no normal, fold-up maps, only topographical maps in giant volumes sitting dusty in the reference section. We found northern West Virginia and searched for roads from Moundsville to Wheeling amidst the topography contours. I found Dolores's road; it passed through a long-gone town called Knoxville, which must be why Dolores called it "the Knoxville Road." I saw the twisting creek and the intersection at Dolores's store. It all made sense now that it was over—a bike trip metaphor for life.

Later that evening, we sat reading in our tent, pitched by the parking lot behind a church just south of Wheeling. A car pulled in. Was someone coming to kick us out?

"Why don't you stay here, and I'll see who it is," I said to Mary. If they only saw me, they wouldn't know that we were both women.

I crawled out of the tent. A crowded car was parked twenty feet away. As I walked over, the teenage guys inside noticed me without interest.

"Do you know where there's a liquor store that won't card us?" one asked as I neared the open window.

"Sorry," I said, shaking my head. "I thought you were from the church, coming to kick us out." I gave an awkward wave and returned to my book.

The book—the first I'd had time to read—was *Tisha,* the true story of a young woman teaching in the Alaskan wilderness in the 1920s. After sitting on my bookshelf for years, the worn paperback had caught my eye when I was packing for the trip. I'd started it a few days ago, reading of Tisha's decision to go to Alaska and the trek to her post in a remote town. So far, the weather and wild animals were her enemies, not other people. But I wondered: were people worse now than they used to be?

When the light faded, Mary lay down and went to sleep. I couldn't read any longer, but I couldn't sleep, either. I listened for prowlers, or for another car pulling in. Mary's presence didn't calm me. The rest of the night passed quietly, but I never slept for long.

WE SPENT THE NEXT MORNING in Wheelcraft, the bike shop in Wheeling, and then set off toward the Ohio River. But then my tire went flat. I walked back to Wheelcraft to get it fixed, to save time. Then a library distracted us, followed by a Mexican restaurant just as raindrops started to fall; by the time we got underway, it was midafternoon and drizzling steadily.

I turned onto the historic suspension bridge over the Ohio River, vibrating down the open-grate roadway. Thick, rusty cables supported the bridge from archaic stone towers. Old houses, churches, and brick factories peeked out from the greenery on the opposite shore. I dropped off the end with a thunk, and low buildings sprang up on both sides as the road climbed away from the river, winding back and forth as it slithered into Ohio.

Our map, photocopied from the library in Moundsville, ran out a few miles into Ohio. Yesterday, I hadn't worried when we rode off the Pennsylvania map. It had been morning, and I had been flying high from crossing the border. But today, in an afternoon drizzle, I anxiously scanned the roadside for a convenience store or gas station, seeing only "useless" businesses like auto parts places, hair salons, and lamp stores. Ohio loomed like a vast wilderness.

We kept going, always uphill, with traffic at our shoulders until finally the road widened. The pavement changed to fresh black, bordered with patches of new grass. An overpass and exit ramps appeared ahead. Just past the interstate, a modern gas station stood on a hill. I pushed myself up this final incline.

As I rolled into a parking spot, a truck pulled in next to me. A woman rolled down the window. Barrettes held back her brown hair, which exploded with frizz behind them. "Where are you coming from?" she asked, leaning out her window and staring. She didn't turn off her engine; had she pulled over just to talk to me?

"New Jersey."

"Where you headed?"

Should I tell a stranger where we'd be camping? Not that I knew. "The Pacific!" I said. "But today, we don't know. Our map just ran out."

She reached beside her and picked up a map, opening it on the steering wheel. "See here is Barkcamp State Park, just twenty miles down the road. You can camp at my site. I'm Amanda." She folded the map, leaving open the section we were in, and handed it to me, saying, "Keep it." Mary had arrived, and we both thanked Amanda

As we biked through the rainy afternoon, I marveled over my encounter with Amanda. The universe had conspired to keep us in Wheeling, first with my flat tire, then with the library and Mexican restaurant, making our timing perfect to meet Amanda. I hadn't connected with her, but her offer to share her site felt fortuitous, as if we were on track, at the right place and time.

I kept thinking how miserable we'd be if we hadn't had a destination. It was hard enough deciding where to sleep in clear weather; rain made it worse. And when we reached the park office, the rangers grinned and said, "It's the bikers!" I grinned back as they handed us a map of the campground and marked the way to Amanda's site. Amanda built a fire, which made standing in the drizzle almost pleasant. She even let us drive her truck to the bathhouse, across the campground, so we'd stay warm and dry after showering.

The next morning, we said goodbye to Amanda and rode west into Ohio. I hadn't expected the landscape to change at the border, but it was flatter, rolling gently up and down. I imagined myself flying across the prairies in the Midwest, unhindered by hills.

Thirty-five miles later, well past noon, we coasted into a pastoral valley. Forested hills rose around us, with patches of cleared farmland and stretches of fence. I hoped for a restaurant to refill my water bottles, but then I spotted the sign for Sarahsville: a few houses at an empty intersection.

Mary had stopped on the grass. "What should we do?" I asked. It was five miles to the next town, but without lunch, five miles could take forever.

"What time is it?"

"One-thirty."

"Let's eat here."

I dug out my food: a yogurt from the grocery store we'd visited earlier, a slightly green banana (just how I liked them), crackers with baba ganouj (made from a powder by adding water), and the last of the nuns' cookies. Since I didn't have much water, I only made a little baba ganouj.

Sitting on the scant grass, I fretted over my water. Usually I hoarded it so I wouldn't run out; but it had started to bug me that I often had water for cooking and doing dishes when Mary didn't. (I hadn't said anything, just secretly resented that I provided water after not drinking enough all day.) So today, I'd drunk more, trying not to worry about the future. But now Sarahsville had no restaurant.

Mary biked on after finishing lunch, but I lagged. "I can sit here until I feel better," I told myself. I hadn't made a mistake in drinking all my water. *I'm falling behind.* I kept sitting. I said a short prayer, asking for help at not worrying about water. I didn't feel better.

After five minutes, I sighed and remounted my bike. As I pedaled over a small hill, a new view of the valley opened. By the road ahead were three girls with a table. They had a cooler.

It was a lemonade stand.

I couldn't tell whether I was about to laugh or cry. I rolled to the table and stopped, smiling as the girls greeted me.

The lemonade stand reminded me of something I'd read in *Tisha*—a discussion of Native American faith. Tisha questions why the native Alaskans, forced to live in settlements, don't pile wood for the winter and then freeze to death. The tribe's leader tells her that his people think like hunters, who assume that something to eat will turn up. A white man offers a more detailed explanation, saying that the tribe's former, migratory lifestyle in such a wild, difficult place required a faith to keep them going, faith that they'll get what they need. He compares this to the faith of a wolf. White men, on the other hand, think like beavers, always saving something for the future.[3]

I'd never considered this: what white settlers perceived as laziness was an expression of faith! How ironic that the white settlers set about "converting" the Native Americans to Christianity while the Native Americans already possessed the faith that the Bible instructs Christians to have—gathering only the manna they can eat and trusting God to send them more each morning, instead of gathering lots and hoarding it.

What did this mean for me? If I biked along drinking my water, expecting God to send me more, I had faith? What if God wanted me to be responsible and plan ahead, carrying water? How did I know which action was right?

I'd brought a foldable gallon jug, and I decided to start filling it. Regardless of what it said about faith, if I had a supply of water, I'd drink more, and staying hydrated was important. Distances between towns would increase as we moved westward, and the weather would be hotter; it might be stupid not to carry water.

Carrying water would help me stop worrying. Worrying accomplished nothing; it didn't protect me from disaster. It was just a series of thoughts about what might happen, all of it bad. So why did I keep worrying—what made it so appealing? It seemed like if I *didn't* worry, I'd stop paying attention, and more things would go wrong. Maybe worrying gave me an illusion of control.

Worry was the opposite of having faith. But I didn't know if I could stop worrying, and carrying water might be a good idea regardless.

## Eastern Ohio, in which I wait for clarity before making decisions

AFTER SARAHSVILLE, THE ROAD CLIMBED past a farm, overlooking a gorgeous view of the valley. The sun shone, grasses waved, and all was quiet except for the rustlings of the wind.

Mary waited in Caldwell. It seemed early to stop so we continued, but then the sun sank faster. We resolved to stop in Sharon.

Two miles later we passed the green sign announcing Sharon, then a few houses, and then the opposite direction's "Welcome to Sharon" sign. Sharon was another non-town, and all the upcoming towns had the same tiny dot on the map. It was twenty-four miles to the next big town.

We continued riding. "Where will we sleep?" I wondered for the hundredth time that week. I remembered my resolution to stop worrying, but it was hard at the end of the day.

The road began to roll downhill, narrow and lined with trees. Suddenly the trees on my right parted, and I whizzed past a gravel drive with a flagpole and an open space behind it. I slowed to read the large, white sign standing in the clearing:

# Wreckage Site
# Number 3
of the Navy Airship
## Shenandoah
Ernest Nichols Farm
September 3, 1925
Noble County, Ohio

*What?* I braked harder and turned in.

The sign stood behind a granite marker surrounded by daylilies. A limp American flag hung on the pole. Behind the sign, a grassy slope led up to the trees. At the side of the clearing, a red picnic table stood on a concrete patio.

"Wreckage Site Number 3." It was some kind of memorial. A car flew past on the road, but the clearing emanated peace. The picnic table beckoned. But was it disrespectful to pitch a tent here?

I read the sign again. So a plane had crashed, and this was the third place wreckage had fallen. How many wreckage sites were there?[4]

Mary pulled in. "Do you think we can camp here?" I asked. We deliberated, going in circles: there was a picnic table, encouraging us to stay. But did it indicate permission to camp? We decided to stop and see what happened.

We pushed our bikes up the slope, leaned them on the ends of the table, and got out supplies for dinner. I liked this strategy: waiting for a clearer direction instead of forcing a decision. At the end of the day, I'd often rebel against anything Mary suggested, or doubt my own ideas. It was a strain to review our options, again and again, trying to assess them. This was better.

Cars passed on the road. None of the drivers looked over at us. As Mary cooked her spaghetti, I began to suspect that no one would mind if we camped. I cooked the last Thai noodle soup package I had from home, added spinach, and spread peanut butter on crackers.

Usually at this time of day, our camping routine occupied us: pitching the tent, washing up, repacking bags, changing clothes, rinsing laundry. But today we both sat still. Without the distraction of activity, thoughts came to the surface: *The trip's not how I imagined. I thought I'd sit meditatively every morning and write in my journal every evening. I pictured Mary and I biking side by side, stopping for fun pictures or to explore bizarre roadside shops. Instead, I'm always trying to keep up with her. The trip isn't fun.* Frodo Baggins popped into my head, as he speaks with his Uncle Bilbo in Rivendell in *Lord of the Rings*: "I spent all my childhood pretending I was off somewhere else—off with you on one of your adventures. But my own adventure turned out to be quite different," Frodo says wistfully in the movie.[5]

I wasn't sure I could fix my trip; Mary didn't have to operate my way or appreciate the same things. But at least we could talk. We were sitting still for once; I should speak.

*But what if it makes things worse? What if we argue? What if she decides not to continue on the trip?* These worries seemed rational. But the alternative—silently eating my noodle soup, knowing the next day would have the same problems—seemed worse.

"Are you having fun?" I blurted out.

Mary looked up from her pasta. "I feel like I'm always waiting."

"I feel like I'm always rushing." A thought leapt into my head: "Perfect! She agrees!" But there wasn't a solution. Mary was always ahead and wanted to move faster, while I was always behind and wished to slow down.

But at least I'd said something. Even without a solution, talking felt good.

We decided to sleep at the wreckage site, and the next morning when I woke, I got right up. Usually I lay still, scared to move. I wanted to enjoy camp, attempt to meditate, or write in my journal, but I feared that if I woke Mary, she'd get up and soon be ready to go. As soon as I moved, the day would start *going*. So I'd lay quietly in my sleeping bag and inevitably fall asleep again, missing my chance for free time.

But today, when I awoke at six AM, I wiggled out of my sleeping bag and left it lying in the tent. A haze covered the grass, and overhead the waning moon shone in the sky. I snapped a picture of our tent, like I'd done at every campsite, as well as the wreckage site sign and the moon over the American flag. But then I stopped. Now was my time to be still. I sat at the picnic table and resisted the urges to keep doing something.

WE HAD ONLY A FEW miles to go to New Lexington. The land had leveled off to rolling forest. The distant hills had odd, stumpy shapes.[6]

I barely noticed the mild ache in my wrists and knees.

We passed the sign announcing New Lexington. These green town signs stimulated a Pavlovian response of joy as I anticipated the town's contents: A bookstore? A coffee shop? A park to sleep in?

A row of storefronts began and the road inclined upward. I chugged up the hill, taking it all in: a car lot, a church, a bank, the city hall, real estate, fitness. Cars accelerated past me. At the top, a turreted courthouse faced a small park filled with trees and sidewalks.

The businesses continued for another block before the downtown gave way to houses, and the road dropped downhill. I braked. I hadn't noticed anything good—no misplaced vegetarian restaurant or arty coffee shop, no grassy churchyards for sleeping. When Mary caught up, we turned onto a side street. The backside of downtown offered nothing.

Disconsolate, we returned to the park. "It's our only option," I said. *But we can't just sleep in the middle of town!* Mary walked in to check it out, but a statue caught my attention: striding across a slab of white rock in the center of the park was a fierce metal man. He towered larger than life. In his left hand he carried a book, and in his right a pen, held as if he signed documents as he walked. Carved into the base, in all capital letters, it read,

## JANUARIUS A. MACGAHAN
### 1844          1878
### CHAMPION OF BULGARIAN FREEDOM

Bulgarian freedom? In Small Town, Ohio?[7]

We had to sleep here! Januarius made this another wacky campsite to add to our list.

But behind the statue, a sign read, "Park Closing Hours 10 PM – 7 AM," followed by the number of a city ordinance. I'd worry all night about the police telling us to leave. Plus it seemed rude to violate the rule, as if it didn't apply to us.

Mary walked over. She scanned Januarius as she spoke. "There's a spot by the picnic shelter."

"Let's ask," I said. "They'll see us, and that sign says the park is closed."

"Okay." I suspected she was humoring me.

We found the police station back by the city hall. We entered with our helmets on. I hoped they'd convey our situation quickly, and make us look like dorky bike geeks, not like we'd get drunk or litter in the park.

The receptionist called for the chief, who came out from a back office. "You want to camp in the park?" he said. "Okay—I'll let the officers know you'll be there." Just like that, we had permission.

I glowed with appreciation as the hopelessness of finding a campsite dissolved. My whole world shifted. Permission! And the park felt safe, with the police knowing we were there.

"We get to sleep with Januarius!" I sang as we left the station. Mary didn't reply.

We walked our bikes back to the park and wheeled them into the picnic shelter. Mary unloaded the tent while I dug out the camp stove, and then we pitched the tent without speaking. Was Mary okay? Usually she talked.

"What do you have for dinner?" I asked to break the silence.

"Chili," she said, "if you want that."

"Okay." I'd tolerate spicy chili if it might cheer her up.

She set water to boil with a bag of Boil-in-Bag rice and dumped a can of beans and a can of Mexican-spiced tomatoes into the other pot. "What did I do wrong?" I wondered. "Was I too goofy about Januarius, making a fuss over 'sleeping with' him?" I'd thought it was funny, but maybe I'd overdone it. She pulled the rice off the stove and heated the beans, and then we ate in silence. The traffic light turned, and cars swished past at the edge of the park. I remembered the gum ball I'd bought to cheer Mary up in Pennsylvania. We'd moved beyond those tricks.

When Mary finished, she went for a walk. I sat with my empty bowl in the shelter, wondering what was up. "We got permission to camp," I reminded myself, trying to recapture my elation.

The dishes got exponentially harder to clean the longer they sat. The park had no water spigot, so I took them to the bushes and crouched underneath, scrubbing and then rinsing with my water bottle. I hoped the police wouldn't receive complaints about a sudden influx of raccoons.

After a while, Mary returned, smiling. "I found a Catholic church," she said. "It was unlocked so I sat inside."

"She'd needed that," I realized. Her bad mood hadn't been my fault.

"Will you take a picture of me and Januarius?" I asked.

"Sure." She didn't seem to mind.

I found a pay phone and called the Athas, the parents of a friend who'd offered their house as a rest and shower stop. It looked like we'd arrive tomorrow.

"You're in New Lexington?" Mrs. Atha said. "You're so close! Why don't you come tonight?"

"We're really tired, and we've already pitched our tent in the park. The police gave us permission, and there's this awesome statue of the liberator of Bulgaria."

She paused for a split second, then said, "Okay, whatever works for you."

The only problem left was the lack of a restroom. Fortunately, one narrow storefront glowed with neon signs, slightly downhill in the direction of the police station. I swallowed my guilt over using a restroom without buying anything and followed Mary in.

A circular bar filled the dark room, pushing toward the walls where small tables cowered in fear. Large patrons sat hunchbacked at the bar, while a female bartender, trapped in the circle, moved listlessly from one to another like the slow-moving ball in Pong.

I imagined eyes turning on us, but the burly men continued to watch the overhead TVs. Mary walked to the side, squeezing herself behind the backs of the men. I stuck behind her like a shadow, hoping no one would notice me. I couldn't decide between keeping my head down, as if this made me invisible, and trying to catch someone's eye to smile. Once we'd circumnavigated the bar, the restrooms were easy to spot, and we took care of business and got out.

The next morning, I again left the tent when I awoke. I sat on a bench in the morning air with my next book, *Dune*. I never read sci-fi, but a coworker had recommended *Dune*.

It began with the protagonist, Paul, waking up in bed and sensing his tension as his family prepares to move to the desert planet, Dune. Aware of his tension, Paul practices one of the "mind-body lessons" his mother has taught him. He avoids the "unfocused mechanism of consciousness" so he can "be conscious by choice."

"He's fifteen," I thought. "I'm almost thirty, and I can't even sit still for two minutes." By the end of the first chapter, Paul has used the "Litany against Fear" to pass a painful test of his willpower. "Fear is the mind-killer," I repeated. I'd have to remember that the next time I heard noises outside the tent.[8]

I lowered the book and looked around; my brain slowly returned to New Lexington, Ohio. I struggled to absorb the book's ideas. They felt like a divine truth, like the author received insight into everything and then, instead of writing a new Bible or a philosophy doctrine, he wrote a sci-fi fantasy. And the ideas seemed relevant, like the book had come along at just the right time.

## Sugar Grove, Ohio, or the end of the beginning

THE ATHAS WERE THE PARENTS of Meg, who'd married my high school buddy Brian. Meg had offered their house as a place to sleep, but we didn't know anything about them except that they'd recently moved to somewhere called Sugar Grove. (Meg had kind of snorted when she said the name, as if the actual existence of Sugar Grove were in question.) Amanda, who'd given us her map at the Ohio border, had circled Sugar Grove, but her dying pen's faint circle disappeared every time I looked for it. I had to find New Lexington and trace a route southwest to Amanda's pale, uneven circle on a north-south road surrounded by blankness.

Now, as we turned onto that north-south road, I pondered why we left our path to stay with a family we didn't know. When Meg had offered it months earlier, I'd snapped up the opportunity to have a shower and a bed. Nights had seemed uncertain and potentially costly or dangerous: Would we be forced to stay at hotels? Kicked out of parks by the police? Harassed in our tent by local hoodlums? At least one night, we'd have a safe place.

But then the trip started, and we found places to sleep; a guaranteed spot lost its importance. And now we understood the time and effort it took to bike ten miles off our westward path. We didn't know if the Athas were looking forward to having us or just feeling parental obligation. If it were the latter, we'd have done better to keep heading west, no doubt finding another park to sleep in.

It began to rain, and the road grew hilly. We passed through Bremen, the last town before our turn, which was not on the map. There was nothing on the map for twelve miles. If we missed the turn, we'd ride for an hour before realizing it.

You might think it would be hard to miss a turn on a slow-moving bike, but my brain couldn't stay focused on the monotonous task of looking. As the unchanging scenery of scrubby regrowth trees rolled by, my mind wandered. I snapped back to the present, scanning the roadside for any break in the wall of uneven trees. Had I missed something? Surely I'd have noticed a road, right? Mary had fallen behind me. *What if she turned down a road I missed?*

"You won't miss the turn," I told myself. "You'll see it, even if you're daydreaming."

No mile markers punctuated the roadside, and my pace varied with the hills so I couldn't gauge distance using time. I scoured the surroundings, taking in every post and gravel trail, looking twice to make sure nothing could possibly be a road. My mind drifted again. Five minutes later, I snapped awake and repeated my paranoid routine.

I chugged up another hill, my breath visible as the wet air grew colder. Rain fell more heavily now, and the rough pavement of the country roads rumbled under my tires. A bird on the low branches lifted my spirits, but they sank right back a moment later.

At last I saw a green sign ahead. A break in the scrub transformed into a road—our turn. I pulled to a stop and looked around. There was Mary, biking up behind me. Everything had worked out fine.

According to Meg's directions, this road turned into her parents' road, and then the Athas' house was first on the right. Dampness had crept into my shoes, and my bare fingers tingled, but I ignored it because we'd soon arrive.

We set off down. I couldn't stop scanning for road signs, now that I'd been doing it for hours. My damp hands became wet; my feet began to slosh. The road wound on and on. After several miles, we came to a sharp bend where the new road began. It dropped downhill and flattened into a straight strip between the trees.

Now we needed the first house on the right. But the trees continued endlessly. Why had I let my hands get wet? It was too late to fix it now. Would we ever arrive? Several miles chugged by. Then gravel splayed into the road ahead, and we reached an unpaved drive. My thankfulness dwindled as my gaze followed the driveway, winding uphill into the trees.

Once I stopped pedaling, my legs ached. My arms were sore, and my whole body was stiff in the cold. I couldn't ride another inch, especially not uphill on gravel, so I got off and began to push my bike. Mary did the same. This used different muscles, but those muscles were tired, too; every ten seconds, my arms began to burn so badly that I'd stop to rest. The burning would fade, then return when I resumed pushing.

A house appeared behind the trees at the top of the hill. Then frantic barking began. We both stopped, watching the curve in the driveway ahead. A big brown dog stampeded around the corner and skidded to a halt, barking nonstop. At least they'd know we'd arrived. I wheeled slowly forward. A smaller dog toddled out, issuing screechy yelps amid the barking. The dogs backed off as we approached.

Several cars were parked on the dirt in front of the house, and wooden pallets lay over the mud by the front steps. Stray cinderblocks and buckets were strewn around. Boards and piping lay stacked to one side, along with a tall ladder. No shrubs or plants lined the foundation, only wet red dirt.

Then the door opened and a mom-like woman with short blonde hair came out. She took one look at us and said, "You're on bikes?!"

She'd thought we were driving! No wonder she'd suggested we arrive the previous night. Now she'd know we weren't weirdoes who just really wanted to sleep in the park in New Lexington.

She continued as she stepped into boots. "Meg just said you were going cross-country! I didn't know you were on bikes. We could've come get you."

"We wanted to ride," I said. It sounded ridiculous after how miserable the morning had been.

She introduced herself as Gay Atha and led us to the garage to park our bikes. "We just moved in a week ago," she said, indicating the house on its bare foundation. "We lived in the garage apartment for the past six months."

I unclipped the camping gear and dropped it onto the floor to access the bags underneath. "The food and maps can stay here for now," I thought, eliminating them from my to-do list. I found some clothes, my toothbrush, and my journal and followed Gay and Mary out. At the front door, we left our wet shoes on the mat with half a dozen muddy pairs.

Inside, food covered the kitchen counter: boxes of crackers, lettuce, bags of chips, and cartons of milk and juice. For a second I wondered, "Do they just leave the food out like this?"

"I just went shopping," Gay said. "Are you hungry?" Mary slid onto a stool at the counter. I started to follow but then spoke instead.

"Could I take a shower?"

"Of *course!*" Gay motioned to Mary to eat and led me down a hallway to the stairs.

Steaming in the shower, I silently thanked Mary for talking to our host. I shed the day's grit and dampness and the tumble of tired thoughts in my head. We'd found the road; we'd made it. I no longer needed to be vigilant, to worry about wrong turns and losing Mary. Coming here hadn't been a mistake; we'd been welcomed.

After the shower, I dressed in my cleanest clothes—the outfit I didn't ride in.[9] Voices drifted up from the kitchen. Would anyone call up to me? I tiptoed across the hall to the bedroom Gay had shown me, with a low, slanted ceiling. A quilt-covered bed stood by a short window. Outside swayed the wet tops of pine trees. Tugging up the edge of the quilt, but not the sheets, I crawled under, rested my head on the pillow, and fell asleep.

Mary and I stayed with the Athas two nights. On our day off, Meg's little sister drove us to Columbus. First we visited the Topiary Garden in Old Deaf School Park. The garden portrayed the French painting *Sunday Afternoon on the Island of la Grande Jatte* by Georges Seurat. Bushes had been trained and cut to form the figures of the painting: if you stood at one end of the park, the figures lined up to match the scene. After walking through the garden, we ate lunch; Gay had sent money to treat. Then we saw a matinee about a young woman disobeying her parents to pursue her dreams.

At home, Mary and I joined Gay in the kitchen so she could give us the Myers-Briggs test, a "personality indicator." She'd suggested we do it after hearing about our differences. I'd taken the test before and was still an "INFJ." Mary was an "ENFP." The results explained some of our behaviors: Mary always wanted to talk to our hosts because she was an extrovert (E), while as an introvert (I), I needed alone time to regroup before I could socialize happily. In the absence of a host family, Mary often tried to talk to me. As an organized "J," I sought order where Mary (P) didn't. For example, she didn't notice that she packed the stove differently than she'd found it. But in my mind, there was a right way to pack it, and Mary was doing it wrong.

After dinner, people adjourned to the family room to watch TV. Reluctantly, I trekked out to my bike to repack my bags. Mary and I would leave in the morning. Now that we were with a family, the thought of being on the road depressed me.

But something felt different, too, like the first part of the trip had ended and we now entered Phase Two. So far, the eastern American scenery of forests, fields, highways, and towns had been familiar. Now we moved on to the flat plains of the Midwest. Maybe there wouldn't be winding, narrow roads with sudden intersections. I'd miss those. But the flat openness excited me: if anything could clear the clutter of my brain, it would be the landscape of the Midwest.

# PART 2:
# The Midwest,
# in Which the Road Flattens
# and We Play
# Connect the Dots

## Western Ohio, in which there is
## traffic, and calm, and traffic, and calm . . .
## both on the roads and in my head

I SAT ON A GRASSY SLOPE across from a quiet T intersection. The day hadn't been fun or scenic, not horrible or wet, just dull and trafficky.

We'd lost our route in Lancaster, Ohio, in spite of the stacks of signs at each intersection. After a harrowing left turn with cars whizzing by, we'd biked a mile out of town before discovering we were on Route 188 instead of 33. We'd decided to keep going on the new route.

Now the faint dampness of the grass came through my shorts; I'd been sitting awhile. I took one last baby carrot and gingerly inserted it into the peanut butter jar. It was like playing Operation, trying not to hit the edges. Peanut butter speckled the sides of my hand. I ate my carrot and then licked my hand, unwilling to use a napkin and create trash. My tongue worked better, anyway.

I met Mary at the library in Lithopolis. The traffic returned as we skirted south of Columbus, pausing every five minutes to check the map against the confusing roads. By the time we reached Pleasant Corners, run over by Route 665 and its strip malls, my brain jittered with exhaustion. In the mini-mart, I quivered in the aisles, trying to make decisions about what to eat, jumpy when I rounded a corner to face another customer.

Outside, a gravel road labeled "Main Street" led into the trees. "Let's go eat down there," Mary said. We remounted our bikes and pushed off against the gravel. As the trees closed in overhead, the noise behind us dimmed.

After a few hundred feet, the road emerged at a deserted intersection. A lone church stood against a backdrop of fields, as if the sprawl of 665 couldn't pierce the shield of trees. We hadn't planned to stop for the day, but it was so peaceful that we changed our minds.

After dinner, I sat on the grass to read. Something was missing, though. "I keep expecting to hear Gay Atha talking," I realized. Was it just this morning that she'd made me an extra-large milky omelet for breakfast, with cantaloupe and two English muffins and juice? For a moment, I wished I were back in her house instead of here in a strange churchyard, hiding from the congestion of the road.

The sun woke me at six-fifteen the next morning. Five minutes later, I was walking back to the Pleasant Corners mini-mart. I hadn't planned to go. I could have used "the restroom" behind the churchyard bushes as we'd done the night before. I just found myself walking there.

As I went to the coffeepot, my brain fussed about spending money when I could make tea at camp. "I'll save time—I won't have to bother with the stove," I told myself as I poured decaf into a small paper cup. Besides, coffee only cost sixty cents. I took half a cup and brought it to the counter.

"That's just fifty cents, there," said the cashier, an older man in a plaid flannel shirt. "You didn't fill it up all the way."

I smiled a real smile. "Thank you."

"How are you this morning?" he continued, even though the time for obligatory small talk had passed.

"I'm okay." I smiled again but looked down.

I walked back to camp, sipping my coffee in the bright morning. I felt calm, the opposite of how jittery I'd been last night. My day already had a special moment: I'd received a ten-cent gift and kind words from the man at the mini-mart. I retrieved my book and a granola bar and sat on the steps of the church as the sun rose over the quiet fields. The cup of coffee stood next to me, far enough away that I wouldn't knock it over, and I read *Dune* and forgot about it.

WE LEFT BEHIND THE STRIP malls and headed across dirty plowed fields that stretched to the horizons. At first, I liked it: I could see in every direction and felt wideness and freedom. At one point, a train chugged alongside me, moving only slightly faster than I did, with a line of cars so long it disappeared in a haze.

In spite of the wideness, something always marred the scenery: a billboard advertising another steakhouse or hair salon, or litter, or blank buildings of unknown purpose. The flatness made it easy to see the power lines, their towers marching across the fields and out of sight.

After lunch, I fell behind Mary as more farmland passed. I'd longed for flatness, imagining it would clear my head. I'd thought worries and sadness would evaporate as I rode west, leaving behind their causes in North Carolina. But they hadn't.

I'd once learned, in a wellness program, that all feelings stem from thoughts. I hadn't believed it at first, but I'd slowly realized it was true. Sometimes it's hard to see the thought, when the feeling results quickly, but it's there. After that, when I got upset, I'd try to identify the thought that had caused it and assess whether the thought was rational. If I could banish irrational thoughts, I could cut back on unhappy reactions. But I often forgot to do it or realized that I'd missed my chance. Most of the time, I watched the irrational thoughts when it was too late to combat them.

Lately I'd recognized that no matter where I went, even in the flat Midwest, incessant thoughts ran though my head. Maybe this was why depression had not evaporated. Maybe the causes weren't in North Carolina. I couldn't just bike away from them: they were in my head.

And the flatness of the Midwest was growing dull.

Springfield neared, with more strip malls. After navigating the city to find a Mexican restaurant, Mary and I escaped on a quiet road, biking the final ten miles to New Carlisle. When we rolled in, we circled the handful of streets, seeing only paved lots and buildings. Then we spotted a Catholic church. A lawn spread behind it, with a picnic shelter, trees, and a stone shrine with a Virgin Mary statue. A woman loaded her car in the parking lot. Instead of asking permission to camp, I said, "If we camped here, would anyone mind?" She didn't think so. We thanked her and wheeled our bikes onto the grass.

My thoughts bounced chaotically. I made a list: help Mary pitch the tent, walk around town, get ready for bed while the church was still unlocked, sit by the grotto with my journal. Then I did it all, rushing through my walk only to find that someone from the church had propped a door for us. Finally I reached the last item: I sat on a bench facing the Virgin in her alcove. Angels smiled down from the stone wall behind her.

Sitting there, I finally started to lose the hectic feeling that had built all day. Then I remembered Cory, the guy I'd been thinking of when I'd left North Carolina—I hadn't thought of him in days! After wondering with frustration when the thoughts would stop, I'd lost them and hadn't noticed.

What *had* I been thinking about that day? I'd been daydreaming about the actor who played Sam in the movie we'd seen in Columbus. His name was Nicholas Something-or-other. In my daydream, the real person (Nicholas) kept the personality of Sam. I'd started with Nicholas/Sam as my husband, but that plot was too mundane: I became tangled up in unromantic scenes like taking out the trash.

So I'd started over with Nicholas/Sam coming to Chapel Hill to film his next movie. I'd returned from the bike trip. I met him at work when, full of confidence and covered with flour, I wheeled a rack of bread I'd just baked out into the store. We had a date at the historic Carolina Inn where he was staying; I loved the Carolina Inn's rose-patterned rug and the fact that guests got cookies at check-in, unless they arrived late at night, in which case they got a cookie coupon. Nicholas/Sam gave me his cookie coupon. Then he kept in touch and mailed me an invitation to the movie's opening in Hollywood, along with a plane ticket. When Nicholas/Sam and I arrived at the event, he helped me out of the limo, and then continued to hold my hand as cameras flashed us down the long red carpet . . .

The romantic daydreams had given me a wonderful feeling of being loved. But I'd returned to desolate reality amid the strip malls of Ohio. I remembered the day in Pennsylvania when daydreams had led to a bad mood. Today they'd led to a good mood, but it hadn't been sustainable. Maybe today would have been better if I hadn't gone off into daydreams. Maybe I could have focused on carrying the peace of my morning coffee into the day.

WITH THE SUN BARELY UP, I set off down the sidewalk, then cut across a deserted parking lot. On my walk the night before, I'd discovered a restaurant that opened at seven. I'd been enjoying breakfast at camp: hot cereal and tea. And cooking would save money. But I loved the idea of eggs and hash browns, and there wasn't always a restaurant available. If Mary were setting up the camp stove for her breakfast, it seemed a waste not to use it. "But what if I'm avoiding the restaurant," I wondered, "because it's a new place?" I often shied away from new experiences. "And what if I feel pressure to cook because Mary's cooking?" I didn't want to miss the restaurant just because Mary wasn't into it. What did I actually want?

The morning hadn't brought clarity, and I'd made the decision to go. The reasons in favor overrode my desire to cook at camp. Just yesterday, I'd thoughtlessly gone for coffee at the mini-mart. This morning felt completely different: I'd thought about it way too much.

Now I neared the restaurant. The lot was full. My heart fluttered: I'd feel exposed inside with all those people. But that was part of why I was here, to overcome those anxieties. I crossed the lot, weaving between pickup trucks. With a deep breath, I tugged open the door.

A bell dinged as steamy air met me—not steamy enough to fog my glasses, thankfully, which always left me fumbling to find a spot in my shirt to wipe them. A bustling filled the room as a waitress carried plates and a customer called to her. When she returned to the kitchen, pushing the swinging door open with her hip, more noise drifted out.

Another waitress appeared, menu in hand. "Just one?" I nodded.

"I'm here," I thought. "Relax and enjoy breakfast." The other customers ignored my arrival, and the prices were cheap. I ordered an egg, a biscuit, and real home fries (not frozen cubes dunked in hot oil). There was nothing bad about the place, no cleaner smell or straw wrappers littering the floor. But the sounds were off: I'd imagined a quiet diner, but customers talked and the kitchen clanged. And I hadn't imagined the air as steamy, or the sunlight in harsh slanted panels across the tables.

While the minutes dragged past, I sat in the booth and wondered why I'd come. Was it just to be different than Mary? So many times I'd done what others wanted; was I now going to the other extreme? "I just wish Mary would eat out," I thought, shifting the blame to her.

Since our talk at the wreckage site in eastern Ohio, Mary and I hadn't talked again about "how things are going," and I felt tension between us. A college friend took teenagers on bike trips, and he had a policy: at camp every night, the group gathered and spewed out everything that bothered them, no matter how petty or irrational.

Mary and I didn't have such a procedure. Instead, I kept problems bottled inside, telling myself they were too insignificant to voice. Did it matter if she crumpled the tent when she packed it, instead of folding it? It was my tent, and I wanted it to last; but it might annoy her if I criticized the way she packed it. What if I caused more tension between us? I didn't know how to express my needs without being critical. And did "packing the tent neatly" even count as a "need"?

But kept inside, little irritations swelled out of proportion; "It's not the mountain that wears you out, but the pebble in your shoe," I'd once read on a tea label.

Back at the church, Mary and I packed and then biked toward the center of town. We needed to find Route 571, the only road heading west. It looked simple on the map, but without signs, we couldn't tell which western-heading road petered out after a mile and which stretched on across Ohio.

Card tables by the road distracted me—a yard sale. I pulled over, smiling at a mom and two girls. I scanned for something I could buy as the girls bounced excitedly. Mary rolled up behind me and asked directions.

"Five seventy-one?" the mom said. "That's the road down there, the one past the church . . . it winds around, you'll see a gas station. Just stay on it." Her hand waved vaguely in a forward direction. I spotted a cat keychain, small enough to carry. I didn't need it, but I couldn't walk away from a yard sale without buying something, with the family watching me, disappointed.

Mary and I quickly became lost. We passed no church or gas station. "Why didn't Mary get better information?" I wondered, as if it had been only her responsibility.

We came to a westward road, and Mary called out, "I think this is it!" I saw no sign; her decision wasn't based on data. But I didn't have a better guess, and if I had, I'd have felt scared of being wrong. I had no cooperative spirit to view the decision as an adventure. As I turned after Mary, my day felt ruined.

A mile down the road, a sign for Route 571 passed.

I settled into the rhythm of my pedals, anticipating Tipp City, ten miles away. But the miles dragged, in spite of the flat road. The wind rushed past my face, the air fresh under a bright, cloudy sky. Could the wind make that much difference? When we finally arrived, we gravitated to the coffee shop and got out our books, postponing our return to the wind.

In spite of the respite, after an hour, I grew antsy to be on the road. Mary looked up just as I did. "Should we go?" I asked.

"I guess so." Mary sighed, closing her book.

I didn't feel the wind as we wheeled our bikes off the curb. Maybe it had gone. But when we left the buildings for the broad fields, it returned, gusting in our faces. "It's just a gust," I thought. "It will die down." But it didn't. Before a mile had passed, I longed for the shelter of the next town. I couldn't stop watching for trees on the horizon, because trees would indicate a town among the endless empty fields.

By midafternoon, we'd only gone twenty-two miles from Tipp City when we arrived in Laura, Ohio. (We'd been excited to see Laura on the map because Mary could take a picture for her sister.) I stopped next to Mary at the green town sign. She lowered her camera. "I don't feel good . . . can we find the park?"

The town didn't even have a traffic light, just some brick ranch houses and a few side streets. A blue water tower rose over the treetops; we found a grassy area with a picnic shelter at its base. The crisscrossed beams overhead reminded me of standing at the base of the Eiffel Tower, where I'd found myself fascinated with the intricate metal legs rather than the tower's height. Laura's water tower wasn't as fancy, but still.

After sitting a minute, Mary wanted to stop for the day.

Asking permission to camp had worked in New Lexington, but Laura had no police station. Boarded-up buildings indicated the downtown; the auto parts store looked like the only place in business, albeit closed at three PM on a Saturday. A neighbor of the park suggested I ask the church pastor, but he wasn't home so I left a note in his door.

Mary set up the tent and lay down inside. I got my journal and *Dune,* not sure which I wanted, and sat on the swing set. Mary felt nauseous, with a head-ache. *What if she doesn't feel better by morning? Will we find a ride to a doctor? What if it's a bug that needs a few days—can we keep camping here?* The only comfort was the name of the town—Laura, like Mary's sister who'd seen us off in New Jersey. It seemed to protect us.

MARY FELT BETTER THE NEXT morning. We sat opposite each other at the picnic table, wearing all our layers in the breezy morning. The sun had just peeked over the horizon.

"Where do you think the pastor is?" I asked. His driveway still stood empty.

"I dunno," Mary replied, pouring milk from a single-serving box into the pot on the stove. I turned to my journal, wishing I'd written yesterday instead of reading *Dune* all afternoon. I was remembering our departure from New Carlisle, and how annoyed I'd felt at Mary when we got momentarily lost, and how I'd daydreamed all the previous day. Prayers never helped, but still I wrote, "Today my prayer is 1. be nicer to Mary. I was <u>critical</u> yesterday and felt unable to change. 2. Be aware of what's around me and not just looking forward (or backward). This seems impossible. Sometimes being nice does, too."

I looked at my breakfast: I'd boiled water for tea and now kept one hand wrapped around my mug for warmth. I'd cut up a Granny Smith apple, and I had an energy bar. I hadn't had enough water left to make hot cereal *and* do dishes afterward. I could've asked to share Mary's pot but hadn't wanted to ask a favor.

Mary's milk began to bubble. Then it surged, overflowing. She jumped up and lifted the pot, stirring the bubbles down as a milky film formed on the stove. A puddle dripped onto the table. Would she clean up the mess? *What if she doesn't? Will I say something?* I didn't want to repress my thoughts, but I didn't want to sound critical. I could clean it up myself if she didn't—but would that create tension?

I couldn't leave a mess on the park's table, after we'd been guests! And I didn't want the stove in my bags with milk on it!

"Just wait and see what happens," I told myself. I tried to ignore the scenes playing in my head. Mary dished out her cereal.

I looked at my breakfast: the clear plastic mug of hot tea, the energy bar to the right, my pocket knife to the left, and the bright green apple wedges in a row in back. I'd eaten three chunks of apple. The five remaining chunks stood behind the tea, the sun rising in the east behind them. As the sunlight hit my clear mug, the brown tea radiated light, and I realized that I'd created symmetry with my breakfast, like a small altar before me.

The sun rose bright, glaring, and the apple skins turned in the changing light, like a movie played in fast motion, the shadows moving across them as I sat. Their green color matched my green rain jacket that I wore for warmth, and the sunlight made the tea the same color as the energy bar, and everything just suddenly connected.

"I can't stop being grouchy," I said. "I'm sorry I'm being awful."

"It's okay," Mary replied, eating her cereal. I wanted her to reassure me that she didn't think I was awful, that everything wasn't my fault. She didn't, but I felt better anyway.

## Illinois, in which worried thoughts threaten to overwhelm me, but keep reading because I prevail

I WHEELED MY BIKE INTO THE garage. I wouldn't ride it again for a week.

Mary and I had biked from Ohio into Indiana. We'd stayed with friends in Indianapolis, where I'd spent our day off biking around the city visiting sites, only to end the day feeling unrested and regretful. We'd continued on to Crawfordsville, the home of the Ben-Hur Museum. I had hoped for photos and props from the 1959 movie, but instead the museum housed the papers and belongings of Lew Wallace, the author of *Ben-Hur* the novel. The only item of interest in the entire museum was a series of letters between Lew, who served as governor of New Mexico in the 1870s, and Billy the Kid. Lew had made a deal with Billy (testimony in exchange for a pardon) and then betrayed him.

Mary and I had set out at seven AM that morning to cover the seventy miles to Champaign, Illinois. We'd arrived at my friend Stef's house as the sun neared the horizon. Tomorrow, Mary's boyfriend, from St. Louis, would swing by on his way to Chicago for the weekend. I'd never met him, but I knew they'd met in Americorps and been good friends and had recently started dating long distance. I figured Mary must be excited to see him. He'd bring her to Chicago, while I'd spend a few days in Champaign, and then Stef would drive me to Chicago as well.

That night, while I recorded the day's notes in my planner, Mary used a calculator to add up the miles we'd biked since Cape May. Somewhere east of Champaign, we'd completed one thousand miles; we were a third of the way there.

Our first day in Champaign was May 30th, and Mary stayed in the kitchen all morning, baking a carrot cake for her boyfriend's birthday. I avoided the kitchen. I felt awkward around her. I hadn't wanted to admit it, but now when I wrote in my journal, thoughts surfaced like "things just aren't good between us." I could see a pattern: Tension would build. If we talked (like we had at the wreckage site, where we'd discussed our different travel speeds) or even acknowledged the tension (like I had at breakfast in Laura), it got better. But we didn't keep talking. The tension rebuilt, a new hurdle to talking again.

Being apart would be a relief, but a tiny voice wondered if Mary would give up on the trip—if I'd been so un-fun that she would quit. I knew she wouldn't give up because of the challenge of biking, but she might quit if she didn't want to be around me anymore. If she did, I'd have to keep going alone. I'd be too embarrassed to abort the trip, plus I didn't feel ready to go home.

A van pulled in early in the afternoon, and Mary went outside. Her boyfriend was tall and cute and smiled when he saw her, but I didn't hover near the door to learn more. Soon she came in for her bags, and I helped load my bike and gear into the van, along with Mary's. When we'd loaded it all, and the frosted carrot cake sat on the front seat, Mary came to hug me bye, a brief, hard hug. Then they got in the van and left. I kept standing in the driveway, and the world quieted around me.

The next day, the last day of May, I explored Champaign. Just like in Indianapolis, I stayed busy all day instead of resting. I mapped out a route around the city that prioritized the places I "needed" to go: the university, the bike shop, the bookstore, the art museum. After lunch my list continued—the campus bookstore, the post office, the Champaign surplus. Finally I made it to the coffee shop and ordered a Cafe Caramel. I eyed the outdoor tables, the choice place to sit on such a beautiful almost-summer day, but outside there was noise and traffic and pedestrians, and the wind would blow my hair into my face. Something nudged me toward the peacefulness indoors.

Sitting in the coffee shop I suddenly felt beautiful and self-aware. I'd been efficient and productive, checking items off my list and buying things! And I sat in a coffee shop, writing in my journal. This was the bike trip I'd imagined.

Accomplishing tasks made me happy, but it wasn't sustainable. By the next afternoon, my thoughts had begun to spiral downhill.

I'd see Mary in a few days—I wasn't ready! I didn't miss her. What if Mary felt this negative about me? *What if she takes it out on my bike, by dropping it out of the van, or leaving it unlocked?* I told myself that my bike would be fine, not damaged or stolen, but the thought had upset me.

Mary had said she'd call to arrange meeting in Chicago, but she hadn't called all morning. *Why isn't she calling? How hard is it to make one phone call?* I couldn't relax. *What if she doesn't want to continue?* My thoughts looped in circles.

I tried to think of something else. Stef and her partner's calm domestic life made me wonder if I wanted to meet someone and marry. I'd always assumed I did. But would I have gone on this trip if I'd had a partner? Probably not. Which was worse, being single forever, or not pursuing dreams like the bike trip because of a relationship? I couldn't envision any kind of balance. My head was stuffy. The house was closing in. I hated being unhappy; why had my mood changed?

"Twenty-four hours ago," I reminded myself, "I was completely happy as I sipped my Cafe Caramel and wrote in my journal." Nothing had changed. But something had.

I'd read about thoughts surfacing when you meditate, as the chatter of your brain stops. You feel bad temporarily, but then all the crap gets out and doesn't hurt you anymore. Regular meditation keeps the garbage flowing out, keeping you clear inside. Maybe something similar was happening. I'd thought biking would be meditative, and it had been at first; but after the initial shock of the "nothingness" of biking all day, my brain had adjusted and figured out how to stop the painful thoughts and stress from surfacing and being released. But now, *stopping biking* had brought a new kind of nothingness, and the release was happening again. My emotions swung like a broken weathervane, trying to escape as my brain searched for a way to shut them down.

I couldn't embrace the upset feelings and accept them as part of life. Instead, I hated being distressed: worried about my bike, angry with Mary for not calling, confused about being single, uncomfortably trapped in a house. And frustrated with myself: staying in Champaign was my chance to rest, and I was blowing it! Being upset with myself exacerbated everything.

"I have to fix things," I decided. I called my parents. When they answered, I launched right in: "Mary hasn't called, and everything's really bad between us!"

Mom cut me off. "You just imagine it!"

Why didn't she believe me? She thought my mind invented it—*like something's wrong with me.* Mom began a new topic before I could fix the first one.

Then Dad asked if I'd done any sightseeing. *He doesn't care about my problems with Mary, either.* I wished I hadn't called.

After I hung up, I sat on the bed, willing myself to feel better, but I didn't. And then the phone rang. I reached for it. "Hello?"

"Hey, it's Mary." My bad feelings evaporated. Mary hadn't given up on me!

Mary directed me to her friend's apartment in Chicago, where we'd meet in a few days. She didn't sound enthused to talk to me, but at least she'd called.

By bedtime, my depression had returned. I still fought it. This time, I called my friends in Chapel Hill who'd ridden cross-country last summer.

"Whoa, we were just talking about you!" one of them said. That lifted my spirits.

But then I began talking. "I just can't stop feeling bad. And I don't feel ready to see Mary again." As I continued to list the trip's failings, I could feel her disappointment with me. Everyone wanted me to be happy and have fun; no one wanted to hear that I was sad.

As if to confirm my thoughts, she replied, "Oh, Emily, you *have* to be having fun!" I was more of a failure than ever. Here I was on the trip of a lifetime; only I could ruin it.

I lay in bed that night, my thoughts desperately seeking a way to feel better. "The trip is only a third over," I thought. "It took a while to get used to life on the road. There's still time for things to work out."

"Especially if I travel alone at the end of the summer." Images of tranquil solitude filled my head. By pinning my hopes on the future, I didn't mind things being imperfect now.

I STOOD ON THE SIDEWALK outside my friends' apartment building in Evanston, a suburb of Chicago. They wouldn't be home until five, but I'd had Stef drop me here so I'd know where it was. Even in June, a cool breeze blew off Lake Michigan, a few blocks north. I hoisted up my bag and turned south, sure I'd find a coffee shop in the storefronts we'd passed.

The bag was one of the four panniers that hung on the racks of my bike; I was using it as a suitcase. Its short handle dug painfully into my hand, and the metal hooks that hung it on the rack scraped against my leg as I walked. I tried to hold it away from me, but it was too heavy. After a block, my arm ached, so I switched arms, but after another block the new arm ached, too. The tolerance of each arm diminished until I exchanged the bag between hands every few buildings.

At last I reached the street with the shops. It made me think of my grandma's neighborhood in Queens, with takeout menus littering the gutter and storefronts with shoe displays that hadn't been changed in years. On a side street I found Cafe Express, where I ordered a hot cider and spinach pie. I tried to relax at my tiny table under the cafe's glass windows. After how upset I'd been yesterday, I felt vulnerable, like I'd cry if anyone was rude. Would they ask me to leave if I stayed too long? *Maybe my bag makes me look homeless.* I tried to relax, but I couldn't focus on my book.

Maybe I could go to the beach at Lake Michigan. But if I left, I couldn't return. (Well, I could; but I'd have to buy something else, and I'd feel stupid with the staff noticing my return and wondering who I was, with my weird bag.) It was cold out, and I still had a few hours to wait. Did I really want to go?

The lure of the beach was strong. So I cleared my table, bundled up in my fleece hoody and coat, picked up my bag, and lurched toward the door.

I made it the several blocks north, past the apartment building, to the sandy shore of Lake Michigan. As I hit the sand, walking became more difficult and the bag banged my leg harder. I staggered to a bench, thumping the bag on the sand and sinking down. I didn't feel cold, but I kept myself bundled, knowing the cold would sink in now that I'd stopped moving.

Lake Michigan stretched to the horizon. I had no affinity for lakes, but this one looked like the ocean, with no far shore and with small waves rolling onto a beach. Seagulls stalked around on the sand as if they, too, thought it was the ocean. As I watched the seagulls, it suddenly seemed like a good time to say a prayer, so I tried but only felt more desolate inside. But the desolation wasn't terrible, just a dull sort of loneliness. After yesterday, I welcomed the relative emptiness of my feelings. It was a new and interesting state of existence.

Without warning, every seagull on the beach opened its wings and took off. The flock rose into the sky and disappeared behind the trees. I kept sitting until I grew too cold, and then I picked up the bag and heaved it along, back to the apartment. It was almost five.

I buzzed the door buzzer, just in case they were home early. Then I sat on the stoop to wait. Long, cold minutes passed. Did they want me to visit? Or did they feel obliged? *What if they're inside—maybe the buzzer doesn't work, or I didn't push hard enough.* I stood and pushed the buzzer hard so I couldn't be mistaken. No one answered. I sat back down.

*What if they never come home? What if they've forgotten I'm coming and made plans in the city, and I sit here waiting and darkness comes? How long should I sit here? What would I do?* I wanted to cry.

And then someone walked around the end of the building and in the gate. It was my friend Eric, and he was already grinning. "Buehls!" he exclaimed, striding up the walk. I realized I was grinning, too. "Sorry you had to wait!" he said, getting out his key.

"It's okay, I went to the beach."

"Man, I can't believe you biked here! Buehler, that's awesome!"

I'd just biked from New Jersey to Chicago. I lugged my bag inside.

THE NEXT MORNING I RODE downtown with Eric and his wife, Christina-Mai. They parked in a parking deck where each level had a different color to help commuters remember where they'd left their cars. In addition, a different song played on each level.

"I always try to find a spot on the yellow deck," Eric said as we cruised up past pink, orange, and blue and then slowed to crawl through yellow. We pulled into a spot and got out. I could hear faint music: "*Tie a yel-low rib-bon . . .*"

Eric bopped his head in time as we walked to the elevator. "A yel-low rib-bon!" he sang along, his voice flat.

"That's why he likes this floor," Christina-Mai said.

"Well you don't wanna have 'She'll be comin' round the mountain' stuck in your head all day, do ya?" Eric replied, pretend-punching her arm.

We planned to meet for lunch. Then I headed to the stained glass museum at Navy Pier. After walking through the hallway of stained glass, I visited the Terra Museum, a small American art museum, and quickly viewed the whole collection. Aware of how I'd wasted my chances to slow down in Indianapolis and Champaign, I monitored my mood. But I felt good, energetic; I didn't need a time-out.

After meeting Eric and Christina-Mai for lunch, I parted from them at the farmers' market. The bleak day discouraged sitting outside, so I got in line for a free tourist trolley that ran south to the peninsula with the aquarium, the history museum, and the planetarium. I only had time for one museum. Ideas about visiting each clogged my head. Looking at fish would be fun, and history might be interesting.

*But I've always liked stars. And I've been to aquariums plenty of times. And I hated history in school.* I felt like a five-year-old whose mom insists, "You *like* this movie!" just because she liked it once, as if something's wrong with her for growing up.

Outside the trolley, the wind off the lake howled. To the north stretched the gray silhouettes of skyscrapers. I stood in the cold, unsure which museum to visit, then walked to the planetarium. I *had* always loved the planetarium in grade school.

Inside, I bought a star show ticket even though it cost as much as the museum entry fee. I went straight to the theater for the next show. I wanted to relax in the dim theater and watch the sun set and the stars come out, as the lecturer pointed out constellations with his laser pointer.

But instead of a simulated sunset, the lights snapped off. Rock music began as slides flashed on the domed ceiling and a recorded voice boomed out, "THE NIGHT SKY! AN INCREDIBLE JOURNEY!" The planetarium stars lit the backdrop, fading in the slideshow's light pollution. When had planetariums come to this? Didn't kids stargaze anymore, or did they need these television-like images to maintain their interest?

After the "star" show, I entered an exhibit, "From Night Sky to Big Bang." I read the displays and immediately forgot what I'd read. I tried to grasp the vastness of the Universe, which always made me forget to breathe. The displays progressed to a discussion of the future: the inevitable loss of everything familiar, and the impermanence and therefore pointlessness of human life. "What will happen to the Universe?" the loudspeaker voice boomed overhead as I walked through the desolate reaches of space. "Scientists predict that it will keep expanding. The stars will run out of energy and go out. Someday, the Universe will be a quiet, dark, and cold place." I imagined floating past the lifeless planets, utterly alone.

After an hour, I'd grown weary and dejected. I hadn't thought I needed a break after lunch, but maybe I should have taken one anyway. Maybe I needed to be proactive about taking time-outs, to avoid getting drained and depressed. I passed the doorway to "Telescopes, Then and Now" and decided to skip it.

With a heart like lead, I fought the heavy exit door and staggered out into the wind whipping off the gray lake. Across the choppy water, giant shark fins circled the aquarium's dome to advertise a new exhibit. I wished I had gone there.[10]

BEFORE I CALLED MARY THAT night, I focused, whittling down the words in my head so I wouldn't be overwhelming. "I won't anticipate her answers," I told myself, "or overplan or explain too much." I'd just say what I wanted.

I dialed. "Hey, it's Emily," I said when she answered.

"Hi."

"Want to meet for lunch tomorrow in Pilsen?" Pilsen was the Mexican neighborhood, on the same side of the city as her friend's apartment.

"I can't, I haven't heard from Curt yet." Curt was her friend who was picking us up tomorrow, and taking us to Milwaukee. We'd bike west from there.

Her rejection pricked, but I ignored it. "Okay, I'll just come to the apartment after lunch then?" I rearranged my day to form a new plan: maybe I'd eat lunch alone in Pilsen, or at the Art Institute.

The next day, after a few hours in the Art Institute's galleries and cafe, I suddenly felt antsy to go. I skipped the remaining galleries and took the red line train across the city, then walked from the station to Mary's apartment.

"Here I am walking around Chicago," I thought, surprised by my confident attitude . . . as if I'd always done this.

Mary was alone, her bags clustered around the coffee table. "Curt'll be late," she said.

How had her week been? She'd seen her boyfriend after a month of biking a thousand miles to reach him—how had it gone? What had she done in the past two days, since he'd returned home? It seemed nosy to ask, so I didn't.

Since Curt was late, we walked to a Mexican restaurant. Out on the streets and through lunch, I noticed the lack of the horrible tension I kept expecting. Back at the apartment, Mary pulled out a lump wrapped in plastic wrap: the remains of the carrot cake she'd baked in Champaign. She offered me half.

*Is my piece slightly smaller than hers?*

"So what if it is?" I told myself. It was her cake, she was nice to give me some.

*Did she want to share it, or did she feel obliged? Should I have refused it?* I didn't even like carrot cake; I hadn't wanted to hurt her feelings by refusing.

I wished the thoughts would shut up. I tried to erase them from my mind.

## Madison, Wisconsin, in which I desperately try to stop thinking and meet with unexpected success

THE NEW BERLIN TRAIL HEADED west in a perfect line. A train track ran along one side, wooden power poles along the other. All around, fields baked in the eighty degree heat; a mile off, trees crowded the horizon.

At first I felt glad to be away from traffic. But the straight trail quickly grew tiresome. No matter how long I rode, it looked exactly the same! The hot sunlight made my back damp. Finally the trail ended, in Waukesha, where we visited a supermarket. In addition to dinner supplies, I bought cheese slices, yogurt, a banana, and a bagel. I started with the bagel and half the slices of cheese, sitting on the curb outside the store.

We left town on the Glacial Drumlin Trail. The name came from the shape of the land: "drumlins" were asymmetric hills, and the ones in Wisconsin were "glacial" because they'd been left behind by retreating glaciers. The new trail ran straight, too, but looked more interesting and felt less hot and oppressive. Maybe the scenery had subtly changed, or maybe it was the effect of a rest and a bagel with cheese.

Mary and I rode together, not pulling ahead or falling behind. I felt aware of my actions and words, keeping everything pleasant; I didn't want to do anything antagonistic. When we stopped at a trailside park, Mary agreed to pose "driving" the car-shaped climber, as if she were making an effort, too. I wondered at my pleasantness; my heart felt empty, like it wasn't even there. It was how I'd felt on the beach in Chicago, like a new state of being. And it was a relief to be this way with Mary, after feeling tension for so long. Would the emptiness last? I liked it but didn't think it an ideal solution.

The power lines and train tracks disappeared. Now a wide irrigation ditch ran below us, like a canal, with still water reflecting the cloud-dotted sky. Beyond spread fields with bright green rows in newly turned earth the color of used coffee grounds. I imagined stepping on the field: my foot would sink ten inches into the rich soil.

The mild afternoon passed, one field after another. We came to another park, full of trees, in Sullivan, Wisconsin. We'd entered Wisconsin! When had that happened? Yesterday—it seemed like days ago—in the car with Curt, driving from Chicago to Milwaukee.

"This is nice," Mary said, surveying the shady park. The trees hid it from the trail.

I rolled to a halt beside her. "Should we stop?"

"Yeah." She lifted a leg over her bike and I followed, wheeling mine off the trail and onto the grass to lean against the rough bark of a tree. I hadn't set up camp in a week but it came right back: help pitch the tent, find the stove and gas, wash up, change clothes.

That night, I wrote in my journal, describing the empty feeling that had replaced the tension I'd been feeling around Mary. I got this idea that I could work on being happy regardless of what happened around me. Instead of focusing on fixing external things, like my relationship with Mary, I'd focus on how I could be a better person. I listed my ideas: I'd accept people, I'd let go of anger and judgment, I'd cultivate patience. I'd say prayers every morning to create a positive mindset for the day, and at the end of the day to give thanks.

I'd been seeing only the negatives. What were the things I liked about Mary, that I'd stopped noticing since we'd been on the trip? "She sees the good in people," I wrote. "She tries to live by her beliefs even if it is scary. She's easy going. She's honest—or tries to be. She accepts my ideas—that is, she lets me have them. She understands insecurity. She is willing to keep going. She will make herself do tough things. She respects lifestyles—eating habits, prayer. She tries to respect what she doesn't understand."

I went to bed hopeful.

BY NOW IT WAS JUNE 6th—almost summer—and the Glacial Drumlin Trail was alive with wildflowers. I'd never thought much of wildflowers. They're a nice idea, but really they're dinky and disappointing, lost among the green. But here they gathered along the trail, thriving in the sunshine that reached down into the clearing. Beds of white or lavender phlox flowed down from the trees to the edge of the hard-packed dirt. I kept stopping for photos: The green back petals of an unopened daisy splayed like miniature sun rays. Perfect white balls of dandelion bobbed. The lobster-colored coattails of a wild columbine drooped over its pale yellow vest.

Then the trees cleared and we rolled out into a field of straw, where bunches of powder-blue flax blossoms shimmied in the breeze. A hill rose up to a red barn. A blackbird swooped low, and I watched for the flash of red and yellow from his wing. The redwing blackbirds had persisted as we'd moved west, like good omens.

The trail ran through a town before diving back into the woods. Gargantuan Queen Anne's lace towered over me. Then I spotted a small signpost: "Beware of Wild Parsnip! It burns exposed skin!" A line sketch showed the now-menacing plant. Had I touched any?

Midday, the trail left the woods again and ran alongside a road before dead-ending at a guardrail. A cleared strip continued with train tracks instead of a trail. We found ourselves back on the map, on a highway toward Madison, following directions to the house of my friends Meg and Brian.

ON OUR FIRST DAY IN Madison, Meg and Brian took us to the sprawling farmers' market and then to the community garden, where we weeded their daisy-filled plot. Brian had a surprise planned for the afternoon.

"We're going to the Forevertron!" he said. "It's so totally Buehler! As soon as we saw this place, we were like, we have to take Buehler here! Oh man, you're gonna love it." He used a tripped-out '70s voice and waggled his fingers in my face. "It's far out, dude!" He smoked an imaginary joint. I smiled, the way you smile when people are singing you "Happy Birthday" and you don't know what to do.

The Forevertron turned out to be a scrap-metal sculpture the size of a mansion, with towers, bridges, and whirligigs. Queues of spider-like metal creatures marched down its exit ramps. In the woods and fields surrounding the Forevertron stood other scrap-metal artwork, like the Bird Band, an entire symphony of bird creatures with bodies of tubas and euphoniums, and sprays of old horns for tail feathers. I didn't see any rules about not touching or not climbing on the sculptures.

Brian led us to a trailer where the artist, Dr. Evermor, sat in the shade, white hair poking out from under a black cowboy hat. Dr. Evermor invited us to sit and sent his wife to make us popcorn. He told us he'd traveled through time in the Forevertron, starting in England in the time of Victoria and Albert. The Forevertron was a time machine.

That evening, I got out my stationery and began to write. I hadn't been writing as many letters; I'd realized they were like an addiction. Every time I finished one, a small burst of elation satisfied me, but it didn't last; the need to write another letter returned. But the Forevertron had been so awesome that I wanted to share it with everyone I knew.

Mary worked quietly in another room. She'd seemed to enjoy the Forevertron, and I'd seen her laughing at Brian's goofing. And she'd played cribbage with him before dinner. But we'd only spent one night with her friends in Milwaukee—would she mind that we were spending three here? What if she felt disconnected as I had at Curt's? Should I ask if she was okay? I felt awkward, and asking might make it worse.

Should I try to fix our relationship, or accept it the way it was? I'd decided to focus on fixing myself . . . *but doesn't that equal ignoring Mary? Isn't that wrong?*

"Maybe nothing's wrong with her—maybe she doesn't want me trying to fix anything," I thought. "Maybe she has her own issues."

Thinking just confused me; I tried to clear away the thoughts.

Instead, I considered the end of the trip—where and when we'd reach the coast. Our path across America had changed from the large zigzag I'd imagined (through places I'd picked based on *Rough Guide* descriptions) to a mildly zigzagging line connecting our friends' houses. After our final stop to visit Mary's sister in Minnesota, our direction would be unclear. I still had some major zigs and zags in mind but saw our route becoming shorter and straighter. If we rode straight west from Minnesota, we'd end up in Portland or Seattle.

Originally, we'd had a vague idea about ending in San Francisco, and I'd booked a ride home on the Green Tortoise, an adventure travel bus. I'd taken one of their trips five years earlier and loved it: The vintage buses had had their seats replaced by a cushioned platform. Two drivers took turns, while about thirty passengers hung out talking, playing cards, writing in journals, or just gazing out the windows. The bus stopped for meals and day hikes; most driving happened at night while the passengers slept like sardines on the platform or in the overhead luggage racks. That first trip was especially relevant because Mary and I would ride some of the same roads I'd traveled then.

This year's trip left San Francisco on September 19th. Mary hadn't settled on an end date. She wanted time with her family before starting her new job in the fall. Today, Mary had mentioned that she might want to finish biking on August 7th in Seattle, because her boyfriend would be there and could give her a ride back east. Plane tickets to North Carolina were four hundred dollars, she'd said, so the ride would save money.

She hadn't planned, and the Universe had sent her a free ride, whereas I bought my ride home instead of having faith. I defended my actions: *I saved up for this trip! What's wrong with taking the Green Tortoise home? Besides, I don't have a boyfriend to give me a ride; I have to make things happen for myself.* The arguing went in circles.

"Stop!" I told my brain. "Stop obsessing!" Maybe Mary wasn't criticizing me for taking the Green Tortoise. Probably she was just glad of her own free ride.

"This is a challenge," I thought later, lying on the sofa bed with my knees tucked up to stretch my lower back. Mary lay quietly next to me.

"I should be nice even if Mary is criticizing me." But wouldn't that be patronizing? This left me where I'd been earlier, trying to fix things.

It was impossible! I wouldn't think on it anymore. I prayed for help instead.

SUNDAY MORNING, I CRAWLED OUT from the covers and took my journal to the plant room. I thought of it as the "Morning Room" even though it faced west because the multiple windows let in clear morning light. They were open, too, letting in a fresh June breeze. I made myself sit still for several minutes before writing.

After breakfast, I went outside to put new brake pads on my bike. The cool, cloudy air welcomed me. There was solitude outdoors. I rolled my bike out of the white shed and got to work. A few minutes later, a warning raindrop hit me. I moved into the shed's open doorway as more raindrops fell, pattering heavier on the early summer canopy of leaves, until a regular shower drummed down. I stood sheltered and dry, but still right out in the rainstorm, breathing it in.

Meg caught sight of me from the kitchen window and pushed it wide open. "Need a rescue?" she called out. "I've got an umbrella!"

"No, I'm fine!" I smiled and waved through the downpour. She smiled back, and it seemed that at that moment, each of us was in her own space, the place where she needed to be. I looked at the white shed, the rain-soaked grass, the slick wet tree trunk. The colors vibrated, intense. The phrase "glazed with rain" popped into my head. I recognized it immediately: William Carlos Williams's poem, "The Red Wheelbarrow." I imagined the white chickens' tail feathers poking up from the green grass.[11]

I finished my brake pad installation; the rain ended. But when I returned to the house, I carried quiet with me. I went back to the Morning Room to write in my journal.

Later that afternoon, we drove downtown to see a movie at the beautiful old Orpheum Theater. We sat in the balcony, and I smiled when the movie began with a small African boy wobbling along a dirt road on a rusty old bicycle. The movie was called *Nowhere in Africa,* and watching it, I soon lost track of myself completely. For some reason, we'd left empty seats between us, so I had no neighbor to pull me back to reality with a rustle or cough.

As the credits rolled and I came back to the theater, I forced myself to remain still. Usually I made excuses to justify lingering: "I want to see the credits" or "I want to see the soundtrack information." But really, I just wanted to sit, to let the movie finish absorbing. Today, I didn't make excuses. I just sat.

At last the heavy curtain dropped over the screen, and the lights brightened with an imperceptible hum. I looked around; I sat alone in the balcony! I hadn't noticed the others leaving, or worried that they'd be waiting for me.

I stood up. An odd, aware feeling filled me, like I was more present in the world than usual. I took a minute to look over the empty balcony, and the deep theater beyond, wishing I could soak in the feeling, and kept looking even as I stepped toward the door. Then I blew silent kisses out over the theater and left.

## Western Wisconsin, in which we are where we're meant to be

I SAT ACROSS FROM MARY, DOING nothing. We'd stopped to read a historical marker and, drawn by the peace of the park behind it, gone to sit at a picnic table. We couldn't camp here, exposed to the busy road. But I wanted to stay.

This park, I'd read on the marker, was the former site of Dover, Wisconsin, home of John Appleby, who'd designed a "knotter" for the grain binder based on the movements of his mom's knitting hands. The town had died when the railroad chose a different town for a station stop.

I took a bite of my banana. "I just want to keep sitting here."

"I know." Mary popped another almond into her mouth. I finished my banana and folded the peel onto the table. Then I stretched my arms, pressing them into the top of the table to also stretch my back. A minute ticked past, then another.

A car slowed and pulled into the turnout. It churned up dust, advancing until it stopped alongside us. The driver rolled down his window.

"Where you from?" he called, leaning with his elbow out the window.

"New Jersey!" Mary said. His eyes widened and his head bobbed. On the seat next to him, a preteen boy stared out his closed window, while another sat in back.

"Will you be here in five minutes? I've gotta drop them off." He indicated the boys. We nodded, and he drove away. I looked at Mary; she shrugged.

A few minutes later, the car returned and the driver, Bill, joined us, bringing a well-worn map. After a brief mention of our trip, he launched into stories of day trips he'd taken and the area's roads. The Wisconsin map he carried had special patterns for bike-friendly roads—Bill offered to lend it if we'd mail it back. Mary thanked him and took it.

Bill's truisms, like that physical adversity would make us stronger, didn't inspire me. But I tried to look attentive and nod periodically.

"You can camp at my church," Bill said when he learned we had no plan for that night. "It's just a few miles."

"So we weren't meant to camp in this park," I thought as Mary and I said goodbye and returned to our bikes. "But there was a reason for us to keep sitting here: it led to Bill and his church."

We headed on, watching for the route. The state map showed a town, but we found only a gas station before our turn.

The new road wound through a valley, perfectly flat. Fluffy cottonwood seeds blew across the roadway, and redwing blackbirds flitted in the fields. The dot of a white church appeared. Behind the church stood silos, and then trees rose up on a hillside. Meeting Bill had led us off the main road, and this smaller road was all-around more beautiful: more peaceful, more green, idyllic. The main roads, the ones on the state map, were often a watered-down version of beautiful, seen through a filter of car dealerships and fences.

We arrived at the church and wheeled our bikes around back. A fence surrounded the churchyard, a porta-potty stood in the center, and a water pump came out of the grass near the building. Across the fence towered three concrete silos near an asymmetric red barn, surrounded by low buildings and a rail fence. We pitched the tent, and I unloaded the cooking supplies, but then I sat in the shade on the church's front steps. It was only five-thirty.

After the traffic on the main road, my ears rang in the silence. But as I sat, the silence seeped in. I noticed birdsong. A car passed, its engine rumbling louder, then fading. A faint hum grew into the roar of the tractor coming home. Amid the noise, I looked up at the sky, where puffy clouds drifted by like a fleet of fluffy airships floating out to combat. The tractor droned past, turning in at a gate by the barn.

"Just this morning," I thought, "I felt sad to leave Meg and Brian, but now I feel perfect." I had that wonderful *alive* feeling again, the one I'd had after the movie. The clouds and fields vibrated in the light. I wished I could soak up enough of the feeling to make it last.

The urge to write letters came, but it seemed at odds with the feeling of being in Wisconsin, on the steps of the church, in the beautiful day. I'd already recognized the addictive nature of letter writing, and how the contented feeling of "getting something done" never lasted. But writing letters was also a distraction, a way to keep life at bay and avoid being present in reality. I hid behind letters the same way I hid behind my camera and my journal. They would defeat the unnerving alive feeling.

But it was hard to do nothing.

After a minute, I gave in and opened my journal. After writing about the day, I picked up my new book, *The Four Loves* by C. S. Lewis. I'd gotten it at a used bookshop, thinking it might have answers about dealing with friendships and relationships and parents.

The first section, though, was "Likings and Loves for the Sub-Human." I struggled to focus on the dense writing, until a passage on the fallacy of worshiping nature stood out: "Say your prayers in a garden early, ignoring steadfastly the dew, the birds and the flowers, and you will come away overwhelmed by its freshness and joy; go there in order to be overwhelmed and, after a certain age, nine times out of ten nothing will happen to you."[12]

It wasn't just me—C. S. Lewis understood! I constantly berated myself for not "having fun" or not feeling things I "should," but my expectations were the problem. On one hand, it was hard not to have expectations about exciting moments (like, for example, the moment when I'd reach the Pacific Ocean); and it was nice to look forward to things (like the peaceful coffee shop I hoped to rest in at each new town). But expectations led me away from accepting a relatively dull reality and enjoying it for what it was, and occasionally being surprised by it.

As the light began to fade, I returned to the churchyard to make dinner: kale mixed into a can of chili-flavored beans. Mary had disappeared into the tent. The sun moved down over the back fence, setting behind hills that bordered the marshy-looking land I glimpsed through the trees. I'd hoped for a good sunset and now here it was, but the alive feeling had faded. I made myself watch the sunset anyway, as I ate dinner. "I have no expectations of feeling moved inside," I told myself. "I am content." But I felt dull.

Then the bushes rustled. I stared in the failing light. Something moaned! Alarmed, I stood, straining my eyes. The top of an animal moved over the fence: black and white.

Cows! Returning home to the barn!

I hadn't expected anything, and something had happened!

I walked to the fence to watch the cows pass. High overhead, a half moon shone in the sky. The cows walked single file, my presence causing a brief back-up as each cow paused to look at me. One let out a loud, "Moooo."

*How long should I stand here watching cows?* I couldn't just enjoy the moonlit farm and the night air and the cows; my brain had to interrupt. But the cow line ended, so I returned to my dinner.

Mary and I kept passing signs for something called "House on the Rock." As far as I knew, House on the Rock was a tourist trap, a giant house full of stuff—musical instruments, lamps, a carousel—with a steep entry fee. I didn't particularly want to see it. But then Mary spoke up.

"We went when I was little. I kind of want to go . . . but it's too expensive!"

"Let's just bike there," I said, "and then you can decide. We'll still be going west, and maybe we'll get a nice view of the house from the road." So we followed the next "House on the Rock" sign, off the main road and off the map.

By now, the glimpses of sun had vanished, defeated by heavy clouds and a hanging mist that threatened rain. Houses lined the road, not scenic farmland. After a while, we passed the entrance to a golf course, and then the road climbed into trees, steeper and steeper. I began feeling something was amiss. We hadn't seen a "House on the Rock" sign in a while, and the road had narrowed. Or maybe I just didn't want to go up the hill.

Mary and I both stopped. "I think we took a wrong turn."

Mary's sigh seemed to agree. I pulled out my map while she got out Bill's, and we both spent a minute staring, hoping for an answer. Not knowing which way to go, we chose downhill.

As we coasted back toward the golf course, I saw the sign at the entrance:

## House on the Rock Resort
### & Golf Course

It had a logo like the House on the Rock logo. We'd been following the wrong signs.

"Oh, no!" Mary said as we both began to laugh.

We pulled into the driveway. "Can we get a picture?" I asked. Mary got her camera and set the timer, balancing it on the decorative stone opposite the sign. I kneeled in front, and she ran to join me before the camera snapped.

We now had no idea where the actual House on the Rock was, so we decided to continue on. Mary got us back to a main road, where we turned west under gloomy skies that drained the surrounding farms of beauty.

The road led to Gotham, where we found the Pine River Trail. The trail ran alongside newly planted fields bordered by trees. In the quiet, desolation sank in. We didn't pass a single person. "There were quiet afternoons in Indiana and Illinois," I thought, "but I never felt lonely with the wide open spaces." Here, with trees overhanging the trail, I felt lost. The tiny plants made me imagine we moved back in time—the crops shrank back into the earth, growing younger as we headed west. Some fields hadn't been planted yet; weedy grasses choked the dry husks of last year's crop.

The trail ended at Richland Center. After a break for lunch, ice cream, and email, we were back on Route 14, our original route before the House on the Rock detour. The road rolled up and down. We hadn't seen hills in so long, I'd forgotten about them. But the ice cream filled me with energy.

At the library in Richland Center, I'd gotten some emails that upset me. "I won't think about them," I told myself. "I'm not home, I am out here on the bike trip." But as the afternoon wore on, my brain no longer occupied the peaceful place of that morning. I couldn't resist thinking about the emails.

Before leaving on the trip, I'd attended a monthly sweat lodge: a group of people met to sit in the dark heat of the lodge and to share prayers. I valued the experience, but one of the group's members irritated me with his long-winded ramblings and self-important "teachings." He had begun to complain that our group lacked commitment—some people didn't attend every month. Now he had emailed that he couldn't come to the June lodge because he wanted to spend Father's Day with his dad. Although this *was* a good reason, it was also an excuse to avoid an event he'd lost interest in.

"It's not my problem," I repeated. "I'm on the bike trip."

But a second email bothered me as well: someone had forwarded an email from the leader of a Lakota tribe who declared that non-natives could no longer participate in native ceremonies. They ruined the energy of the ceremony, he wrote, and introduced inappropriate new-age elements. He concluded by writing that each person should find his own way to God.

I picked apart his email. On one hand, barring a whole group of people because of the behavior of a few seemed unfair. But on the other hand, I could imagine behaviors that ruined the energy of a religious ceremony, like talking too much, or acting like you've had all sorts of revelations while everyone else just sits hoping. Banning outsiders might diminish these behaviors, but surely some "non-natives" participated appropriately. Couldn't they be allowed?

The leader seemed to assume that no non-Native-American's way to God would be through Native American ceremonies. But I didn't want to be stuck with Christianity as my only way to God, simply because I'd been born with it. Christianity didn't feel totally right, and I hoped to add to it or find a religion that did. Native American spirituality had appealed to me, as if I had something to learn from it. Following that call couldn't be a bad thing.

"He's just one person," I reminded myself as I tried to calm my thoughts. "Not all tribal leaders will feel this way."

Route 14 curved north, and we turned onto 171 to keep heading west. We found the cutest park in Boaz; I wanted to stay. Maybe if I sat like we had in Dover, someone would offer us a place to sleep. But Mary was leaving, so I contented myself with reading the park's historical marker: Richard Brewer was a Boaz resident who moved west to work at a ranch in Lincoln, New Mexico. When "rival cattlemen" killed his boss, he deputized the ranch workers to arrest the murderers. One worker was William Bonney—Billy the Kid! Brewer died in a resulting shootout, and the many scuffles that followed (in which neither party seemed entirely right or wrong) eventually brought the law to Lincoln in the form of Governor Lew Wallace. I already knew this part of the story from reading Billy's letters at the Ben-Hur Museum: when Billy saw a chance to clear his name by cooperating with the investigation, Lew agreed to the plan and then betrayed him.

I took a last look around the park and pushed onward. By now the sky had cleared to blue, with puffy walls of cloud on the horizons. Green hills rose around me, all farmland with few houses. I'd forget the sky, seeing only the foreground of hills and trees, but then the clouds would jump out. I began to look for patterns, remembering paintings I'd seen in art history class where the giant clouds mirrored the shapes of the treetops below.

A car passed with a bike on its roof rack, and a hand waved out the window. I waved back; she'd known not to honk and scare us. The car drove out of sight.

A minute later, a car with a bike on the roof approached—the same car. She slowed as she neared. Mary and I stopped.

"I just passed you," said the driver, a woman in Spandex, "and then I thought, 'Where are they going to sleep?!' There's nothing for miles!"

Mary shrugged and smiled. "We just sleep by the side of the road."

"You can sleep at our house," the woman said. "I'm Katie." We introduced ourselves, and she told us how to recognize her driveway, a few miles on. Then she U-turned and drove off.

The hills increased, but the promise of a place to sleep kept me going. Katie was right: I didn't see any good spots to camp. I began to feel the listlessness of hunger, as if the energy in my legs was draining out into the road. My lunch and ice cream had long ago worn off; each pedal stroke became tiresome. I began to feel slightly nauseous.

"I hope she makes us dinner," I thought. It was too much to ask; we'd already gotten an easy place to camp. But it would be so wonderful to arrive and have dinner waiting! Chugging up a hill, I called up to Mary, "I know I shouldn't think this, but I hope she makes us dinner!"

"I know!" Mary shouted back.

*What if she makes dinner, and it has meat?* Would it be rude to pick the meat out?

At last we turned onto Katie's gravel drive. When it began to climb, my tired legs threatened to rebel. I pushed harder, willing myself to the top. From the crest, the driveway dropped and rose in another hill, somewhat bigger. I mentally groaned. The driveway continued like this, rolling up and down, and my legs ached to stop but we had to be almost there. And the faster I got there, the faster I'd get dinner—whether Katie made it or I did.

At last the trees opened and we pedaled up the final hill toward a fence, with a pristine red barn surrounded by several outbuildings. The driveway curved sharply, still heading uphill. I stopped, got off, and pushed my bike toward the brown house at the top, with its porch and fancy trim.

As we leaned our bikes on the porch railing, Katie came outside. "You made it!"

We nodded. "The driveway was rough," I said, smiling.

"Well, come on in and rest. I made some dinner." My smile permeated my face. "I guessed you're vegetarians," she added, and we nodded. "My daughter's a vegetarian."

Inside we met Dorothy, an elderly friend visiting from Florida, who motioned us to seats at the kitchen counter. Dorothy drank iced tea out of a Blue Willow mug—my mom's china pattern, which I took to be a good omen. Bowls sat on the counter next to a pot of lentil soup, and Katie returned to stirring vegetables in a frying pan and then poured them into a bowl of pasta. "I only had eggplant and peppers," she apologized, "and the soup's from last night."

"It's great," I said. She'd made a salad and put out a loaf of bread with hummus.

Katie's daughter (who was about our age) wanted to do a bike trip, so Katie pumped us for information. "Do you have a route planned?"

"Nah, we kind of make it up day to day."

"We thought about buying the GoBike maps," I explained, "but they cost a lot and they didn't go some of the places we wanted."

"GoBike?"

"They publish routes, and the maps tell you where there's food and campgrounds. They're really great, it's a great idea. But I'm glad we didn't get them, cause finding places to sleep has been one of the best parts."

"Where DO you sleep?"

"Where DON'T we sleep is more like it!" Mary laughed. We began listing our campsites. "The convent was the best—"

"No, the wreckage site! And Januarius."

"State parks . . . city parks . . . behind churches."

"Lots of churches."

"We found some nice parks along bike trails."

"So you're able to take trails a lot?" Katie asked.

"We were on the Pine River Trail this morning." She nodded. "We had one great one in Pennsylvania, and one from Milwaukee almost to Madison. Usually they're just short little bits going in our direction."

The door opened and a big man came in—Katie's husband, Bud. After shaking our hands and smiling, he said, "So I've got a question—don't you girls have *parents?*"

Mary chuckled while I replied. "Yes. They're not happy about this trip. Although, they seem pretty excited every time I call: they're like, 'Where are you now?' Mom's keeping a map, and they announce our location every week at church."

By the time dinner wrapped up, the sun hung at the horizon. Mary had gone with Katie to turn on the sauna in one of the outbuildings, and I got out my phone card to call home. They picked up on the second ring.

"Hi, it's me."

"Hi, Emily! Where are you?"

"Soldiers Grove. At the home of Bud and Katie."

"Hi, kid." Dad had picked up the portable phone. "Where are you?"

"Soldiers Grove."

"I just asked her that. Get with the program!" Mom said to Dad. Then to me, "Where are you—whose house?"

"Bud and Katie. Katie passed us on her way home from a bike ride—she had her bike on her car—and then she came back. She said she thought, 'Where will they sleep?!' She made us dinner."

"Be sure you thank her," my mom said.

"Tell them thanks from me," Dad added.

Bud walked past the doorway of the bedroom where I sat. "My dad says, 'Thanks!'" I called out.

"We'll put her on the next plane home!" he yelled to my parents. "Just say the word!"

"Did you hear that? He says, they'll put me on the next plane home."

"Okay, behave yourself." I imagined Dad grinning as he hung up his phone.

Mom was finding Soldiers Grove on the map. I itched to get out to the sauna, even though I'd been in one as a child and hadn't thought much of it.

(I'd thought there'd be jets of water or a pool, not just heat. Where's the fun in that?) Now a sauna seemed extravagant and fun to show off, so I said, "Okay, well, Mary's waiting for me . . . *in the sauna*."

"Oh brother! The sawww-na!" Mom said.

"Yeah, I wanna go."

"Okay, okay. Well, enjoy your evening. Say thank you."

"Okay, Mom."

I abandoned my puny camp towel for one of Katie and Bud's plushy bath towels and went outside. Pink color drained from the sky, leaving black silhouettes of the trees and barns. A faint breeze reached me as I trod downhill to the sauna barn.

Later that night, I sat with my journal in the softest bed ever, in the flowered spare room. Mary radiated contentment beside me, and I felt relief in thinking she was happy. I'd had a social evening, participating in the conversation instead of withdrawing into my head. I'd sat in the sauna with Mary, unsure of the point of sitting in a hot, damp room, but afterward feeling clean and relaxed.[13] I'd exited the hot sauna into the most beautiful night, cool, in the middle of outside! Even though we were sleeping in the house, I felt infused with fresh Wisconsin air.

Too tired to write, I took notes so I'd remember the day. It hadn't been "fun" until we'd arrived at Katie's, but now I wondered about my expectations. I couldn't meet a Katie and sit in a sauna every day; and the long afternoon of biking had been necessary to get us here. I remembered when I was twelve, I'd tried to write a story that was all love scenes. Because love scenes were my favorite part of stories, I'd thought a story composed *entirely* of love scenes would be amazing. But it hadn't worked; it was boring. Maybe we needed the long stretches of tired biking to make us appreciate the highlights.

## Iowa to Minnesota, in which
## I become one with my depression
## in a town called Harmony

KATIE ACCOMPANIED MARY AND ME to the town of Soldiers Grove, the first "solar village" in America, rebuilt after a flood in 1978. We set off past quiet farmland and forest under a low, cloudy sky. I was not sore, not hungry, not bored, not tired . . . I was actually just enjoying riding, not looking forward to getting somewhere.

Around lunchtime we crossed the Mississippi River; it was narrow and swampy. We turned north alongside it. Scrubby bushes and white daisies lined the roadside, and stands of trees stood out across the swamp to our right. Occasionally the marshes turned to farmland, with dilapidated barns standing in misty grass. In spite of the new humidity, I again enjoyed riding, and I stopped to take pictures without worrying about the time it took.

We rode eleven miles upriver to New Albin, Iowa, a small grid of downtown streets like a movie set. People waved from cars as we explored. In the middle of town, a giant bell stood on a green with a gazebo; the green was too exposed for camping. An elderly woman on a bike directed us to the park, and a police officer, straight out of Mayberry, looped past every thirty minutes and assured us, "You won't have any trouble! The park closes at ten, so you won't be bothered. Let me know if you need anything!" The park felt safe and peaceful, even with carloads of teenagers driving past on their way to the river. I even left my wallet in my bags, thinking, "I can't imagine anyone robbing us here."

Now we sat, enjoying breakfast at our picnic table in the shade. Yesterday, for the first time, I'd washed up with my soap—a sparkly, yellow sunshine-shaped soap that I'd gotten last Christmas. I'd used soap in restrooms or at houses but not at campsites, because it took more water to use it; but last night, with a pump available, soap had seemed manageable. Now the soap's mild scent graced the air as I sipped my tea. I hadn't checked out the restaurants in town, realizing I wanted to make Cream of Rice for breakfast.

"I can still go for a walk around town," I'd thought, "to mail my letters."

*Or I can go just to walk.*

I sat quietly as Mary finished her breakfast across from me. Slowly my brain soaked up the fact that birds cheeped overhead in the trees. I noticed the quiet marshes and the pleasantness of the sunlight and shade.

A car rounded the corner and moved slowly down Fifth Street, crunching on the gravel until it stopped opposite us. "Are we in trouble?" I thought automatically. It didn't matter—we were leaving anyway. A woman hefted herself out of the car, pulling her large coat around her shoulders as she shut the door. She turned and marched toward us, wobbling on her heels when she hit the grass but striding on. Mary and I stood to meet her.

"I'm Dora Witherspoon from the New Albin Town Board," she began, holding out a ring-laden hand. "I just wanted to thank you for spending the night in our town!"

Was she for real? "Oh, thank *you!*" Mary replied, shaking her hand.

"It's been wonderful here," I said.

"I have a little something for you to remember us by," Dora continued, and her other hand opened to reveal two round pewter key chains.

"Thanks!" we said in unison, taking them. One side showed the gazebo in the middle of town. "New Albin Centennial" said the other side, "1895–1995 New Albin, IA." We thanked her again, and she tottered away.

THE ROAD TO THE IOWA-MINNESOTA border wound through a river valley. Cultivated fields stretched to rounded hills. A picture-perfect barn passed. White daisies danced in the breeze. I stopped once to pull off my hoody as the sun rose, and once to have oatmeal chocolate chip cookies. Mom had mailed the cookies to Madison. They were individually wrapped in Christmas-green plastic wrap to keep them fresh. "I should tell her to wrap two cookies togeth-er," I thought. I never ate just one.

I saw Mary ahead, waiting by a route marker. Our back road didn't warrant a "Welcome to Minnesota" sign; the marker simply announced Minnesota Route 26, and the pavement changed slightly, as if Iowa had paved more recently than Minnesota. Mary's family was from Minnesota. She had me take a picture as she rolled across the line.

A few sunny miles later, we ascended a steep hill into Spring Grove. An oversize bronze Viking statue hinted of the town's Scandinavian heritage. After lunch, on the walk to the grocery store, we passed a statue of two men arguing. I thought the statue would be fun to take pictures with.

"I can stay longer," I told myself. "I can catch up with Mary later." So after the grocery store, we looked at the map and picked a town called Harmony, thirty miles away, as our meeting place.

After Mary rode off, I walked back to the statue: a life-size bronze farmer (in overalls, with a pitchfork) arguing with a bank man (in a derby hat and coat-tails, a cigar stump jutting out of his mouth) who for some reason wielded a plumber's wrench. They depicted a historic conflict in Spring Grove; I wished I could pose with them! I snapped a picture. Then I walked up the street to the Viking and took his picture, too. Was that all I'd wanted to do? It hadn't been very fulfilling.

I retrieved my bike and followed Route 44 signs back into the hot, sunny farmland. "At least I tried," I told myself. "I was assertive about what I wanted." But six miles down the road (about an hour later), when I passed a sign for Mabel, I regretted using my free time to take meaningless pictures. "Mabel" made me imagine an old-fashioned ice cream parlor in a cute downtown. But I didn't have time to stop. Had Mary stopped in Mabel? Had she met friendly locals in the ice cream parlor? Gritting my teeth, I passed the turn.

After another hour, I passed Canton without stopping. The sun beat down. Another hour passed as my legs grew tired. I just wanted to reach Harmony. At last I saw buildings.

By late afternoon, we'd pitched the tent in Selvig Park, a grassy square in the center of a grid of streets. The sleepy town and our reception in New Albin the previous night made me think no one would mind us camping. But an antsy feeling stopped me from sitting down. Something unpleasant stirred in my breast, and if I stopped moving, it might surface.

What would make me feel better? I'd call a friend after checking in with my parents. A pay phone stood on the corner.

"How's the trip going?" my friend asked after greeting me.

"It's okay," I said. "How are things there?" As he started to tell about last weekend's rock show, my mind drifted, isolated with my oncoming depression.

I made myself listen to the chatter, but I wasn't really there anymore. It was a relief when we hung up.

I didn't have the energy to explore Harmony's historic sites. Trudging back to the park, I could think of no more distractions: I'd called home, I'd been to a grocery store, and I'd recently written letters. I didn't feel hungry, and the high sun meant plenty of time for cooking later. The antsy feeling had diminished, though; now I had a dull, empty feeling in my chest.

I wandered across the grass to a gazebo and lay on the floor inside, staring woodenly at the ceiling. My spine stretched and flattened against the hard floor. I felt like nothing. *Something must be wrong with me. Why can't I just be happy like other people?*

Eventually, still not hungry but motivated by the sinking sun, I pulled myself up and returned to our picnic table. Mary ate her dinner nearby. I made a box of mac and cheese and added all the broccoli I'd bought that morning—I didn't need to ration it because I could go to Harmony's grocery store tomorrow. With the broccoli, I had dinner and leftovers. Then I took my dessert—yogurt with honey, banana, and nectarine, and more of Mom's cookies—and headed back toward the gazebo. But halfway there, I changed my mind and went to the swing set.

As soon as I sat, a lump swelled in my throat. I ate some yogurt anyway, swallowing hard to get down a piece of banana. Then I began to unwrap a cookie, fumbling with the green plastic wrap, and I thought of Mom wrapping them. She wrapped each cookie individually, to keep them fresh. And she'd made the cookies I liked. I started to cry.

Sometimes she mailed granola. I didn't like it that much, with its raisins. I told her I didn't like raisins, but she still added them, as if she didn't believe me. Why wouldn't she listen to me? I cried harder.

Then I thought about the time she got me a notepad with a dog on the cover instead of the black- and white-speckled journal I'd needed. The store hadn't had journals, and she'd been excited about the dog; but the notepad wasn't useful and I'd wished she just hadn't bought anything. Or I wished I'd acted excited about the dog notebook for her sake. And there was the time I asked for "boy underwear" for Christmas and she got me large, granny-style underwear instead. "Well, you didn't really want men's underwear, did you?" she'd said. I'd gotten upset, and my sister had laughed, making it all worse.

Tears dropped off my soaked cheeks onto the packed swing set dirt as my thoughts veered. My parents worried about this trip . . . they worried if I went to the movies! "It's dark out! Be careful! It's the other drivers we're worried about!" It was hard enough being brave about new things without their worries.

How many things had I not done because of them? I felt a flash of resentment, and immediately it became guilt.

I tried to catch my breath without making noise and hiccuped. A deep breath slowed the tears, but then I looked at the halfway-unwrapped cookie in my hand, in Mom's green plastic wrap, and a new wave of crying began. Was I wrong to try to grow up, hurting my parents in the process? Was I wrong to go on the bike trip? I could tell my parents I appreciated them—but weren't words cheap after I'd gone against their wishes, going on the trip?

I sagged on the swing as my thoughts reached their lowest ebb. These problems seemed so hopeless, and I felt so miserable, that I wished I could be dead. My thoughts launched into the funeral scene, with family and friends saying nice things about me and finally understanding that they had never understood me. "But I don't want to be dead!" I interjected, just in case someone was actually listening to prayers that day. I'd never kill myself while Mom and Dad were alive.

*But what if they weren't here?* The thought crept in. *They'll grow old and die. What if after they're gone, I get so depressed that I no longer have a rational side?*

I shook the thoughts away, wiping my eyes and looking around. Maybe someone would come along to talk to—maybe some cute guy who lived in Harmony. But inside I knew: no one ever came along at these moments. My most-depressed moments always made me think of that sappy "Footprints" poem that people hang in their bathrooms, that claims there's only one set of footprints at the tough times of life because God, instead of walking beside you, carries you. It seemed to me that there was only one set of footprints because God left me to flounder alone, so I could learn some lesson.

I cried until the tears ran out. Then I sat in my post-crying daze, rocking back and forth on the swing set. Did Mary notice me across the park? How was *she* feeling? Had she had secret cries, too? *This could be PMS,* I realized, counting the days in my head. I looked again at the green-wrapped cookie in my hand, and a small lump swelled in my throat, but it passed with no more tears.

I took a breath and sighed it out, picking up the spoon in my yogurt and scooping up a piece of nectarine. It was sweet! The sweetest piece of nectarine I'd ever had, and the nectarine hadn't felt all that ripe. I imagined God reaching down through the clouds to touch that piece of nectarine, sweetening it, perhaps trying to make amends for abandoning me earlier.

A loud bark sounded behind me. A dalmatian tied on the lawn across the street watched me intently. She sat at the end of her tether, tail wagging. I stood and placed my dessert on the swing.

The dog wagged and wiggled more furiously as I crossed the road and stepped into her yard. "Hi," I said, and she wiggled her butt right off the ground, prancing in excitement before making herself sit again. I held out a hand for her to sniff and then scratched behind her ears.

The bad moment had ended. They always did. And now that it was over, I didn't mind that it had happened. Maybe there *had* been some lesson achieved through that trial. And it seemed better somehow to go through it, rather than to avoid it. Avoiding it would not make it go away; it would still be there to deal with later.

## Eastern Minnesota, in which hot days and straight roads are filled with revelation

WISPY CLOUDS FEATHERED THE BLUE sky, and I inhaled the fresh air. Like yesterday, the road ran due west with no towns, but today the grassy fields and lonely barns looked prettier. Yesterday, we'd biked thirty-five miles of long, straight nothingness as the temperature climbed to ninety. I'd been lucky to have leftovers for lunch, because we hadn't passed a gas station, much less a restaurant. But we'd found a park in the town of Lyle, where I'd washed up and enjoyed the shade while the locals played ball nearby.

Probably the scenery was the same, but today I was able to appreciate it because it was morning and I had clean hair. I'd washed my hair that morning under the pump in Lyle's park, scrubbing and rinsing until it squeaked.

Coiling my hair under my rinsed-clean bandana, stiff with the imprint of the picnic table where it had hung to dry, had given me a feeling that my hair would stay clean forever. This made me think of the hills we'd climbed in Pennsylvania—how I hadn't accepted climbing hills as a regular part of life, but had wanted each hill to be the last, with reaching the top my final reward. Or how, after we dried out our gear in the sun, I resented the next rain shower for wetting it again. Now I wanted my hair to stay clean indefinitely.

But it was easy to move on from the top of a hill, or to keep biking when it rained, or to continue living after washing my hair. It was harder when I "got stuck" in life. Like when I had a group of friends that worked well together, and I kept trying to make plans with only them even as they made new friends. Or when I'd hang on to an exciting crush on one guy, keeping my buoyant feelings secret so I'd never have a definite response from him. When life felt particularly happy, I wanted to freeze it, and I didn't recognize when it was time to move on. Then, when I finally let go of how things had been, I had to make an unsettling transition to the new present, only to become stuck again. So, life advanced in unpleasant leaps forward instead of one smooth progression.

Did I miss things in the present while I clung to the past?

Fifteen miles passed uneventfully, with Mary pulling ahead and out of sight. I came to the larger (but still deserted) Route 65, which ran northwest for eleven miles to Albert Lea. Sure that Albert Lea would have a restaurant, I kept going even when a gnawing began in my stomach. But as I grew hungrier, I grew sad, and familiar thoughts moved in. *Why am I not having fun?* I was away from work and the crushes that made me feel sad at home; why was I still sad?

I tried to work out what thoughts had led to feeling sad, but nothing clicked. The sun felt hot, and I was hungry . . . why did I have to feel so bad? *And how much farther is Albert Lea?*

A large tree approached, over a bridge. Shade covered the wide cement walls, at a perfect height for sitting. I could easily lean my bike on the wall, well off the road. I braked without thinking.

Overhead, leaves swirled in the hot breeze. A silent stream flowed under the bridge. I got out peanut butter and a spoon and sat on the wall, scooching my butt backward until my legs dangled and rested.

In the shade, breezes cooled me as the sun's heat radiated off. I sucked on a spoonful of peanut butter and watched the road. *Does the peanut allergy ever develop midlife? What if I suddenly can't breathe? Would a car come along in time?*

"I'm not allergic to peanuts," I told myself.

I looked left down the long stretch of deserted road. I studied the wood posts supporting the metal guardrail, the backs of the road signs. As the minutes ticked past, my skin cooled. The peanut butter placated my hunger. I again looked down the road. "The view backward down the road," popped into my head, and the air grew clearer. Unexpectedly, I felt aware of myself sitting on the bridge, as if I were thinking, "I'm on the bridge, I'm in the shade," only I was not thinking at all. Stray thoughts and feelings spiraled together into an exact moment. It was like the feeling I'd had in the movie theater in Madison.

This time it unnerved me, but I still wanted it to last. But I couldn't resist:

gently, as if the moment could be scared off like a deer, I reached into my bag for my camera and snapped a picture looking backward down the road.

I felt better, but I made myself keep sitting. I wanted to be sure. There was no need to rush to Albert Lea.

"I shouldn't be so hard on myself," I thought, "upset at myself for feeling upset. And the tension that keeps popping up between Mary and me . . . it's not my fault or Mary's fault. It's just the way it is."

And then suddenly my stress had gone. The world had calmed, quieted. I looked at the road. I was awake and ready to go.

MARY AND I SPLIT UP for lunch in Albert Lea, so afterward, I left town alone. Mary was surely ahead; disappointed with lunch, I'd gone to Dairy Queen.

The sunlight beat down. The roadside offered no shade; any trees were behind a fence. Route 46 paralleled Interstate 90, but I couldn't see or hear the interstate.

Ten miles slowly passed. I bought juice at a gas station, the only building I'd seen. Route 46 joined Route 22. There was nothing to mark the intersection but grass and the fence. I turned.

And then I saw a tree: a gigantic tree, sprawled over a driveway. The fence broke for the driveway: I could reach the shade! With a burst of pedaling, I rolled onto the gravel. The shade enveloped me. I lay my bike down and collapsed next to it, panting as heat wafted off. While I rested, I scratched a heart into the dust caked on my sweaty legs.

The final spot on the day's itinerary was Brushy Creek. I found nothing but a crossroads with two houses: one standing and another, catty-corner, falling down. As usual, the trees were behind fencing, the shade a foot away. I sat as close as I could, as if being near the shade would somehow help. My knees and thighs gave their familiar twangy ache as I lowered myself to the ground, where I leaned against the fence and closed my eyes. Damp grass stuck to the bottoms of my legs. Ants crawled on the dirt.

When I dragged myself up for the last ten miles of the day, my exhaustion magnified the ache of my sore knees and the stiffness of my shoulders. The energy in my legs waned as soon as I started pedaling. I watched for the two crossroads I had to pass as the miles crawled by. Finally, after a total of sixty-two miles, I arrived in Blue Earth, Minnesota.

Blue Earth radiated quietness, with more cars parked than driving. I pulled over at a visitor center. My stiff body unfolded off my bike, which I leaned on the wall before plodding toward the door. Cool air hit me as I entered, and a woman looked up from her desk and smiled.

"Hi." I hesitated. "Has my friend been here?" She didn't reply. "Another woman on a bike?"

"Oh, no, I haven't seen her."

"Oh, okay, she's probably at the library. Is there a library?"

She gave me directions while my brain slowly began functioning in the cool air. "Are there any parks in town?" I asked next. "Like somewhere we could camp?"

"There's Putnam Park, but a lot of people camp at the fairgrounds."

"How do I get to the fairgrounds?"

"They're on the far side of town, just go up the main street and it'll be on the right."

I found Mary at the library, and we rode to the fairgrounds. The driveway rolled in past deserted buildings. We crested a hill and the grounds spread before us: green hills, sheds, tall light poles, a horse barn, and far across it all, something that looked like a life-size replica of the Jolly Green Giant.

I stared. It couldn't be anything else. "Oh my God, do you see that?" I called.

"Yup." Towering fifty feet tall, two-toned green in the late sun, he stood hands on hips, muscular biceps flexed, just like on the bags of frozen peas. I was so glad we were camping here.

I kept glancing at the Giant as Mary and I chose a picnic table. A family filled a nearby table, grilling and drinking beer, talking loudly while the kids ran around unsupervised. The sunlight had taken on its late golden hue so we hurried to set up the tent.

I got out the stove and began ripping spinach for a salad. Mary made her own dinner across from me. Then, out of nowhere, she said, "Do you wish I weren't here?" I stared, and she continued. "I feel like you'd rather be alone, or doing this with someone else."

My brain limped helplessly along, struggling to find a response. My first impulse was to make her feel better. But I wanted to tell the truth. What was the truth? Of course I didn't want to be alone—I'd be scared to be alone. But did I want *Mary* with me, or did I just want someone? I complained to myself about her, but I never wished she were someone else, did I? All the same, I never appreciated her. I felt thankful for the lady at Dairy Queen today who chatted with me, but not for Mary. Now I felt ashamed.

I'd been staring at my spinach for five seconds. If I said the things I'd *like* to feel, maybe lying wasn't so bad.

"No," I mumbled, "I couldn't do this without you." I looked up but couldn't make my eyes meet Mary's.

She began talking about how we didn't communicate or support each other. It was good to talk. We hadn't really talked since Madison.

"It just seems like we're so tired by the end of the day, we don't discuss anything," Mary was saying.

"I know," I replied. "I don't know why, when something bothers me it's so hard to speak up about it. I know you won't be mad, but instead I convince myself it's not a big deal and that I can just deal with it on my own instead of saying something."

We felt like friends again. After dinner, we walked to the Green Giant, laughing at the unlikely landmark. I thought again of happiness and "having fun," the terms I'd been trying to define while I'd sat on the bridge that morning. I thought of my friends who'd ridden cross-country the previous summer and told me fun stories. Then I thought of another friend, Jo, who'd left Chapel Hill and flown to San Francisco with no money and no plan. She'd ended up crying in a train station until some strangers took her home.

"Maybe my trip isn't the same kind of trip those bike friends were on," I wrote in my journal later. They'd been on a honeymoon sort of trip, whereas Jo had seemed to be on a search for personal growth. "Maybe mine is a Jo-crying-in-the-train-station kind of trip."

# Part 3:
# South Dakota,
# the Spiritually Moving Part
# of the Trip

## Minnesota into South Dakota, in which I start to let go of the trip I thought I'd be on

I WATCHED INTERSTATE 90 FLASH PAST from the back seat of Kathy's truck. Our last day on the road, we'd covered a boring, hot stretch of seventy-seven miles straight west to Worthington, Minnesota, where Mary's sister Kathy lived with her husband and three kids. We hadn't spotted the buildings on the horizon until the sun was sinking low over the grasslands.

We'd spent three days in Worthington. While Mary had taken her niece and nephews to the pool and enjoyed their ball games, I'd wandered by myself to the lake or stayed home to write emails. At the thrift store, I'd bought a book by John Steinbeck called *Travels with Charley: In Search of America*. The back cover described Steinbeck's cross-country road trip with Charley, his French poodle. It gave examples of his adventures, like dining with truckers and encountering bears, that struck me as similar to our adventures, even though they weren't. And it described Steinbeck's thoughts on the American identity, including racism, loneliness, and kindness. If the back cover put a lump in my throat, I could only imagine what the story inside would do.

I'd also bought a skirt of airy blue material with red flowers. I'd cut it off at the knee and hemmed it on Kathy's sewing machine. And Kathy had given

Mary and me two halves of a blue checkered sheet to sleep under on hot nights when we didn't want to use our sleeping bags.

I felt anxious about the land ahead—larger and wilder places. A woman at the pool had tried to reassure me, saying, "Don't worry, the people of South Dakota are great . . . except for the Indians." When I'd stared, she'd amended her comment: "Well, the drunk Indians, which is like 90 percent of them."

That was racist, wasn't it? How should I react? Should I argue? I could only defend the maligned Native Americans based on ignorant, idealized pictures in my head—what if the locals knew something I didn't? And what would I do as we traveled? I wanted to be open-minded about everyone, but I couldn't hang on to the "inherent goodness of people" when the people were drunk. Would I feel safe in South Dakota?

At Kathy's, I'd felt disoriented indoors. On the road, I often thought I must be dirty, but now I realized how tan my skin had become; it felt too tough in the still air of a house. And Kathy had commented on the large amounts Mary and I ate.

I didn't feel stronger, but I felt sort of solid . . . except for my knees, which still periodically twitched in pain. I had stopped my daily knee exercises, thinking that I stressed my knees enough with all the biking. I tried to push with less force when they hurt. The rest of my body hurt constantly: wrists, forearms, seat. Some muscles didn't hurt while biking but pained me when I climbed steps or sat. But I'd grown used to all that.

Mary had decided to finish biking by the end of July: we only had forty-three biking days left, and we had about eighteen hundred miles to go to reach the West Coast. This meant an average of forty-two miles per day, which wasn't bad; but we'd stop to see places, and we had to cross the Rocky Mountains. Also, our tentative route still included a major zigzag south to Cheyenne, Wyoming.

Before the trip, I'd flipped through a *Rough Guide* to America for ideas of places to see. The description of Cheyenne had caught my attention: "The approach into Cheyenne, dropping into a wide dip in the plains, leaves enduring memories for most travelers. With the snow-crested Rockies looming in the distance and short, sun-bleached grass encircling the town, the sky suddenly appears gargantuan, dwarfing the city's leafy suburbs and everything else below it."[14] I'd added Cheyenne to my list.

Once we'd started biking, our route had practically straightened, and I'd let go of many places I'd hoped to see. I'd held on to Cheyenne as the one place I *had* to go. I kept imagining our arrival, just like in the *Rough Guide,* and my feeling of awe when I saw the view. Later, after I'd met the love of my life while buying a cowboy hat in downtown Cheyenne, I'd tell friends how I'd read of Cheyenne in the *Rough Guide* and felt pulled to go.

Now, with Mary's new departure date, it seemed unlikely that Mary and I could reach the West Coast on time. Kathy offered to drive us part way across South Dakota; we'd miss some dull landscape and could still arrive at the Pacific together. But I balked at the idea of a ride—it was cheating! We wouldn't be riding across the whole country! I wouldn't be able to tell people, "I've ridden my bike across the country," without adding the caveat, "except for a third of South Dakota."[15]

But the alternative—not reaching the West Coast with Mary—was bad, too. I imagined the depressing Pacific Ocean photo I'd take without anyone in it. And it seemed wrong for Mary to travel so far and not see the Pacific.

Mary and Kathy left the decision to me. I didn't feel a clear pull toward one path, so I weighed the pros and cons:

> con: ride = cheating
> pro: eastern South Dakota seems pretty dull
> pro: arrive at the beach with Mary; Mary gets to see the beach
> pro: ride in the truck with Kathy; time with Kathy = fun
> pro: I'd feel less guilty about taking us out of the way to Cheyenne
> pro: there's a good-looking road toward the Badlands; Kathy could drop us there

The pros indicated we should take the ride, but cheating was a big stumbling block.

But who were we cheating on? Taking a ride was just different than what I thought the trip would be, but the real trip hadn't been like the trip I'd imagined, anyway. But part of me clung to the remnants of my vision.

Also, I wanted to see the Corn Palace in Mitchell, South Dakota. The *Rough Guide* called it "the World's Largest Bird Feeder." If we took a ride, we'd bypass it. I mentioned this to Kathy.

"Oh, we go right by it!" she said. "We can stop and see it, no problem!"

It hadn't occurred to me that we could *drive* to the Corn Palace. The fortuitousness decided me, and I agreed to take a ride.

Once I'd made the decision, my old plan seemed hollow, whereas the new plan resonated, clear and vibrant. It felt like when I cleaned out my closet, struggling to remove "the dress I used to love" or "the skirt that still fits so well." Once the old clothes were gone, I never missed them.

Now I watched the mile markers flit by, the scenery one endless yellow field. I was glad we were not out there biking. I hadn't slept well last night, and a knot of nervousness clung in my chest each time I remembered that tonight we'd be on the road again.

What would happen at the end of the trip? The night before, via email, a friend had backed out of plans to ride with me in August. My mind had dealt with the rejection by shifting gears: suddenly traveling with her didn't seem all that great. I'd be better off traveling alone, or with the guy I'd meet when I bought my cowboy hat in Cheyenne.

"Think about today," I told myself. I had this odd feeling that the *real* trip was about to begin. The Midwest had been different than the East but easy to adjust to—all those town parks to camp in, and predictable flatness and wind. Now there'd be long stretches without towns, then the Rocky Mountains, desert basins, bears . . . I didn't know what we'd encounter.

The South Dakota border flashed by. We had another hour of dry landscape to go before the Mitchell exit. I hoped it would pass slowly.

FORTY-NINE MILES PAST MITCHELL, KATHY exited the interstate onto Route 45, heading south. After a mile, she pulled into a gravel rest area. We were a quarter of the way across South Dakota; we'd head south for twenty miles to Platte, and then turn west onto Route 44, the road that would take us across the Missouri River, through the Badlands, and into Rapid City and the Black Hills.

The departure felt like Cape May all over again. Kathy helped unload our bikes, and I secured my panniers, then stacked my sleeping gear and fastened bungee cords over it. All around spread fields of dry, waving grasses. I'd been in South Dakota before, but not to bike across it. It seemed wider than ever.

The moment of departure came. Kathy gave me a hug, and then she gave Mary a hug that went on and on, and I wished Kathy had been my sister, too, so I could've gotten a longer hug. Then there was no option but to leave. With a final goodbye, I pushed off and rolled over the gravel and out onto the road. Mary followed. The truck door slammed behind me, and I heard its engine start. It crunched across the gravel, paused, then ground its tires and pulled out. The truck's sounds quickly faded.

The road disappeared ahead in the hot sun, no cars in sight. The fields were the flattest thing I'd ever seen. They couldn't be flatter than the Midwest, but maybe the lack of trees accentuated the flatness—with only waving grasses, nothing broke the horizontal. *I like it here,* I thought involuntarily. I liked it in spite of the sameness of the view. I felt something I struggled to define. "The Midwest had a clearness to it," I thought, "but South Dakota has an *openness.*"

MY WATCH HAD DIED DURING my swim in the river; after a day of biking past waving grassland and wheat fields, we'd arrived at a campground on the edge of the wide, shimmering Missouri River. (All that worrying about where we'd sleep, and we'd ended up with a river view!) Ironically, Mary had received her watch in the mail in Worthington. She'd forgotten it at home and had been asking the time for the past six weeks. It had grated on me: why couldn't she just buy a new watch? Now her watch had arrived, and mine was dead. I wouldn't ask the time unless absolutely necessary.

So that morning, I wondered how late it was getting as I sipped my tea. I'd made a slow breakfast of hot cereal with sliced nectarine to prolong the time at our beautiful beachfront campsite. I pulled out the South Dakota map even though I knew we'd be on Route 44 all day. The road paralleled the gridlines across the bottom of the map, over the Missouri River and onward.

When Mary began to pack, I followed. She set out, and a minute later, I biked past the ranger hut and stopped at the quiet road. Morning sun filled the sky to my left, lighting up the pavement that turned reddish where the land dropped away and the road continued onto the bridge. The bridge looked about two miles long and had only three-foot Jersey barriers as a railing.

I pushed off and rolled down, gaining speed, until I rolled onto the bridge. The shoulder disappeared so I moved to the middle of my lane, glad there was no traffic. Gusts of wind buffeted me as I pedaled out over the blue water, churning far below. The wind blew from all directions at once.

I kept my eyes on the red-tinted roadway and the green hills ahead. When I stole a glance over the river, I saw white caps scudding its surface. What if I fell? I was near the middle of the road; I wouldn't fall. *But what if a car knocks me?* My heart thumped. "Look at the hills," I told myself. They danced in a wall before me, slowly drawing nearer. The bridge hurtled symmetrically away.

I was halfway there. I could see the banks of the opposite shore, the gray road climbing up the hillside. Then the water ended and land slid under me, and I calmed right down. I could still fall over the edge and break my neck, but at least I wouldn't drown.

The blue of the river gave way to gray-purple waves that lapped at a narrow, muddy shore walled in by waist-high, grass-topped bluffs. I clunked down off the bridge, and the road immediately began to climb. Feathery grasses waved on the hills that towered over me on both sides. The road climbed and climbed, but it wasn't hard this early in the morning. At last I saw Mary, sitting cross-legged on the shoulder, gazing back at the river. The road leveled behind her. She didn't move as I passed.

I stopped by Mary's bike, leaning against a metal post. The rigid soles of my biking shoes clopped on the pavement. How oddly quiet it was, with only rustling grasses. The wind had stayed down at the water, or else it blew somewhere over our heads. Mary kept staring at the river that ran silently below, white in the sunlight. I hated to leave it behind. But ahead, the road dove into the green hills, and disappeared tantalizingly around a bend. I had no idea what to expect.

## The Pine Ridge Reservation, on which nothing is as I expected

THE WIND GUSTED ALL MORNING until it blew steadily, one long gust. Once, Route 44 made a turn, and the wind disappeared for four heavenly miles as I rode north. I entertained a hope that it had stopped, but when the road turned back to the west, I found it waiting for me, bursting with disapproval in my face. It seemed to attack me, eroding me like the river eroded the muddy cliffs. What would be left of the mud version of Emily when the wind was done?

It was impossible not to think about the wind, about how hard it made biking. And there was no end in sight: the wind didn't end like an uphill; it just continued relentlessly. But as I thought about how much I hated the wind, at least I wasn't daydreaming. In its own way, the wind kept me present.

The same wind flowed harmlessly over the grasses. "That's another difference," I thought. "Midwestern fields had plants in neat rows. Here it's just grass." There was something more real about the fields in South Dakota.

In Winner, I asked the girl in the bakery about places to camp. "Don't stop in Mission!" she said. "You don't want to sleep in Mission, it's not safe." As soon as I left, I unfolded our map and found Mission: west of us, on the shaded rectangle labeled "Rosebud Indian Reservation." Another warning about Native Americans . . . what should I think? But Route 44 skirted the reservation, so we wouldn't go through Mission. We'd cross the Pine Ridge Reservation instead.

I'd never been on a reservation except for once, on the Green Tortoise bus trip. Somewhere in South Dakota, we'd stopped for "Indian tacos" at Nellie Cuny's cafe. Years earlier, Nellie had rescued a Green Tortoise bus mired in mud by pulling it out with her tractor. Ever since, the cross-country tours had stopped at her cafe.

The bus had rumbled down a long, unmarked drive to a plain brown building with only the word "CAFE" painted on the side, and I'd wondered how it attracted visitors since you couldn't see it from the road. There weren't any other customers. Inside, I waited to give my order—meat or bean tacos were our only options. I reached the front, where a rosy-cheeked woman with white curls sat taking money. I disguised my surprise and ordered; that was Nellie Cuny? She looked like my Grandma Solari!

Dex, the bus driver, caught me on my way out. "Not what you were expecting, eh?" She was right: the Native Americans in history textbooks all had straight black hair in braids. They'd never looked like Grandma Solari. And the textbooks never went beyond wigwams and teepees; I'd never considered that reservations had more permanent buildings.

We ate outside Nellie's as the sun set over the grasslands. After dinner, we drove to a campsite that the Green Tortoise used with Nellie's permission. Dex said we were only allowed to camp because of Nellie, which left me with the impression that one needed permission to sleep on a reservation.

Now I remembered Dex's statement and worried because Mary and I didn't have permission to camp on the Pine Ridge Reservation. Maybe reservations had different rules than the rest of America, and we couldn't pitch our tent by the road or in a park. Plus, I didn't want to sleep on reservation land without permission because it seemed disrespectful.

But the reservation was forty-five miles across. It seemed likely we'd sleep on it.

THAT SUNDAY MORNING, CLOUDS BROODED overhead. This was my new favorite biking weather: clouds that shielded the sun but never gave way to rain. The flat roads flew by, easy going without the wind blowing. Yesterday, ridges had appeared to the north, dark against the sky.

Two of the towns west of Winner didn't exist anymore. The next possibility was White River, followed by Cedar Butte.

The scenery unrolled like one long painting, undulating grassy fields with patches of feathery burnt sienna, all of it ending at the horizon with the green-gray ridges whose shapes mirrored the uneven clouds in the sky. Yuccas grew by the road, their spiky leaves pointing up while heavy white flowers hung down. Tiny sunflowers and white morning glories poked up from the dwindling grass at the road's edge. A fence, almost lost in the tall grass, still ran twenty feet from the road. I'd been sure that once we were "out west" the fence would go away, but it hadn't.

After two hours of biking, a blue water tower appeared with "White River" on it in stick letters. Dust covered the road into town as if no one had entered in a long time; we rode in through a big metal gate. With its hard-packed dirt road and dusty air, White River looked like Mos Eisley minus the aliens.

We turned left at a windowless concrete building. A grocery sign hung ahead. A group of tattered men waited by the wall outside, standing or sitting on crates. We weren't yet on the reservation, but the men had dark skin and hair and features that seemed Native American. They looked up and watched me ride past, unsmiling, and a tiny thrill of fear went through me. Would they bother me? As I parked against the wall, one of them stood and ambled over.

"Can you spare fifty cents?" he asked. I smelled alcohol.

"I'm sorry, I don't give money to people." He nodded and turned away. Was I wrong to refuse? In Chapel Hill, the police recommended not giving— the money went for crack, they said. And the homeless shelter served three meals a day. But things were probably different here.

I sneaked my wallet out of my bag and tried not to worry about leaving my bike as I hurried after Mary to the door.

Inside, the swept floor and clean counter reassured me, as did the female clerk. I didn't see fresh produce or cheese; it was more like a convenience store. I got some cans of beans and approached the register.

"Is there anything in Cedar Butte, like a grocery store?" I asked the clerk.

"No, not really."

"Is there anything between here and Wanblee?"

"There's Corn Creek, up at the next intersection. They have a little store."

"Is there a park there? Or somewhere we can camp?" Maybe she'd let me know if the Pine Ridge Reservation had any "no camping" rules.

"There's a family—just past Corn Creek. The Daniels. They'd let you camp." She described their driveway.

"Okay, thanks." I took my cans and exited to load them into my bags, watching the group of men out of the corner of my eye. I checked the map; I saw one intersection between here and the reservation, but it wasn't labeled. Nothing was labeled "Corn Creek." When Mary returned, we rode away, looping through town toward the road we'd come in on.

The clouds had cleared, and we rode out of White River with hot sun beating down. The road looked flat, but I coasted without pedaling, a long descent into trees and across the Little White River. I flew out of the trees and began pedaling up the other side, slowing until my momentum had gone. Then slow minutes ticked by as I worked my way up the long, gradual hill.

We rode into the afternoon, looking forward to a rest in the town of Cedar Butte. But when we arrived, the crumbling buildings of Cedar Butte might've been an abandoned outpost on the moon. I pulled into the shade of a white concrete wall. A silent air-conditioner stuck out overhead, and tall weeds grew through the cracks at the ground. A few phone poles stood over the buildings; a stiff-looking wire came down to attach at one corner. One car was parked far back from the road.

The only new-looking thing in Cedar Butte was a silver post office box, subdivided into twenty mailboxes. Mary and I parked next to it and got out snacks and water bottles. Then I lowered myself to the hard ground, wincing as my knees bent and small pebbles pressed into my palms. Once sitting, I tried to find the place where my knees didn't hurt, halfway between cross-legged and straight out in front. Sitting that way, with half-bent frog legs, made me feel like a large, dumb baby.

I dusted gravel bits off my palms and reached for my peanut butter. A slight breeze cooled the back of my neck, and restfulness seeped into my legs. The stillness surrounded us like a ghost town, except for the shiny metallic mailboxes that almost rang out in their newness.

We rested for fifteen minutes and had just gotten up to go when a scuffling caught my attention. A stocky dog with multicolored fur trotted around the corner of a nearby building. The dog didn't alter his trot when he saw us. He jogged over and cursorily sniffed me as I scratched his head. Then he moved to the mailboxes and sat.

Then a man came around the same corner, thin and stooped and clutching a white envelope in his hand. The man noticed us but returned his focus to walking, and we watched his slow approach as the dog jogged over to him and then back to the mailbox, encouraging (or perhaps herding) him. Did he live here all alone? The postal box had twenty mailboxes, but maybe that was the smallest size the postal service had.

"Hello!" the man called when he neared.

"Hi!"

"You must be on a trip!" His voice wobbled.

"We're from North Carolina."

"What's that?"

"NORTH CAROLINA," I said loudly. "WE'RE BIKING CROSS-COUNTRY." He just looked at me.

"I'm MARY," Mary said. He looked at her and then me.

"EMILY," I said, putting my hand on my chest.

"Henry," he said. "I was just coming to check the mail." He slipped his letter into the slot and used a key to open one of the boxes. It was empty.

The dog flopped down on the pavement and lay panting. Henry closed his box and turned back to us. He didn't say anything.

"WHAT'S YOUR DOG'S NAME?" I said.

"What's that?"

"YOUR DOG!" I pointed.

"Oh, that's Coop," Henry said. "He's okay. I had another dog, but he ran off. I had to go in the hospital, and when I got out he'd gone. So my family got me this one. He's okay." He spoke doubtfully, as if Coop just didn't compare with that other dog.

I imagined Henry's family coming to visit: a long journey, perhaps by covered wagon. But they could probably drive here in five minutes. And probably Henry had a phone, although it was hard to imagine anything as advanced as a phone working in this decrepit place. *Why didn't his family feed his dog while he was in the hospital?*

"IS IT NICE HERE?" He looked at me. "IT'S NICE AND QUIET."

"It's nice," he said. "I liked it better 'fore they built the hog plant. Right over the hill—I can smell it when the wind blows. Indians built it so they can't do anything about it. Doesn't seem fair."

I didn't reply, sorry for him and not wanting to debate what was fair.[16] Henry continued to stand there. I didn't know what to ask, and we couldn't stay, so I stretched and leaned over my bike, zipping a bag. Henry watched us prepare to leave. Coop lay panting.

"Can I take your picture?" Mary had her camera in her hands.

"What? Oh!" He saw the camera. I moved next to Henry, and he straightened and put an arm around my waist. When my arm touched his shoulder, I almost jerked back: I felt hard bone. It flashed through my mind, "Maybe he has shrapnel embedded in him from some war," but then I realized he was just very thin. A lump formed in my throat, and my eyes filled with tears. I was glad I had sunglasses on.

Mary snapped the picture.

"Well, bye, it was nice meeting you," Mary said.

"BYE." I waved. Henry stood in the shade as if we weren't leaving, or maybe we were the only thing likely to happen that day, and he wanted to make the most of it. We wheeled our bikes to the road and pushed off.

As I rolled downhill, the world started to move again, the air whipping by, and I started to cry. I let Mary pull ahead. Tears washed my cheeks, mixing with my sunscreen, which then crept into my eyes, stinging. If I began to calm down, one thought of Henry in Cedar Butte brought on new spasms of tears. Was Henry still trudging home with Coop, the less-than-great dog, trotting nearby? Had he reached his crumbling house and gone into the dismal interior? Did he now sit at a dirty kitchen table, eating a pathetic lunch of stale crackers and questionable cottage cheese?

Then so many tears came that they kept the sunscreen at bay.

Hot and tired, I chugged along toward the Pine Ridge Reservation. Once we passed the sign and entered the reservation, would we find somewhere to camp? Would we find the Daniels'? I tried to distract myself by recalling a dream from last night, but my exhausting thoughts kept returning to their hopeless circles.

"If I were really good at meditating," I thought, "would I be able to empty my brain and ride along peacefully?" It seemed impossible. I remembered something a manager at the co-op where I baked had said. We'd been discussing the arrival of another big-box chain superstore in a neighboring town, and its effect on the local businesses, and I'd asked, "How do you stop the big chains?"

"You can't stop them," he'd said. "But you can have something good already in place, so that they won't want to come."

Maybe my thoughts were like those superstores. It was too hard to stop them, but if I could find something else to think about, maybe they wouldn't come. I'd already recognized that daydreams weren't a good solution because they removed me from my surroundings and reality. I could try singing. I could notice the scenery, but it was easy to be distracted from that. Maybe I could just repeat, "I am biking through South Dakota," over and over.

At last I spotted a building ahead, another windowless box. No trees shaded the gravel lot with its one car. Route signs marked the adjacent crossroads. On the map, this crossroads was about two miles outside the reservation.

Inside, a large woman stood by a register. Two children ran around, yelling and laughing. When they saw me, they ran to the safety of the counter. The woman smiled, and I waved hello. I crossed the concrete floor to the sparse shelves, hunting for something I could buy. I settled for peanut butter cups and approached the counter. "Could you fill my water bottles?" I still hated to ask.

"Sure!" She smiled, and I thanked her as she took them and turned to the sink. The kids stared up at me from behind the counter. The boy clutched a partly eaten cookie and had chocolate smeared on his face. I smiled, but they just kept staring. The woman handed me the full bottles. "Where are you from?"

"North Carolina." I no longer explained that we'd started in New Jersey. After a thousand miles, it didn't seem to matter.

Mary arrived, and we headed on, looking for the Daniels' place. The sun shone high in the sky. We had plenty of time to find a campsite. But there were no driveways that matched the store clerk's description, just endless grasslands. We pedaled on and on. We must've gone two miles. Maybe there was no sign at the reservation, and we were already on it.

We reached a drive that looked right, but there was no mailbox. Was this the Daniels'? If we rode down it, we'd be trespassing.

"Do you think this is the Daniels'?" I asked.

"She said it was past Corn Creek."

"So you think that *was* Corn Creek?"

Mary shrugged. "Let's just try it." It made sense; the next driveway could be miles away, and it would probably be unmarked, too.

We bumped onto the gravel. A fence ran on either side. Soon the fields swallowed the road behind us. Then a house came into view, and the fences moved out to encircle it. There was no car in the driveway.

"Should we knock?"

"Yes," Mary said, rolling her bike to lean on the fence. What would we do if no one answered? But three seconds after our second knock, the door cautiously opened to reveal a small dark-haired girl looking up at us.

"Hi, are your parents home?" Mary said. I winced inside as more creepy lines popped into my head: "I'm a friend of your mom," or "Want one of my peanut butter cups?"

"No, my dad's out," the girl said. A slightly older girl lingered in a doorway in back.

"We were hoping we could camp in your yard," I said. "Could we wait and ask your dad's permission?" She made a motion sort of like a nod.

Mary and I returned to our bikes, got our water bottles, and sat on the grass. If the dad said "no," we'd just have to set off again.

But he didn't return, even when dinnertime came. "If I were home alone at her age, I wouldn't tell a stranger, 'My dad's not coming home tonight,'" I thought. Of course, I probably wouldn't have opened the door in the first place.

"I don't think her dad's coming."

"I know," Mary said.

"Maybe we should ask her if we can camp."

We returned to the door. I hated that our presence might be ruining the girls' sleepover.

This time the door opened right away.

"Do you think your dad would mind if we camped here?" Mary said. The girl hesitantly shook her head back and forth.

"We'll just pitch our tent by the driveway. I'm Mary."

"I'm Emily." I waved.

"I'm Cindy," she said, "and that's my friend Rachel."

"It's nice to meet you. Thank you." We backed off the steps.

Once the tent was up, I dug out the stove and set it up on the gravel, which seemed like the safest place. I didn't want Cindy's dad to return to a burnt-down house. While I fiddled with the stove, the front door opened, and Cindy came out, followed by Rachel. She unwound the hose off its rack on the side of the house and began to pull the end toward us. I went over to thank her.

As the sun got closer to the ridge of the field, longhorn cattle drifted in. I assumed they were longhorn cattle: they had long horns that stuck out sideways and turned up at the tips. Low clouds of pink and blue hung over the fields, and the setting sun pierced through as if one of the steers' horns had pricked a hole.

I sat on the gravel to write in my journal. As the sunset passed and faded, lights twinkled at the horizon—could it be Rapid City, a hundred miles away? More likely it was Interstate 90, thirty miles to the north, but I liked it better as a city glittering under the twilight. Only a narrow band of turquoise remained in the sky, over the horizon and the twinkling city, with dark clouds pressing down from above.

Wind began to stir the grasses. What was coming? I wanted to keep writing. After another half page, though, the wind blew more insistently. The cattle didn't seem alarmed, standing and grazing. I grabbed the solar flashlight and crawled into the tent.

Inside the tent, where Mary slept, I wrote another half page, but then the flashlight began to fade. I wrote faster and faster, trying to record it all: the comments we'd heard about Native Americans, the warnings about Mission . . . then the flashlight failed, so I switched it off and closed my journal.

Outside, the wind now gusted and the tent jerked back and forth. "It's such a good little tent," I thought, lying down in my sleeping bag and looking up at the shuddering ceiling. Thunder rumbled, and soon came the first flash of lightning. Were the cattle still grazing? Were cattle a good indicator of safety, or did they lack the instincts to get out of a storm? "The cows are not scared," I told myself. Besides, surely lightning would strike those long horns before it hit our tent.

The gusts grew constant, and the flashes came faster. I lay awake listening to the thunder, my body jumping with each flash or rumble. Then a pitter-patter began that increased into a downpour, and again I prayed that our tent could handle the weather, the wind and driving rain, and that we wouldn't be struck by lightning.

I lay listening for ages, unable to close my eyes until at last the rain abated, and then I found myself yawning. With the promise of the end of the storm, I drifted off to sleep.

But the storms returned throughout the night, and every time I awoke to them, I wondered what we'd do if it still stormed in the morning. I couldn't bear the thought of packing and eating in a downpour. But it grew quiet as the sky lightened, and I lay awake hoping. At seven o'clock, I got up.

Pale clouds filled the sky, pressing down on the damp, yellow fields. The mild scene lacked all the glory and terror of last night's sunset and storms. The cattle still stood in the field across the driveway, in which someone had parked a blue Datsun.

A few minutes after I'd gotten up, a man came out with a small yellow dog. I overrode my instincts to avoid him and walked over.

"Hi," I called. "I hope it's okay that we camped here. We didn't want to get the girls in trouble."

"It's fine." He extended a hand. "I'm Tom Denver." So we weren't at the Daniels'!

"We've had bikers before. I told her she did the right thing."

"Well, thank you," I said, and he nodded and went back inside.

AFTER ALL THE WARNINGS AND fear about the reservation, crossing it was completely anticlimactic. It felt just like the rest of South Dakota. All we found in Wanblee was another windowless grocery store. I bought a bean burrito and nuked it in the microwave, and then sat on the curb outside to eat. A few trucks pulled in and out. The men tipped their cowboy hats as they entered the store, and I grinned back.

The only hint of danger was a road sign pocked with bullet holes. "But that might not suggest danger," I told myself, "maybe just bored teenagers." *Bored teenagers with guns.*

I'd hoped to learn something about the reservation, to participate somehow. I'd imagined striking up a conversation and getting invited to a meal, or spotting a plume of smoke rising over a field and recognizing the shape of a sweat lodge like the one my friends had built back home. But now, biking past fenced-in fields and the occasional house or trailer, my daydreams seemed ridiculous.

The only thing that happened that fit my ignorant daydreams was I found a bead necklace by the side of the road. But the beads were large, white tubes and pink hearts—not the teeny, brightly colored beads that we'd called "Indian beads" as kids. The "Indian beads" I'd expected seemed to represent what I'd learned about Native Americans in school, that they lived in teepees and wigwams and wore braids and leather clothing; the necklace I found represented a modern, realistic view of Native American life.

Had there been beadwork before plastic, perhaps made of shell or bone? Had the beads been dyed bright colors, or been as tiny as the ones I'd had? Maybe the original beads represented another history of Native American life, other than what I'd read in a textbook.

I picked up the necklace and tied it under my handlebar. A few miles later, I came to the turn that led off the reservation.

## The Badlands, in which I find the barren landscape that I'd thought I wanted

A REDDISH-BROWN WALL APPEARED OVER THE grass, blocking the horizon like a miniature mountain range with jagged mud peaks. Horizontal stripes indicated the layers of mud, deposited eons ago, then exposed by erosion. Then we passed a sign, "Badlands National Park," and a thrill ran through me.

As we rode into the campground, I scanned dozens of empty sites. Apparently, not everyone shared my love of the Badlands; having geology as its main attraction made the Badlands the nerdy loser of national parks. Or maybe no sane person wanted to camp with the wind. It rushed over the treeless campsites, undeterred by the curved, wooden screens attempting to shelter the picnic tables. It blew through my brain. But the backdrop of mud hills loomed over us; I wanted to camp right in the park.

It was five o'clock, so I had plenty of time before the ranger talk at nine. The visitor center and amphitheater were just up the road. Mary and I pitched the tent, pushing in the stakes as the wind tugged against us. While we made our dinners, a young man came bobbing around the loop drive. He asked about our bikes, then introduced himself as Dave, pointed out his parents' camper, and asked to take our picture. He took our email addresses so he could send it.

After dinner, I carried my pot and utensils to the nearest pump to wash, then laid them to dry and moved the stove under the table for the night. I just had to spread my sleeping gear in the tent, reorganize my bags, wash up, and change clothes, and then I'd be able to write in my journal.

A ranger approached. "Hi, just advertising my paleontology talk over in the amphitheater."

"Thanks, I'm planning to go," I said. "Is there a pay phone somewhere?"

"There's one outside the visitor center."

"What time is it now?" It had to be past seven, with the sun so low.

"Eight-fifteen." She moved on.

Eight-fifteen! How could it be eight-fifteen? I'd thought I'd have time for my journal. And I wanted to call home.

Mary stood. "I'm gonna go call Linda. I'll see you at the talk."

She always had time!

"Okay, calm down," I told myself, unrolling my sleeping pad. "I'll just get this done and go. I can wash up after."

I piled my gear into the tent and set off. I passed the amphitheater, where people gathered on long benches. A short line waited to use the pay phone. Mary wasn't there.

My irrational fuming resumed as I waited. *Mary always has enough time. She's always relaxed and enjoying herself, and she manages to do all the things I want to do—writing a journal, reading—in addition to making dinner and washing up.*

"Well, maybe I'm just slower," I thought. "It's not that I'm doing something wrong." But the solution was to travel more slowly, and Mary and I had already talked about that: she always felt like she waited for me.

This was my chance-of-a-lifetime vacation, and I wasn't having fun. And it didn't seem fixable. A lump swelled in my throat as the person in front of me hung up. I pushed the lump back and picked up the phone.

Dad answered. "Hi," I said. "I can't talk because there's a ranger talk at nine. What time is it now?"

"What? Oh, uh, hang on . . . it's just about eleven here," he said.

"Okay, well, I should go. We're in the Badlands, in the campground."

"Oh, uh, okay."

"Okay?"

"Okay, talk to you soon."

"Bye."

"Bye now."

As I jogged to the amphitheater, I imagined Mom walking in from her sewing room, anticipating me on the phone. Why had I even called? I'd con-fused Dad and upset Mom. The lump in my throat reappeared.

In the amphitheater, the ranger stood in front of an illuminated screen. Her voice carried over the audience as I joined Mary. The Badlands clay, she said, had washed off the Black Hills as they thrust upward, millions of years ago. Animals stuck in the mud became the fossils that emerge as the mud erodes.[17] The Badlands erode half an inch per year. Features from the 1920s are gone; the once-menacing "Vampire Rock" is now two measly, dull tips. We learned about "worm sandstone," a rock full of holes left by either gas bubbles or worms. And we learned that fossilized poop is called "Copralite," named after paleontologist John Cope by rival paleontologist John Marsh.

When the talk ended, we filed out of the amphitheater with the crowd. I'd relaxed during the talk, but now my thoughts returned. The trip was passing too fast. I wasn't happy, and I had to do something to fix it.

"Hey, Mary, I feel like the trip is going too fast." Did I imagine a cloud of tension descending? "It's just I always think I'll get to camp and have time to write, and I never do. By the time we get set up, there's never time."

"You can't relax and you're blaming me," Mary said.

I backed down. Was she right?

Mary *had* agreed to spend two nights in the Badlands. I had known I want-ed to stay and asked if we could. But often I didn't know what I wanted. I thought too much and became confused. Like in New Carlisle, Ohio, when I hadn't known whether to go out for breakfast or to cook at camp: pondering didn't help me figure it out.

Maybe I was so in the habit of doing what other people wanted (or what I *thought* they wanted) that I couldn't tell what *I* wanted. Maybe in the immedi-ate moment, I wanted the other person to have what *she* wanted, because this made things comfortable. The root of the problem was my fear of creating an uncomfortable situation. Maybe working through that discomfort, instead of avoiding it, was a better solution, the same way that accepting sadness was better than avoiding it.

I flashed back to seventh grade, when my friend Dana Steele overheard a conversation between her mom and Janet Lowenstein's mom. The way Dana told the story, Mrs. Lowenstein had said, "I ask Emily, 'Do you want tuna fish or peanut butter?' And she says, 'Whichever is easier for you.' And I'm like, 'They're both easy,' and she says, 'I like them both,' and I'm like, 'Just freakin' pick one!'"

Now, leaving the amphitheater, I thought, "I hated tuna fish." Why hadn't I just picked peanut butter?

How could I tell, though? Did the other person really want me to decide, or was she just being polite? If I wasn't honest about my needs, maybe the other person wasn't, either.

When Mary turned for the campground, I followed the crowd to the parking lot, where the pay phone now stood empty. It would be midnight at home, but I called my parents anyway. This time, Dad answered, and Mom got on the other line.

"I argued with Mary again," I said. "I always feel rushed, and I asked if we could slow down, and she said I'm blaming her because I can't relax. I just feel like we're rushing through things. I want to stop and enjoy it."

"You can go back again some other time," Mom said.

"Take lots of pictures," Dad said.

"But I want to enjoy it now," I whined, beginning to squirm. This always happened! Why did they try to fix everything? "Sometimes I just want you to listen, not give advice." It came out steady, without a whine.

"Okay," Mom said.

There was an awkward silence. I exhaled as quietly as I could. I'd asked for what I needed. A weight had lifted, and the world felt calmer.

"How was the ranger talk?" Mom said. I told them about Copralite. Then Mom started telling me about the sewing projects she'd been making for her church group.

When the lights blinked out, leaving the parking lot in blackness, I realized all of the cars had gone. A minute later, something football-size scuffled by on the ground. Its bare tail waddled away in the darkness. I cut Mom off.

"Um, Mom, the lights went out, and I think a giant rat just walked by."

"Oh, you'd better go then. Get a good night's sleep." We said goodnight.

The darkness was so deep that I couldn't see my feet. I inched down the sidewalk as my eyes adjusted. But then I looked up, and the lights of Interior, two miles down the road, stuck in my eyes and blotted out the sidewalk again. Then a car came toward me, its headlights illuminating my legs, socks, shoes. The shadows slid past with the car, and the darkness returned darker than before.

The wind had quieted, but it still blew through the night air. The cloudy sky was devoid of stars. I didn't feel scared. Should I? "I'm completely alone in this open, dark place," I thought. "The rangers are gone, the other campers are back in the campground, it's just me out here . . . and the rat." Across the street, a field receded half a mile to the base of "The Wall," the mud mountain range. I couldn't see The Wall but knew it loomed.

The sidewalk ended at the gravel path that led over the field to the campground. As I stepped onto the gravel, a car approached from behind. My shadow stretched out before me, and all the tiny bits of gravel lit up, each with its own little shadow, and if I squinted it looked like I stepped into a field of stars. Then the car passed, steering a box of light in front, illuminating pavement, road lines, and grasses. Its red taillights receded down the road toward Interior.

THAT NIGHT, I LAY AWAKE, thinking about my faults. Things like not speaking up about what I wanted—shouldn't I have learned to do that years ago? And I kept ruining things between Mary and me, creating tension. Or did I imagine the tension?

The next morning, we puttered around our campsite. Because we were spending a second night, we didn't have to pack. I dug around in my bags for the flashlight I'd needed the night before, and (in a pocket that I'd apparently not opened since Cape May) I found my alarm clock. I hadn't missed it, but finding it made me feel good, like everything would go right from now on. I had a plan for today: nine o'clock ranger talk on geology, three o'clock ranger talk on plants, with plenty of time in between.

Mary and I rode to the restaurant at the visitor center for breakfast. Clouds coated the sky, the air damp with the threat of rain. While we sat, people stopped at our table to ask about our trip. They must have guessed that the bikes parked outside belonged to us, based on our grungy appearance.

Nine o'clock ticked nearer. When my pancakes finally came, I gulped them down and then left Mary reading in our booth. I had to chug uphill with my full belly to the Castle Trail parking lot. I arrived in time to follow the ranger down a trail into the mud spires, but I couldn't focus. He droned on—sedimentation, Cretaceous Period, Rockyford Ash—but it wasn't interesting like last night. When the talk ended, the group spread out, floating back up the trail like gas molecules released from a flask. I stayed behind, willing myself to appreciate the scenery, but after a minute I gave up.

Mary waited in the parking lot. We set off on the long Castle Trail. Within a minute, we'd lost the activity of the parking lot; no one else was out braving the mistiness. In the heavy quiet, I might whisper and be heard a quarter mile away. The air chilled me through my raincoat, and the dampness blended the muted colors of one mud hill into another. Previous rain had swirled the mud floor with streaks of blue and purple, as if the rain had dissolved a pastel sunset and mixed it into the mud. Prickly pear cacti bloomed their yellow, tissue-paper flowers along the trail.

Just as Mary and I reached the place where we could see out over the mud towers to a green valley, it was time to turn back. By the time we neared the parking lot, my legs dragged and my stomach rumbled.

We coasted back to the visitor center. The air felt colder; the mist gathered its forces, threatening to turn into raindrops at any second. With nowhere to go but the restaurant and our campsite, Mary and I hoped we could sit in a booth all afternoon. I ordered "Indian tacos" of beans on fried dough; they came with a recipe.

While we ate, we discussed the end of the trip. Yesterday, Mary had brought up Cheyenne, the city in Wyoming that I wanted to visit. She planned to finish biking possibly sooner than the end of July. With less time to reach the Pacific, the pressure to cut Cheyenne grew. I'd found myself saying we could skip it. I hadn't felt like I'd lost anything. Instead, I'd begun imagining a post-Mary plan that included Cheyenne: maybe I'd ride from our end point (currently Seattle) to see more national parks, then take a bus to Cheyenne before going to San Francisco to meet my Green Tortoise ride home.

Now Mary said she might meet her boyfriend in Seattle even earlier—if we couldn't arrive in time, she'd leave me and take a bus. I'd taken a ride from Mary's sister *and* given up Cheyenne to enable us to reach the Pacific together, and now she said she might skip the ending. Why had I compromised if we weren't going to arrive together after all?

But I didn't feel upset, only a little empty as I imagined arriving on the beach alone—taking a picture of the empty ocean, or having a stranger take my picture. Then more new plans began to form. If Mary left, I'd bike westward alone, but I'd visit parks on the way, taking my time to see them. I'd fill the weeks until my ride home by biking slowly to San Francisco.

After eating, we ordered coffees, which we sipped slowly to make them last. The waitress disappeared, leaving us to our booth; the weather hung wetly outside. Mary decided to write postcards to everyone on her list—both friends and people we'd met. I wrote some cards and in my journal, periodically forcing another sip of cold coffee. The prairie walk left from this parking lot, so I didn't have to worry about getting anywhere on time.

LATER THAT AFTERNOON, THE PRAIRIE walk ventured onto the mud, picking our way between tufts of grass and tall thistles toward The Wall, which towered under the low clouds. We wouldn't get lost—we could see the visitor center— but it felt odd to walk with no path. A dozen tourists followed the ranger, who pointed out plants and talked about survival in the harsh climate, but I again struggled to pay attention. We reached The Wall as the hour ended.

I didn't feel ready to go. I wanted something more to happen. As the group drifted back to the visitor center, I found a protrusion of mud about chair height and sat. The backs of the tourists receded through the waist-high plants, their bright clothing contrasting the dreary surroundings.

Stormy clouds rolled across the sky. Even beside The Wall, the wind blew.

I tried to pray and, as usual, felt nothing. I kept sitting. It didn't help, but it still seemed like the thing to do.

I forced myself to sit for half an hour. Then I gave up and headed back. I tried to notice the rocks and plants and hoped to see some wildlife that would make the trek special. Tiny wildflowers poked up from the rain-smoothed mud, their dirty leaves half drowning, but their white heads opening upward. "Maybe it's not my lot in life to feel joy," I thought. "We've been safe on our trip and met lots of cool people. Maybe I should be glad with that."

But I still wanted lightheartedness. I thought of the feeling as being closer to God. And I prioritized it above falling in love. Shouldn't I be getting some divine support with a goal like that? Whoever was out there didn't seem to care.

With the wind at my back, I stepped up to the road, leaving the muddy prairie. On the pavement, the wind increased. I retrieved my bike from the restaurant and walked back to camp, where the wind howled and gusted. Our tent strained against its stakes, one end blown in so far that it flattened against the ground. I didn't want to sit out in the wind, but I'd already spent hours in the restaurant; the campsite was my only option. I pulled out pasta leftovers and, rather than light the stove in the wind, ate them cold along with a piece of carrot cake.

It wasn't just the wind that made it hard to be there. The Badlands didn't have any woodland benches or mountain vistas, just open spaces and barren mud. Even if the weather had been clear and calm, just *being* in the Badlands was hard because all distractions were stripped away, leaving just you and your internal crap.

*That's what I wanted!* I remembered now: I'd wanted to escape the distractions of life by going on this trip, to clear my head and sort things out. But this was not how I'd imagined it: unsettling, upsetting, hard to exist.

But maybe something was happening on the inside; maybe I was learning something I hadn't yet realized, and life would get easier soon. Maybe having a clear head meant working through this badness, the same way I'd experienced sadness in Harmony, Minnesota, instead of seeking to avoid it.

The moment darkness appeared, I crawled into the tent. I lay awake, listening to the wind rage, until finally the rain came down.

# The Black Hills, in which I become immersed in the moment

I CHUGGED UP ANOTHER HILL, MY legs weak. I'd lost sight of Mary; the road curved around a reddish rock outcrop, bright in the dreary air. Yucca poked from cracks, along with tufts of dry grass and wildflowers. A field stretched away on my left, ending at a tree-covered ridge under the cloudy sky.

Yesterday we'd arrived in Rapid City. After our days in the desolate Badlands, followed by a national grassland and the tiny town of Scenic, Rapid City had assaulted my senses with its traffic and strip malls. We'd found a department store where I'd bought a new watch with Winnie-the-Pooh on it. Then we'd tried to camp at the fairgrounds, only to stumble into the middle of the state's High School Rodeo Championship. After wading through horses to the exit, we'd found a park. Rain this morning had delayed our departure.

Now on a back road to Keystone, I appreciated the quiet scenery, but the sudden, steep hills annoyed me. Hadn't we biked up enough hills on this trip? It didn't help that I hadn't gotten much sleep: a sudden downpour had awoken me in the middle of the night, only to taper off a minute later, and then return. I'd finally realized a sprinkler was dousing our tent. No wonder the park had had such plush grass.

I reached the top. A row of gray-blue peaks rose beyond the forested hills. The clouds grew darker. Even on this straight stretch, I didn't see Mary. Then trees closed in and all was silent, just the tall trees and my breathing as I pedaled another mile, then struggled up yet another hill.

I caught up with Mary resting at the sign for Black Hills National Forest. Ahead, the trees framed a Tiffany window of blue peaks. We set off together, but when the road started to climb, Mary again pulled ahead. As I labored up the new hill, I inhaled pine scent, only a snatch. The hill wound on. When I finally reached the top, I stopped to catch my breath.

I leaned my bike on a rock, then clambered up beside it. My legs dangled. Opposite me, a baby pine tree grew atop a cliff. Raindrops tickled my face, but I was too exhausted to move. I looked up into the rain as it fell harder. The pine tree's clumps of needles were like black stars against the white sky.

The shower spent itself, and the sky brightened, and brightened, and then a stretch of rainbow blossomed on the clouds. It was a touch of magic, like I'd been given a gift. Mary might always be ahead, but for once my slow pace had paid off—I'd seen a rainbow. The clouds and rainbow dissolved into clear sky. Now the little pine tree's sunlit branches were framed by a brilliant blue.

The sun brought mugginess, hanging in the air as I dragged myself back onto my bike. But after I'd pedaled for a minute, the road plunged downhill, dropping until it ended at Route 40. Across the intersection flowed a flat stream, and as I turned right, I had a déjà vu of the flat road we'd taken into Moundsville, West Virginia, six weeks earlier.

The new road stayed flat, and although sunlight glinted high on the dark brown wall across the stream, I rode in shade. The stream held a perfect reflection of the sky and trees, broken only by a few small boulders. No cars passed.

After a few miles, a green sign announced, "Keystone, Population 232." Mary's bike stood outside the convenience store, a weathered board building. The other shops were closed. I parked near Mary and went in.

As soon as I found her, I said, "I saw a rainbow!"

"Oh, I know," she said. "Wasn't it great? It was so huge!"

Huge? I'd only seen a little rainbow. "What you saw is still good," I told myself. "You were happy with it."

"They have tofu," Mary said, holding up a package from a cooler. "Want to split it?" At least there was tofu.

MORNING IN THE BATTLE CREEK Campground dawned sunny with clouds spotting the sky, a perfect day to visit Mount Rushmore. I had always wanted to see it—an American icon. To the south, George Washington's profile shone bright on the gray mountain, visible as Samantha had promised. (We'd met Samantha on our last morning in the Badlands; she and her friend Heather had insisted we camp here and enjoy hot showers, and given us money to do it.)

Sunlight gleamed on the RVs lining the driveway below. A row of trees dappled our campsite in shade. We didn't hurry, savoring the luxury of being clean with shampooed hair.

"Want to share a load of laundry?" Mary asked.

"Sure." I dug through my bags for my dirty clothes—which was all of my clothes—and accompanied her to the laundry room. Then, while our laundry washed and dried, I wrote and ate breakfast—grits and rice hot cereal mixed, with pear and apricot, hot tea, and banana bread that some campers had given us. When I'd caught up in my journal, I continued reading the book I'd bought in the Badlands, *Mother Earth Spirituality*. It was about Native American beliefs and mentioned the Black Hills in the second chapter.

I thought I could see why the Black Hills were sacred to Native Americans: their craggy rocks reached toward the heavens, vertical and bare, making ascent a challenge. And they had a majestic presence. As I'd biked yesterday, in some places, I'd felt faces watching me out of the stone. But if I'd looked closer, I'd only seen hints: a rock curved like a broad nose, or a crack like a squinted eye. In a brochure from the visitor center, I read a quote from an 1868 treaty that gave ownership of the Black Hills to the Native Americans: "Paha Sapa, the Black Hills, will forever and ever be the sacred land of the Indians." The treaty had been broken.[18]

When our laundry was finished, Mary and I bumped down the gravel driveway back to Keystone. We rode past the tourist strip, quiet in the morning, and onto the connector to Route 244, a four-lane parkway leading up to Mount Rushmore. We passed the monument's sign, and the road began to climb.

I downshifted as I pedaled, then downshifted again. Soon I'd reached my lowest gear. I pumped hard on the pedals to keep my load moving. At least the road had a wide shoulder, away from the traffic, which increased as an hour ticked past. Behind the guardrail, the grassy slope dropped steeply into forest, which extended across the valley to the next hill. My pace was as slow as could be without me falling over.

After another hour, I reached a turnout where drivers had pulled over. I spotted George Washington's profile across a valley. The view wasn't picturesque, but it was the first closeup sighting, so I stopped. Tourists walked in the shoulder with cameras, lining up a good shot. I snapped my picture without leaving my bike and resumed climbing.

Another slow mile brought me around the side of the hill. The next turnout, filled with cars, had a view of all four presidents. But after stopping to snap another uninspired photo, I had so much trouble pushing off and staying upright as I gained speed that I vowed not to stop again.

I crawled on. It couldn't be much farther; the sky was getting bigger and bigger. Now the presidents scowled overhead, their faces whiter than the natural gray rock. Their sharp features contrasted with the peak's round curves. I noticed another face, a grumpy line of mouth, flared nostrils, and round eyes, to the right of the presidents. Below their heads, where forest began, a rockslide of broken boulders sloped away.

The road curved, and Mount Rushmore disappeared. I heard my name. I looked up to see Mary waving behind a guardrail on the next tier, almost directly overhead. I was almost there. I curved around the top of the hill until at last I rolled up to the line of cars at the gate. There was a parking fee, but the guard waved me past.

Mary waited at the entrance. I paused to balance before lifting a stiff leg over my bike to dismount. I wobbled to the wall to lean my bike by Mary's. My legs felt rubbery.

The entrance led into a courtyard with a stone floor, polished shiny like new grave markers. At the far end, tourists disappeared under three giant square arches decorated with narrow hangings like mutated American flags. The four carved presidents glared over the arches. Dark gray rock surrounded the presidents, and there was the face I'd seen from the road. Now I saw another face: to the left of George Washington, a jagged cleft created a heart-shaped face, with a bulbous nose and horizontal slit eyes, high cheekbones, wrinkled cheeks, and a stubborn mouth. This face tapered into a wrinkled neck. I thought of Grandmother Willow in Disney's *Pochahontas* movie. Elsewhere, I caught an eye or the snub of a nose, hints of other faces peeking out of the rock.

We crossed the wide courtyard with the flow of tourists, our riding shoes slapping on the smooth floor. After the arches came a walled-in area, then more arches leading into another long courtyard. At the far side, an opening led into a colonnade between stone pillars with flags on top. "This sure is an elaborate entrance," I thought. "It's like being stuck in the end of a Beethoven symphony, repeatedly thinking I've reached the end only to have another crashing finale." The right angles reminded me of military formations.

The flag gallery exited onto the viewing platform. After glimpsing the monument for hours, seeing it now was anticlimactic. It looked just like it did in pictures. And the impressiveness of carving the monument no longer interested me. Everywhere I saw the *other* faces, the natural ones, peering, smiling, or glaring down from the peaks. The heart-shaped face, on the end of the row, turned toward the sun, basking in the warmth. Next to it, the pale face of George Washington shrank into the cliff, no longer grand but puny.

What faces had been on this peak before the presidents'? I imagined these faces—the faces created by God, or by geological processes if you don't believe in God—blasted away by men trying to glorify their own kind of face. Suddenly I realized what had caused the "rockslide" that sloped down from Mount Rushmore: it was the waste created by the blasting, the debris of the original mountain.

Tourists milled around us, looking up at Mount Rushmore or posing for pictures. Did anyone else feel disillusioned?

After a brief tour of the visitor center, Mary and I returned to our bikes and sat on a bench to eat leftovers. A round rock protruded over the treetops behind the parking lot, like a person squatting behind the trees, head pulled into his shoulders. "He must be wrinkling his nose in disgust at the giant RV parked next to him," I thought. It had the Native-American-sounding name Pace Arrow Vision and towed a trailer with two Jet Skis.

After lunch, we began the descent. Ugly orange fencing lined the guardrail. Rocky crags towered overhead, first on the right, then on the left as the narrow road twisted. At breaks in the rock wall, I looked out over a forest. In the distance, rocky peaks poked out like islands in the sea of treetops.

The rock formations captivated me. The thin shoulder dissuaded me from taking pictures, but then a peak rose so beautifully that I couldn't help myself. I pulled as far off the road as I could and reached quickly for my camera. I hoped the drivers who edged past weren't cursing me for taking pictures when they couldn't.

A sign warned that a "profile view" approached, and the road forced itself wider to provide a turnout for cars. Overhead, George Washington's tiny head poked out from the side of the scarred rock. I looked for the heart face to George's left, but from this angle the rock looked entirely different. Now to his left, a huge oval face stared straight down at me, with tiny holes for eyes, red rust spots on the rocky cheeks, and a slit of mouth. George's head stuck out on the side like a sickly pale tumor.

I continued on, and now as I wound through the hills, everywhere I looked another face peeked out. On the uphill climb, I'd stopped for photos because I thought I should, but now I wanted to.

When my film ran out, I switched to a roll of black-and-white that had been in my bags for the past eight weeks. I didn't want to be stuck with black-and-white film when a good sunset came along, but at the rate I was going, I'd use the whole roll in no time. I got lost in my world of photographing, not worrying about how far ahead Mary might be or where we'd sleep that night, just soaking in the shapes of the rocks and the fresh cloudy air. The faces in the rocks were glaringly apparent, but I had a feeling that not everyone saw them. All the while, the road wound down through long-needled pine trees.

MARY WAITED AT THE END of the road. The pine trees backed off to leave grassy slopes around the intersection. A paved trail paralleled the new road and then disappeared into the woods. "This'll take us the right way," Mary said, pointing down the trail.

The rain held off, but the air felt so wet that I imagined drips echoing down in the mist as we rode through the forest. The trail surfaced along the road, and then it did begin to rain, plopping drops not wholly committed to the effort. I hated the thought of my bags getting wet, and of sleeping in a damp tent; as I willed the rain away, it only came down harder.

Then we saw a sign for the Crazy Horse Memorial.

Until yesterday, I'd never heard of the Crazy Horse Memorial. I'd found the brochure in the Keystone visitor center. The Lakota tribe had proposed the project, a colossal statue of the chief riding his horse. Crazy Horse had been a spirited war leader. When the government had taken his land, and someone had mocked him, "Where are your lands now?" he'd replied, "My lands are where my dead lie buried." Crazy Horse was invincible in battle; the US government captured him by trickery, taking him prisoner when he came for negotiations. They stabbed him in the back when he tried to escape.

The Crazy Horse Memorial, ten times as big as Mount Rushmore, remained unfinished, slowly funded by visitor donations—the artist had twice refused federal funding, believing the project should be "built by the interested public and not the taxpayer."

I'd been excited to visit Crazy Horse, but now, after feeling angry about the carving of the sacred Black Hills by the American government, I wondered how I'd feel about a carving done by Native Americans.

Mary and I reached a tunnel that led under the driveway entrance to Crazy Horse. A dank odor filled the narrow space, but it sheltered our bikes from the steady rain so we left them and walked.

The open land differed from the intense closeness of the hills at Mount Rushmore. As we trudged up the driveway, we looked out on distant hills and forests. The driveway ran on and on. Where was the visitor center? I dragged my tired body along. At last a building appeared.

Inside, we passed through a dark, air-conditioned atrium. I shivered but enjoyed the dry air. On the far side, on a viewing platform, we looked several miles across a tree-covered plain to the massive, tan mountain being carved into Crazy Horse. The head of a horse had been sketched onto the side of the mountain, and Crazy Horse's profile looked out over his pointing arm. A pile of rubble cluttered the ground.

In the visitor center, I read that the original artist, Korczak Ziolkowski, had moved here with his family in 1947 and dedicated the rest of his life to the work. He'd prepared detailed plans of the project before passing away in 1982. Some of his children were supposedly continuing the work, but the photos of blasting that I saw in the visitor center were years old.

It seemed gutsy of the tribe to attempt the carving, clearly making their project grander than Mount Rushmore and picking a hero like the steadfast Crazy Horse. And the mountains here, spread out on the plain, didn't seem as special as the tall peaks I'd seen this morning. But they were still mountains. And there was still a pile of leftover debris. (In sketches of the finished work, complete with an "Indian Museum" and "Indian University of North America" on the plain below the carving, the rubble had been cleared away.)

Mary and I hung around the visitor center, sipping free coffee with vanilla-flavored creamer. When we saw that the restaurant offered veggie burgers, we decided to eat an early dinner. If we ended up camping in the rain, at least we wouldn't have to cook. Our friendly waitress and chocolate cake for dessert made me feel better, and I warmed up and dried out.

But back in the chilly rain, my spirits sank and my feet dragged on the long walk back to our bikes. The day's hard biking had drained my muscles. The trail wound into woods again, and we rode five or six flat miles as the afternoon stretched on. The rain dwindled, but the air remained damp. Had evening come? With the thick clouds and bland light, I couldn't tell.

At last we saw a road and houses—we neared the town of Custer. The forested hill on our left ended at a field with goal posts: a school football field. It was quiet, so we stopped and pitched the tent. A car whirred by on the road behind the bleachers. But no one would see us unless they stopped and got out.

With dinner eaten, I had free time, but I felt too damp to bring out my journal or book. My wet socks grated on my nerves, but my shoes were soaked, too, so if I put on dry socks they'd just get wet. As I tried to plan my next move, a bright beam of sunlight hurtled out of the trees in the west and struck me in the face. I couldn't believe it. The clouds overhead began to glow brighter, and the harsh beam spread until its white light suffused the tree tops, erasing their tips, pushing out a wall of light like in movies when a UFO lands in a forest clearing. Overhead, the sky grew brighter and brighter until the thinning clouds just dissolved away, leaving the sky a beautiful blue, the remnant clouds scattered across it in whites, purple-grays, and yellows.

"It's a good thing I finished the black and white film at Crazy Horse!" I thought. I'd never expected to have a sunset today.

I took my camera, climbed the bleachers, and lay down on a metal bench, looking up at the sky, snapping a picture as the yellows deepened to orange and then to pink. I wanted to catch the moment when the dark clouds on bright sky crossed over to bright clouds on dark sky. My socks squished in my shoes, but I was too tired to take them off. Another car passed; this stadium might be where the local teenagers came to smoke and drink after dark. I tried not to think about it and kept watching the sky.

WE'D ONLY SPENT TWO DAYS in the Black Hills, but it felt like a long, difficult journey. We'd made it out the other side.

Custer, South Dakota, teemed with national sites—parks, monuments, forests, grasslands, and museums, like the National Museum of Woodcarving. A giant bison on a brochure advertised nearby Custer State Park. A scenic byway through the Black Hills began just east of town. But the Black Hills felt done. I hated to leave, but it was time to head west.

We left town on Route 16. A network of clouds crossed the blue sky. The wide, sunny view contrasted the damp closeness of trees and rocks in the Black Hills—at first it unnerved me, but I grew to like it. The road wound over domes of waving grass with pine forest at a distance. Barely any traffic passed in spite of the absence of alternate roads. The empty scenery lacked even an abandoned farmhouse, but there was always a hill or bend and the promise of what lay beyond, even if it repeatedly turned out to be more bare scenery.

The road wove through blasted rock. I passed an ominous yellow warning sign: "Narrow Winding Road, No Shoulders, 1 Mile Ahead." As the road coasted down past more rock, I reached another sign: "Falling Rock." And then a third: an arrow bent like a U-turn arrow, only it was the shape of the road ahead. With each new sign, the warnings became funnier, as if I were a cartoon character heading to the haunted house, bypassing the signs that read, "Danger, turn back!" and, "Last chance! Death awaits!"

We stopped for lunch at a picnic area at Jewel Cave National Monument but didn't descend the steep driveway to see the caves. A few miles later, we passed a brown sign surrounded by tall grass and yellow and orange wildflowers: "Leaving Black Hills National Forest."

The road continued over the hills, hot and sunny but bearable, as if I were still drying out from yesterday. After a while, I coasted down a long slope, leaving the hills behind as the forest thinned, reduced to scrubby bushes, and the view grew wider and wider. There was no fence, only markers along the edge of the road. And then, at the bottom of the long downhill where the road flattened, my heart soared when I saw a sign, high on thick wooden posts: "Wyoming."

# PART 4:
# Wyoming,
# the Most Fun Part
# of the Trip

## Eastern Wyoming, in which I succeed at figuring out what I want

G IDDY WITH HAPPINESS, I POSED with Mary by the sign for Wyoming. We also posed with the South Dakota sign, which we'd missed earlier because we'd been with Kathy in the truck—only ten days ago, but it felt like a month. We removed a small plywood sign that read, "No Fireworks" so it wouldn't ruin our picture. I imagined the police swarming in to arrest us; but then I thought, "It's not a big deal—we'll just tell them we wanted a nice picture." Would they care? "No," I decided, "they wouldn't—we're in Wyoming!" I felt a wild sense of freedom.

On the map, bright colors spread across the state: flat yellow basins and blue and green rivulets of mountains. The first town, Newcastle, was only half an inch from the border, but tiny red numerals indicated ten miles—the maps stayed the same size as we moved west, but the states were getting bigger.

The last remnants of evergreens died out as we left the border, until we rode across a rolling grassy landscape. Twenty feet from the road, a wire fence began. All the dampness of yesterday had gone.

BY THE NEXT AFTERNOON, I'D grown used to the landscape: treeless hills, scrubby grass, the occasional clay-red rock, and only the tiny shadows under sage bushes for shade. If I saw a bigger shadow, like the asymmetric quadrilateral cast by a highway sign at noon, I'd pull over for a water break. Shade had become a treat, like ice cream. I wished they sold it next to the Gatorade.

We'd spent the previous night with a family in Newcastle. They'd seen me sitting in the churchyard across the street and invited us over. They'd even served us breakfast.

I recalled the giant yellow sign that had startled me as I'd left Newcastle that morning: "16 CLOSED WHEN FLASHING, RETURN TO NEWCASTLE." It was hard to imagine the snow that could close this flat, open road. It was hard to imagine *any* snow, with the temperature creeping toward one hundred degrees. Grime coated my skin, powder stuck on with sweat and sunscreen. At least the wind wasn't bad. I checked my watch and the mile markers and estimated I rode twelve miles per hour.

I'd left Mary in the diner in Upton, a dusty, side-of-the-road town thirty miles from Newcastle. I'd set off with fantasies of reaching Moorcroft and finding somewhere shady to sit and write. Energized by lunch, I'd cruised along the quiet road. But the day had grown hotter, and the energy of lunch had worn off.

At last I saw buildings. A minute later, my road ended at a stoplight. I scanned the stores and spotted a grocery. Downhill, there was grass by the train tracks: maybe a park. Then my gaze shifted, and across the street I saw, like the pot of gold at the end of my rainbow, a bench in the shade.

My muscles ached as I dismounted. I looked at the red light. Did I need a car to make the light turn green? *What if someone comes and sits on the bench before I get there?* "There's no one in sight," I told myself. "Calm down." When I was tired like this, irrational worries were more believable.

The light changed, and I wheeled my bike across the intersection.

The shade cooled my skin. I dug out my journal and plopped down on the bench. At last! I wrote, "6/30 Monday Moorcroft, WY. I left Mary in Remy's diner in Upton—" I glanced up.

There was Mary, with her familiar fluorescent-green panniers, heading slowly into town. I'd been so sure I was flying along, faster than her for once! I looked back to my journal, rushing to express the thought before Mary reached me. "I thought I'd have time to write but she pulled up right after me. Oh well."

Mary rolled over. "Hey."

"Hi," I said. "What do you think? I could keep going, but I don't mind stopping." On the map, nothing lay ahead for twenty-six miles.

"It's hot."

"It seems like a park." I gestured downhill. "I don't see a police station . . ."

"So maybe if we just don't ask?" (We'd asked in Newcastle, and they'd said no.) I nodded and got up, packing away my disappointed journal.

There *was* a park at the bottom of the hill. We left our bikes in the picnic shelter and trudged back. At the grocery store, the cashier told us about a public pool. Mary's eyes lit up. I'd planned to return to my bench and journal.

"I'll go check it out," she said. "I'll call you on the walkie-talkies." (My friends in Indianapolis had lent us walkie-talkies.)

So I returned to the bench.

I'd had the brainwave to buy frozen berries instead of ice cream—a box of frozen berries didn't cost much more than an ice cream bar, and it was healthier and just as cold—so now I rested the cold block of raspberries on my leg. I didn't feel like chiseling away at it.

A breeze crossed the back of my neck; I'd borrowed scissors last night and cut my hair. I twisted my head from side to side, enjoying the swish of my clean, lightweight locks. Whenever my hair got long, I yearned to cut it, but my brain always interfered, telling me that if I let it grow, maybe this time it would become long and lustrous . . . even though it never did. And when I finally cut it, I always felt great.

The block of raspberries created an icy square on my leg. I held it to my forehead. Then I positioned it under my left thigh and opened my journal.

As I wrote, I kept thinking about the pool—should I go? I felt fine sitting where I was. The walkie-talkie crackled. "Calling Emily."

"Emily here."

"There's open swim from six to eight."

"I might stay here." The box of berries dripped condensation onto the ground. "I'll see you in the park?" I hoped she wouldn't take it personally.

"Ten-four, see you later. Over and out."

What is it about walkie-talkies? You can't help talking like a fighter pilot when you use them. "Roger that," I replied.

I put down the walkie-talkie and pulled out the berry box. The edges squished around a solid center. I switched it to my right thigh.

Had I made a mistake? Swimming and getting clean sounded great. But I imagined a deserted, tranquil pool. In reality there'd be crowds of screaming kids, and I'd be self-conscious in my boxer shorts and sports bra. I felt happy where I was. And I could wash up in the park.

Why was it so hard to figure out what I wanted? Pool or bench? Long hair or short hair? I *thought* I wanted one but truly wanted the other. In the Badlands I'd considered that I made decisions based on other people's desires. But these new examples only involved me. How could I not know what I wanted?

I remembered the first art class I took in college. The professor said we had to relearn to draw the way children draw. Children look at a scene and recreate it as best they can with their limited motor skills, so we drew with our left hands, or without looking at the paper, to emulate children and to make us look at the scene. As we age, we stockpile ideas about how things look, and we draw not what we see but the ideas in our head: the sky is blue, the grass is green. The sky is not always blue! But we stop looking.

I had lots of ideas stuck in my head about what I wanted, such as "I like my hair long" and "I should go to the pool to get clean" and "I want ice cream on a hot day" and "I should go out to breakfast because there is a restaurant available." But what I really wanted was different: short hair felt good, I was happy sitting on the bench, frozen raspberries were better than ice cream, and I wanted to cook hot cereal at camp.

I needed to see past my stockpile. I wanted to make decisions based on what I truly wanted, like I had today. I suspected that if I ever managed to meditate regularly, decision making would become easier.

I looked at my journal, thinking I should record the past few days. And I wanted to remember this bench. "I could take a photo of the grocery store and call it, 'View from the Shady Bench,'" I thought. "Or, I could cross the street for 'Shady Bench as I First Saw It.'"

But I was tired of taking pictures. And now that I sat still, my whole body and brain felt utterly exhausted. I just wanted to rest; I didn't even want to write.

So I made a list of things I felt thankful for: the shady bench, the frozen raspberries, small towns with parks, knowing I'd have water from the pump. Then I put aside my journal and retrieved the berry box from under my leg. It had a hard center but squishy sides. I carefully ripped open the top and used my spoon to scoop up the slurry of berries that sloshed along the edges.

THE SUN HAD AN HOUR to go, but clouds were forming. Mary and I sat in the picnic shelter with dinner, watching the sky grow cloudy, then glowering. Off to the west, behind a grain elevator with a slanting, rusted tin roof, darker clouds slowly swirled, set off by the pale yellow strip of sky at the horizon. The blue-gray clouds were the exact color of the grain elevator, making the dark roof float in the air. Dark wisps stretched down from the cloud bank like X-rays of teeth.

Then the sun reached the break at the horizon and gleamed. If someone had told me that a fire raged across the prairie, filling the sky with thick gray smog, I'd have believed him.

Sunset passed and the grain elevator darkened to a silhouette against the brilliant yellow horizon. Above, yellow, orange, purple, and blue tinged the gray clouds in swirling patterns. The dark mass was moving closer. A lone gust of wind ruffled my journal pages and blew a pair of boxers off the end of the picnic table, where our clothes hung to dry. I moved our stove to the floor under the table, and Mary and I stood to zip our bags, stow our papers, and move our laundry to hang off our handlebars. Then I returned to my dinner.

The sunset faded and the clouds continued to build until it began to rain. Laundry swung on the handlebars. Then a gust hit, and the stove skittered across the concrete. I tucked it closer to the table. A plastic bag skated across the floor. Mary and I jumped up. Another gust caught my boxers and lifted them off my handlebar. We grabbed the loose items as the gusts became nonstop. I wolfed down the last bites of dinner just to finish, so I could focus on the storm. Lightning flashed.

The sunset was over. Darkness filled the spaces between flashes. The flashes accelerated until they came continuously, with the thunder a nonstop background.

Mary said goodnight and headed for the tent. I felt safer under the shelter, so I kept watching. Bolts of lightning connected the bank of clouds to the fields below. The wind grew chilly, bringing in bits of rain. I moved to the floor and leaned against my bike, comfortingly solid against my back. Would I know if a tornado came? Everyone said they sounded "like a train." I'd heard two trains that day, but I still couldn't imagine hearing a tornado.

The lightning grew even more frequent, until I could see several bolts at once in my peripheral vision, electric tethers holding the clouds to the earth. The thunder rumbled and boomed from all directions. Sometimes the lightning jumped from cloud to cloud, forming a net across the sky. Sometimes, yellow glowed inside the clouds, starting at one end and running up their length.

My back grew weary of sitting on the concrete. At last I decided to go to bed, in spite of my fear of being out in the tent. But when I stood, my fear dissipated, as if it had built up only because I sat still.

## Spotted Horse, in which I let go

I PLUGGED AWAY IN THE AFTERNOON heat, looking for Spotted Horse on the horizon. We'd reached Gilette, Wyoming, at lunchtime—a sprawl of gas stations, fast food chains, parking lots, and intersections, all of it hot and dusty and not desirable for camping. So after taking refuge at the library and finding cheap Mexican food for lunch, we'd continued on. It was thirty-six miles to the next town, Spotted Horse. It would be a long afternoon.

We'd ridden out into a bleak, grassy landscape. On the map, the road crossed three creeks, but all I saw were watery ditches reflecting the sky. Other than a distant factory with sloping conveyor belts (but no driveway), there were no buildings. The mile markers were our only excitement.

Biking across the rolling hills grew harder as the afternoon wore on. At each crest, I hoped to see Spotted Horse even though I knew I couldn't have covered the miles yet. Few cars passed. I caught up with Mary snacking at a dirt driveway. The location had no benefit as a rest stop, but the intersection made it feel like more of a place than the side of the road.

The western sky grew dazzling as the sun moved behind clouds that glowed white and silver, with beams shining out as if angels were singing inside. For a while, the gray pavement turned red. Then it turned black with a new coat of asphalt and a taxicab-yellow dotted line that smeared off to one side. Soon Mary and I overtook the paint truck, trundling along as workers dropped yellow dashes onto the road. I slipped my bike between two dashes, glad the line wasn't solid, and passed the truck.

But a minute later, Mary and I hit an uphill. The truck gained on us. It couldn't move out to pass because it had to keep painting, so we pulled off the road to let it by. When the road flattened, we overtook the truck again. We played leapfrog until the truck fell behind.

All the while, I kept a constant hope for sight of Spotted Horse. But each time I chugged to the top of a hill or rounded a bend, I scanned the new landscape and saw nothing but bare hills. The sun sank lower. As I came up the next hill, sunbeams radiated from a cluster of clouds, silhouetting a fence above me and a deer, frozen on the hilltop.

From the crest, I saw a few buildings on the next hill. "It might not be the town," I told myself. But as I coasted down and then began to climb again, I saw a horse—a fiberglass horse. White splotches sprawled over its brown sides, and it had a white mane and legs. Maybe it had once stood in an amusement park for kids to pose on. Someone had propped it vertically to make its legs paw at the air.

Overhead, in a mod font, the white oval sign read, "Spotted Horse."

I climbed slowly toward the horse. A white building sat at the back of a tiny parking lot. A tour bus with "Powder River" on the side was parked there. A tree spread overhead, an ice machine stood out front, an American flag hung limply, and an old phone booth stood deserted. Behind the building peeked out a few old-fashioned trailers, a rundown farmhouse, and a shiny, white home. In the lot sat an old car with double headlights, a red truck, and a bigger, white truck pulling a trailer with unidentifiable equipment chained on. As I arrived, I heard the engine of the white truck running. The cab was empty.

I stopped at the sign, then lifted a weary leg over my bike and stood up straight, adjusting my shorts. It felt like a hundred degrees. Ahead, the road dropped, continuing across the barren land. Power lines came through Spotted Horse and skipped off across the hills, not bothering to follow the road.

For a minute, I waited while Mary arrived, but then I thought, "I can ask to camp, instead of hoping Mary will do it." I walked to the building and pulled open the door.

Inside stood a pool table. Dozens of framed pictures covered the walls. Behind the bar stood a woman with short blonde hair, bright in the dark room, and a big man stood across from her. "Here they are!" she said, grinning.

"Hi," I said, suddenly awkward. I forged ahead. "We're biking, and I was wondering if we could camp here."

"No!" Her smile disappeared. I stood with my smile frozen. Then she burst into a cackling laugh and grinned again. "Of course! Come on in! Donnie said, 'You've got a couple of thirsty bikers on the way!'" The man shifted so I smiled at him. He wore a baseball hat and a blue tee shirt with iridescent mirror shades hanging from the neck

Mary came in, and the woman asked our names and introduced herself as Coleen, and the next thing I knew, Coleen had seated us at the bar, and Donnie had shaken our hands in his broad ones, and Mary had ordered a beer. I considered the usual things I ordered in bars (like water or juice) but felt embarrassed. "I'll get whatever Mary had."

"You girls like *fancy* beer," Coleen said, setting down two bottles of something called "Moose Drool." I wondered if fancy beer cost a fortune, and then I glanced at Donnie and suddenly knew he'd pay the tab. Then I was drinking Moose Drool and it was the best thing I'd ever tasted, and it didn't matter that I hadn't eaten in hours, and I didn't worry about talking because Coleen made the conversation happen.

While Mary answered questions about our trip, I looked around at the photos on the walls—rodeo riders, trucks, horses, and people with dogs. A sign framed with rope read, "This isn't Burger King. You get it my way or you don't get it at all!" One fabulous rodeo shot caught my eye, the cowboy hanging on as the bronco kicked high. "That's Paul," Coleen said. "He lives in Interior."

"South Dakota? We were just there!"

"You should look him up," she said. "He's half Sioux. He makes saddles—just ask. People will tell you where he lives."

At a lull in the conversation, Coleen reached behind the bar and pulled out a bundle of rope. "Hey, Donnie!" she said. "Which girl should we tie up first?" A chill went down my spine, and I didn't react. But then she laughed. "I'm just kidding you! Don't be scared of us!"

I wondered, "Am I stupid to be here, drinking beer? I don't *think* so. But Mom and Dad would probably disagree."

A small green sign hung over the bar, like the signs posted at the edge of each town:

### SPOTTED HORSE
### POP    2
### ELEV    3890

"Are you the two?" I asked Coleen and Donnie.

"No, Donnie lives in Ar-vaay-da!" Coleen said, as if Arvada were the snooty side of the mountain. "Arvada is our zip code," she said, and then continued like a cheerleader, "but we know, we live, *IN, SPOTTED, HORSE!*"

The other resident of Spotted Horse shuffled in—Coleen's partner, Jerome. He nodded at us and then puttered quietly behind the bar, the perfect complement to Coleen's socializing. I continued looking around the room. I couldn't stop myself from smiling at the antelope butt mounted like a deer head, with googly eyes glued on to make it a funny face. Nearby, a tacked-up note read "Ty's mom beat him at pool."

"Why do you have a bike?" Mary asked. A dirt bike lay under the pool table.

"We race it around the pool table when we're bored."

I imagined all the evenings they'd had here. Did they ever get a crowd? Tonight, Donnie's hired help played video games in the back room, along with Donnie's yippy little dog.

Donnie was a cattle rancher. He had a wife named Donna and two kids. I kept picturing Donna as a thin city slicker with styled hair, big earrings, and bright lipstick. She couldn't be a suitable wife for a cattle rancher. "Married!" I told myself, because Donnie had started to seem kind of cute, which startled me since I never noticed older men, and besides, a cattle rancher? "You're a vegetarian!" I reminded myself.

Our vegetarian diet hadn't come up, but wolves did: the government had recently reintroduced wolves to Yellowstone National Park, where they'd once roamed. Because the wolves were considered endangered, Donnie said, ranchers couldn't kill them, even if they killed cattle. At home, I would've immediately sided with the wolves, but now, in the face of an actual cattle rancher, I paused.

"It's ridiculous," Donnie said. "People killed them off for a reason, and now they're putting them back?"

Neither Mary nor I replied, and Coleen narrowed her eyes at us. "You're not tree huggers, are you?"

I didn't want to lie, but I didn't want to disagree with Donnie, either. I had no idea what to say. I opened my mouth. "I think we might be." I grimaced, and we all burst out laughing. Coleen held up the rope.

"Which one should we tie up first?!" she hooted, and my heart thudded again. She dropped the rope and continued, "Don't mind us—we're not crazy."

"She's just kidding," I told myself. I was silly to think that Coleen would hurt us; I knew she wouldn't. But a niggling doubt wouldn't leave me alone, that if I let go and had fun, I might end up regretting it.

Coleen was talking again, replacing our beers even though we weakly protested. In truth, I'd wanted a second one; I recognized a familiar (though not often experienced) fuzziness that meant I was drunk.

We all trooped outside to take a photo before the sun set. Mary held the green Spotted Horse sign; next to her, Coleen whooped, swinging her arm overhead like it held a lasso. Jerome just grinned with his arm around Mary, and on the far side, Donnie stood with his hand in his pocket. Then Coleen took one with me in it. I knew it would be blurry—my camera was hard to focus—but the blurriness would fit our drunken evening.

"How many cattle do you have?" I asked Donnie as we trooped back inside.

"Four hundred. Out here they need a lot more land to graze. In Minnesota, where it's grassy, you only need one acre per head."

"How many acres do you have?" I guessed five per cow (two thousand) or maybe ten per cow.

"Twenty-two thousand," he replied.

Twenty-two thousand?! How did he keep track of them on so much land? Then I realized—that's why cowboys have horses! So they can ride to the cattle where there aren't roads. "Wow," I said somewhat stupidly, "You're a real cowboy!"

Donnie's forehead wrinkled. "There's a lotta men in cowboy hats who aren't *real* cowboys . . ." He winked and drawled on, "They walk around in their *clean* boots and *big* hats with their *big* belt buckles and *clean* hands . . . they're not *real* cowboys."

"Drugstore cowboys!" Jerome chimed in.

Picturing Donnie riding around his land on a horse, looking for cattle, made him even sexier. "Married!" I reminded myself again. "Older man who drinks six cans of Coors before dinner! Cattle! Cattle!" I was a tree hugger who'd probably side with the wolves.

Back inside, Coleen passed Mary a guest book, and while she wrote, thoughts gushed into my head for my own inscription, "I love you, Spotted Horse! You're the best!" But I imagined the next visitor reading it and thinking, "Wow, she sounds drunk." I struggled to think of something not-drunk sounding, but honest, and interesting enough to impress future readers. But when Mary handed me the book, all I managed was "the most fun we've had on the trip."

Donnie had to go, and he shook my hand and I wished I could hug him. (Mary later pointed out that his truck had been running the whole time we were in the bar, so I added this to my list of reasons why it was ridiculous to have a crush on a married cattle rancher in Wyoming.) Mary and I were suddenly the only people in the bar with Coleen, who yawned as she let us out the front door and locked it. We wheeled our bikes around the building and took out our toothbrushes. Then we followed Coleen across the grass.

They'd said we could sleep in a camper. But then they'd remembered that they hadn't cleaned up from the most recent party, so Coleen had said we could stay in her house, across the bumpy grass past the campers. I could walk straight; my beers must have worn off. Coleen said she'd make us grilled cheeses, so once inside, I helped her find the bread and a block of cheese and hunted for the frying pan.

Now that we weren't whooping it up in the bar, Coleen's wild hyper-ness disappeared like leprechaun gold. I took my grilled cheese on a paper plate and sat on the sofa, where Coleen flipped through her photo album. "Here's my mother," she said, pointing at a portrait. There was Coleen as a teenager, riding in the high school rodeo. Women were allowed in only one event, something called the "barrel race."

At the end of the book, Coleen said goodnight and drifted off to the room at the front of the house. I took a shower and then joined Mary in the guest room at the back, shutting the door. Except for my occasional uneasiness about Coleen's threats to tie us up, tonight had been so fun! I hadn't worried about anything; I'd just been present in the bar, enjoying the banter and the company. I wished it could always be that way, but without drinking beer.

I lay down next to Mary. In the hazy reaches of my mind, something floated, a quote I'd read once about faith. I tried to remember, but before I could catch it, I was asleep.

I AWOKE IN THE NIGHT. Mary stood by the door, rattling the knob, but the door stayed closed and she didn't leave. I sat up.

"The door won't open."

All my misgivings rushed in, and my heart pounded as Mary tried again. I recalled Coleen's jokes about the rope, but I pushed them aside and got up. The doorknob wouldn't turn either way. There wasn't a lock or a hole or anything. "I have to pee!" Mary whisper-whined in distress.

*They've locked us in!*

"No," I told myself, "the doorknob's just stuck; they're not killers, they're good people."

*But I don't really know them—how do I know they're good people?* I imagined Donnie going home to his kids, and it comforted me.

"Maybe we can get out the window," Mary said. We walked the narrow path around the bed to examine it. The screen didn't come out. I imagined breaking out, wheeling our bikes to the road and leaving in the dark. Would they chase us in the morning? What would they think if they *weren't* killers, if the doorknob was just stuck, and they awoke to find us gone, and the screen busted?

Mary lay back down, flat on top of the bedspread. Here I was, imagining being killed, while she faced a more realistic problem. I lay down, too, trying to calm my crazed, middle-of-the-night fears. The room was hot, with no breeze entering the tiny window, but at least the window was there. "They probably aren't killers," I told myself, "but we can break out the window if we have to. In the meantime, we'll wait until morning."

"Coleen might sleep late," I said. "We have to catch Jerome before he goes out."

Mary fell asleep, but I lay awake, the fear ebbing and returning. "They're good people," I repeated. I tried quoting *Dune* like I'd done when I'd felt scared at the start of the trip, "Fear is the mind-killer." I thought I'd never fall asleep.

Then I awoke. A faint light shone at the window. It was early, but I was wide awake. I lay there, waiting to escape. Minutes ticked past. Then I heard movement in the house, and I stood and moved to the door, calling out, "Jerome?!" Mary sat up, and we listened. What if he hadn't heard me?

"Jerome!" Shuffling steps moved toward our door. "It's stuck! It won't open!" The doorknob gave a rattle.

"Huh." Another rattle. "Hang on a sec." His steps retreated. A minute later they returned, and after a couple of terrific bangs, the door swung open. Jerome stood in the doorway with a hammer. His shirt, an oversize "Fat Tire Ale" shirt, had a big red bicycle on it.

"Did you wear that because of us?" I asked.

"Yes." He smiled.

Suddenly, everything shifted back to normal—my nighttime-crazy-killer thoughts evaporated. The morning light had come, and Jerome had dressed in the tee shirt that had a bike on it, just for us. Mary rushed out to pee, and Jerome went to the bar.

My usual morning tension arrived, the worry about having time to write or sit, but I brushed it off. It came out of habit; last night had broken our routine into a jumble, and the pieces no longer seemed important. We'd never had dinner so the stove wasn't out; there was no tent to pack. I didn't think, "I need time to write," or, "I have to have tea." Instead, I just waited to see what would happen.

Jerome reappeared and said, "I made some sausage."

"Maybe they *didn't* notice that we're tree huggers," I thought. What should I do? I didn't want to hurt his feelings.

"We don't eat sausage," I said, "but we could come eat with you." He nodded.

Later that morning, I suddenly remembered the quote about faith I'd been trying to recall the previous night. I'd read it on a bulletin board in the church where Eric and Christina-Mai, my friends in Chicago, had gotten married. It went something like this: "When it's time to step into the unknown, faith means knowing that you will be given something to stand on, or you will be taught how to fly."[19]

## Ucross to Sheridan, in which I take
## one pedal stroke at a time,
## and we reach two thousand miles

COLEEN HAD TEASED THAT DONNIE lived in Arvada, but it was ten miles past his driveway to the turn, and another three miles to the town. By the time I reached the turn, the damp washcloth I'd tucked under my bungee cords had dried crisp, except for where the bungee crossed it. I yanked it out, leaving it to finish drying while I ate carrots. I felt good, considering last night's "dinner" of beer and grilled cheese, and my lack of sleep.

Three miles south to Arvada was too far off route, I decided, so when I finished my snack, I kept going.

A ridge on my left ended, and beyond, far, far away, I saw faint white shapes. They floated over the earth—were they snow-tipped mountains, or low-lying clouds? I imagined them as the Bighorn Mountains, their hazy blue slopes blending with the atmosphere. But then I imagined them as clouds, and that worked, too.

Eight hours later, I turned down the tree-lined driveway at the Ucross Foundation. The town labeled "Ucross" on the map was in fact just the Ucross

Ranch, whose buildings now housed an artist residency program.[20] Coleen had suggested we stop.

Mary had arrived first and arranged for us to sleep on a grassy lawn outside one of the many bright red buildings. The staff had turned the sprinklers off and even unlocked a door so we could shower.

The next morning, Mary and I checked the map. A mile from Ucross, Routes 14 and 16 split. If we took 16, we'd reach Buffalo in twenty miles. After that, the road climbed over the mountains by the Powder River Pass with no towns until Ten Sleep, sixty-five miles away. Coleen had recommended Ten Sleep's Fourth of July celebration, but it was already July 3rd. Plus, I wasn't sure I could handle a celebration that Coleen recommended—it might be too wild.

Mary and I would instead turn north on Route 14, which curved up along the eastern side of the Bighorn Mountains for thirty miles before reaching Sheridan. A few towns dotted the land north of Sheridan; then the road climbed the mountains for twenty-seven miles to a dot labeled "Burgess Junction," where Route 14 split into 14 and 14-ALT.

Mary had added up our miles—1987! We'd cross 2000 miles today. As we set off, we watched the mile markers pass so that we wouldn't miss it.

At first, the gray road wound over fields, the ribbon ahead showing the contour of the land. Scattered buttes and cliffs in greens and browns rose beyond the fields, and a dull haze muted the blue of the clear sky. Dirt roads and fenced fields hinted of farms. When the obscure white shapes I'd seen yesterday again appeared in the distance, they looked a little more like the Bighorn Mountains. As I rode on, the range began to look clearer: I could see the snowy tops. But the blue base still faded into the air.

I daydreamed about living at Ucross, and how I'd stop to visit the nice people in the office before going to my studio each day. Then I planned the scrapbook I'd make for the bike trip. The road began to climb; a grassy hillside blocked my view. I clicked down to my lowest gear. I wondered what everyone in my bakery was doing, and then realized it was two PM on the East Coast; they'd be done for the day.

Out of habit, I glanced at a marker partway up the hill—I often picked something halfway up to focus on as I climbed. "You can rest when you reach that marker," I'd tell myself. But today, I noticed something different. Instead of looking forward to stopping, I found myself repeating, "Right now, I can keep going" with each pedal stroke.

I neared the top and saw Mary's bike, and then Mary walking toward it with her water bottle. She'd pulled into a gravel turnout. As I crested the hill, I saw that the blue haze had cleared, revealing green hills in front of the snowy peaks of the Bighorn Mountains. Mary pulled out her camera. "This is two thousand miles!" she called. I managed a smile, puffing into the turnout, and rolled to a stop. The wall of mountains stretched before me—somewhere in there was the road we'd take over them. I felt remarkably unworried; I'd climb them just like I'd climbed the hill, one pedal stroke at a time.

Mary walked to the end of the turnout, where the chain-link fence dropped down the hill, leaving a clear view. She balanced her camera on a rock. "Will you go right there?" she said, pointing. I had a drink and walked over.

"Let's hold up fingers to spell two thousand!" I said. I made both my hands into Os.

Mary pressed a button and darted over, holding her hands in a peace sign "two" and another O. The camera snapped.

When we continued on, the land dropped away from the road, which continued along a ridge. Clouds floated into the sky, adding more dimensions to the view, and a valley spread out from us to the mountains. It was like the scene in *Lord of the Rings* where the fellowship of men and hobbits hikes along the mountaintops after leaving Rivendell; I had the same soaring feeling inside that I got when I watched that scene.

Noon passed, and at last I saw houses. I coasted under an interstate. There were no chain restaurants or strip malls, just houses and a scenic inn. Then we rounded a bend onto Sheridan's Main Street: An old Woolworth's building lined one side, facing a row of shops. On the sidewalks, pedestrians mingled with brightly decorated horse statues, a Wyoming version of the 1999 *Cows On Parade* exhibit in Chicago.

I eyed Java Moon on the left. The food would be overpriced, but I wanted the feeling of a coffee shop. Mary and I reached the end of the street and U-turned. "How about the Java Moon?" I said. As we rolled over to it, the people walking past smiled and said hello.

When I pulled open the door of Java Moon, I expected too-small tables and a large menu of expensive espresso drinks. But instead I saw bread: real bread, with floury crusts and burnt-edged cuts. Staring, I gravitated toward the nearest shelf, savoring the familiarity of handmade loaves. "Java Moon Pain au Levain" read one sign. I scanned the ingredients; there was no yeast, only sourdough starter. The title was in French, the wheat had been stone-milled, they'd baked it in a brick oven . . .

"I'm home!" I thought. "After two thousand miles!"

Mary bought a loaf, and I bought a bag of rolls; we got butter packets. I also ordered a salad with mandarin oranges and strawberries on top. I was in heaven. We were done biking for the day; we could sit for hours. I didn't even wonder where we'd sleep—Sheridan was sure to have a park. We'd seen a poster for Shakespeare in the Park. Maybe we could sleep there.

I'd just opened my journal when the bell tinkled at the door and a couple came in. The man wore a huge cowboy hat and boots along with his clean clothes. "He's not a real cowboy," I murmured to Mary, thinking of Jerome and Donnie in Spotted Horse. She nodded. A minute later, the couple took the table next to us and introduced themselves as Jack and Amber.

"We're visiting from LA," Jack said with a Scottish accent, and I resisted making eye contact with Mary. But even though he was a cowboy fraud, I quickly liked them. Maybe it's human nature to want a huge cowboy hat when you're in Wyoming.

We told them about our trip. "What do you do when you're not biking?" Jack asked. I glanced at Mary; her mouth was full of bread.

"I'm a bread baker," I replied, dreading his next question: "So how's *this* bread?" I never knew how to explain that I didn't pay attention to the qualities people judged bread by—flavor, texture, "crumb." I liked that it was made by hand, and cared about.

But instead he exclaimed, "Really?! My father was a bread baker, back in Scotland!" His whole childhood rushed into the room. He started reminiscing, and we talked about the loaves we could see on the shelves.

"It's the first real bread we've had since Pennsylvania," I said, "but I don't know if we'd buy real bread even if we could. We can't really carry butter."

"What about olive oil?"

"I look at the little bottles in the grocery store, but they're so expensive!"

When Jack and Amber finished their coffees, I hunted for a scrap of paper and found a receipt from the Crazy Horse Memorial. They wrote down their address, as well as the name of a friend with a restaurant in Seattle, in case we ended up there. "Go in and demand food," Jack said. "Tell them I sent you." Then they got up. I returned to my journal, which had been lying open since they'd arrived.

I'd written one line when someone walked up. A sapphire-blue bottle smacked down on our table. Jack and Amber stood grinning over us.

"Here you go," he said. It was olive oil.

They left with a wave and I sat speechless, feeling I couldn't get enough words out of my mouth to thank them properly. I wished I hadn't called him a fake cowboy. Mary inched the bottle to the middle of the table. It had a fancy paper wrapper. We couldn't resist finding the price on the other bottles at the counter—it was fourteen dollars!

Then finally I wrote. South Dakota had felt special in a spiritual sort of way. Wyoming just felt fun. Fun things kept happening to us, and I was telling the worries in my head to shut up. I knew I'd get upset again, but at that moment I felt happy with everything. I made a note of it: "Sheridan, 3 PM on my Winnie-the-Pooh watch, July 3rd."

I recognized a feeling of transition. It used to come at the start of a school year, or on New Year's Day or my birthday. Partly it was because I'd reached the end of a journal. (I'd decided to mail it home with three blank pages, to avoid carrying it up the mountains. Plus, the post office in the big town of Sheridan seemed likely to be reliable.) Other things contributed to the feeling of transition as well: I'd cut off my hair, tomorrow was the Fourth of July, and we were about to go up the biggest mountains of the trip. Sheridan was the end of a chapter.

Worthington, Minnesota, where we'd stayed with Mary's sister, had ended a chapter, too. Since we'd left—only two weeks ago!—so much had happened. I'd thought I'd record it all, but new adventures kept piling up. Now, at the end of the chapter, I couldn't go back and write about it. There'd be too much new stuff happening.

## The Bighorn Mountains, in which
## we ascend five thousand feet,
## and I try not to think of the future

JULY 5TH, THE BIG DAY: we were about to start crossing the Rocky Mountains.
Before the trip, I had thought of the Rocky Mountains as a one-time thing, a ridge of mountains that ran down the country somewhere in Colorado. I now realized that the Rocky Mountains included many ranges that ran in parallel strips over the American West and up into Canada. We'd be crossing them for weeks, through Yellowstone National Park and western Montana, finally leaving them when we crossed the Bitterroot Mountains into Idaho.

We'd start with the easternmost range of the Rockies: the Bighorn Mountains. The day before, after resting on benches outside Sheridan's library and seeing a matinee, Mary and I had ridden twenty miles to Ranchester, a town close to the base of the mountains. We'd set up camp in the park and attended the town's July 4th celebration. Today, we'd ride six miles to Dayton (elevation 3926 feet), and then climb twenty-seven miles to Burgess Junction, our biggest climb of the trip. Beyond Burgess Junction an arrow pointed at the road, labeled "Summit El. 9430."

I made hot cereal at our picnic table. Mom had always made us Cream of Wheat on the first day of school, and on days when we had events like the swim races at the beach. Although I'd hated Cream of Wheat, I'd secretly thought she might be right about it helping with whatever challenge I faced; so today I made hot cereal to help me climb the mountains, decorating it with the remnants of the raspberries and blueberries I'd bought yesterday to celebrate the Fourth.

While I ate, I thought about Mom so much that I began to feel the feeling of being around Mom as a child, and I started crying. I remembered Coleen showing me her mother's picture, when we flipped through her photo album. Maybe her mom had passed away. What would happen when *my* mom passed away?

I still hung on to my childhood; I hung on to the way things felt back then—better than now—and the idyllic places I had spent time. It pained me to visit my hometown and see housing developments and buildings on my sacred spots, and favorite shops and hangouts closed as the town slowly changed.

As I grew older, life got harder: friends struggled with serious illnesses, people died. Sometimes I pictured myself old and still alone; my family would be dead, and friends would be dead, moved away, or out of touch. Maybe I'd be too infirm to leave the house, and I'd be desperate to take care of myself so that the government would not seize my property and force me into a nursing home. I imagined myself sitting at the window, watching as life outdoors moved quickly past, the length of a lifetime hanging over me. The daydream always made me feel horrible.

It would be less painful not to imagine the future, and to let go of memories of childhood, and to focus on the present. The present might offer moments and places as nice as the ones I remembered. And there was no telling what the future would be like, but I suspected it would not be as bad as my imaginings. It was like biking toward hills: they always looked worse in the distance than they actually were once you start climbing.

I wiped my tears. Mary was at her bike, arranging her bags. The park had cleared after last night's fireworks, and the other campers hadn't yet stirred from their RVs.

Already the sun beat down. I'd filled all my water bottles. How long would the water last? "It's too bad we can't climb the mountains in the afternoon," I thought, "when the eastern side is shaded." But then we might not make it to Burgess Junction by dark.

When we'd eaten and packed, we left Ranchester on the flat road. We breezed through tiny Dayton. I ignored the urge to explore. I did stop once, for a picture of a huge orange sign that read, "Fresh Buffalo Jerky FREE TASTE 15 mile."

After Dayton, the road stretched ahead to the forested ridge we'd climb; this close, I could no longer see the snow-capped peaks. A rocky, diagonal line zigzagged up the ridge, with a treeless blotch at the top left. Mary and I rode the last flat mile, and then the road began to rise.

The gentle slope soon turned right, growing steeper as it headed up the first diagonal. The biking wasn't hard, though; the grades weren't as steep as the ones we'd ridden in Pennsylvania. "I could do this all day," I thought. I just had to keep going at my slow pace and eventually I'd get there. I had about twelve hours until dark; surely I could make it to Burgess Junction by then.

I "trudged" uphill anticlimactically, slow and steady. I'd been picturing snowy peaks towering overhead, but a pine-covered hillside filled the entire view on my left. The opposite view of the basin was pretty, albeit a little hazy, but it didn't grow more interesting as I ascended, just smaller.

The pine trees broke for some bare rock; blasting to make the roadway had exposed layers. Signs were posted with mysterious text like, "Goose Egg Fm Triassic-Permian 205–290 Million Yrs." Wildflowers grew along the road—tiny blue stars, bits of red and orange, and a few shriveled lupines—but they were sparse, with colors bleached by the bright sun, not like the full colors of a nature calendar.

I reached the first hairpin turn, where the road switched from a zig to a zag. Now the view was on my left. But after a minute I adjusted to the change, and the road felt just like it had before.

I kept climbing, catching up with Mary and then losing her. I stopped to rest a few times, but only because I wanted to be careful not to overdo anything; my legs felt fine. A lack of traffic made the climb pleasant, but periodically dirty pickup trucks passed hauling four-wheelers, making me wonder what we'd find at Burgess Junction.

Hours passed as I climbed, up and up, periodically switching direction to the next diagonal. The view dropped lower and lower, and I'd begun to think I should stop for a picture when I saw a turnout ahead, "Sand Turn." Cars pulled in and out. The road turned right and led west into the mountains.

I pulled in. As I gulped some water, a few people said hi or, "You came up on that?!" as they eyed my bike. My heart swelled with the attention; didn't I deserve it after that climb? But no one asked if I needed anything. If I ran out of water, would I ask for help? I'd been rationing it so that I wouldn't have to.

I walked to the stone wall. Far below, the road snaked across the lower slopes before it reached the edge of the mountain and the sharp switchbacks. I traced it back to a cluster of trees—that would be Dayton. Then I realized, I stood at the rocky, top-left corner I'd seen from below. I'd finished the worst part! I'd just biked up the largest barrier to our cross-country trip.

I sat for a few minutes. Then I got back onto my bike. When I turned onto the road, heading into the mountains and turning my back on the basin, it seemed like I also turned my back on the whole eastern United States, on every road we'd traveled so far that summer. It was like I'd stepped into one of those revolving bookshelves that Scooby Doo and Shaggy are always stumbling into, that spin and deposit them in secret tunnels or rooms full of treasure, or monsters. I'd been facing east, looking over the basin, and then it spun me 180 degrees and I faced west.

Evergreen-covered slopes rose around me; on my left, the land dropped to a tree-filled valley. Bare patches on the slopes and gray chunks of rock piled in the valley suggested rock slides. On one hillside, rocks poked out of trees like the ruins of an ancient city. Ahead, only one twist of the road appeared. The road was still climbing.

Soon I felt winded and stopped to rest. My legs weren't tired, but I'd gotten short of breath. I drank more water, mixing in Gatorade powder I'd bought in Sheridan. Then I set off, but a few minutes later I felt winded again. I rode a little farther and stopped. What was wrong with me—why was I so out of breath? The sun beat down as I drank, but it wasn't sweltering; the mountain air had a crispness that vied with the sunshine.

It was the altitude, I realized. Knowing the cause comforted me.

I reached the buffalo jerky samples, in a trailer parked back from the road on a gravel lot. I'd hoped to find a store where I could get water.

After several more miles, the road leveled. I pulled in at a turnout with a view of a valley. Mary's bike leaned against the fence. White wildflowers dotted the grass that sloped down from the road. I waved at Mary, sitting on the fence, and took my lunch onto the grass. I liked the idea of sitting in the wildflowers, even if they were dinky, disappointing wildflowers.

After lunch, the road rambled through forest. Even with the road flat, I had to stop often. My legs started to tire. The day stretched out like it would never end, as if the thin air had lost the ability to turn dark, or as if our altitude granted us extra hours of daylight.

I thought about the next few days: the road split at Burgess Junction, and I leaned toward taking the alternate Route 14 to see the Medicine Wheel National Historic Landmark. I didn't know what it was, other than a Native American site, but I imagined sleeping at its center and finding all kinds of purpose . . . but probably it would be fenced off.

I didn't know which direction Mary wanted to go.

The traffic increased, and a sign passed for the visitor center at Burgess Junction. Clusters of trees stood back from the road. Should Mary and I pull off the road and camp? I'd read that camping was allowed in national forests, as long as you were a certain distance from the road. But after the long day, camping "in the wild" seemed difficult to manage. Plus, a loneliness permeated the mountains that might increase away from the road.

So after I'd met Mary at the visitor center and used the restroom and re-filled all my water bottles, we headed on to a lodge. We passed the junction, where two highway signs hung overhead: "14 West to Greybull" and "14 ALT West to Lovell." Then the road split, and farther down, a connector completed the triangle, as if someone might drive all the way up from Greybull only to go back down to Lovell. The routes wouldn't rejoin for one hundred miles, where they'd meet again in Cody, Wyoming.

Less than a mile past the junction, a long wooden building came into view, with a wide green roof and "BEAR LODGE RESORT" along the top. Four-wheel-drives lined the front, and pine trees surrounded the back. A badminton net sagged on the grass, and a disarray of docks and benches graced a tiny pond. A few pop-up tents stood over empty picnic tables, like an abandoned party.

Vacationers milled in the lobby with a buzz of chaotic chatter. We ap-proached the desk and asked about camping. They charged for it, but we were so tired we decided to stay.

We pitched the tent on the lawn by a picnic table. As the sun set, a party came alive inside, with dance music pouring from the bar. I pulled out the Wyoming map in the twilight, and Mary and I studied the two routes west.

"I'd kind of like to see the Medicine Wheel," I said, trying for a mix of assertive yet polite.

"I'd like to see Shell Canyon," Mary replied. *She just wants to take the easier road, the one that doesn't have the summit.*

"Shut up," I told myself. "Stop putting her down."

"Maybe we should split up," Mary said.

"I was thinking that. It would be good practice for when I'm alone on the West Coast."

But we only had one tent. We looked at the map again. Mary would reach Greybull in forty-eight miles, while I had sixty to go to Lovell, including a sum-mit and the Medicine Wheel.

"You take the tent," Mary said. "I'll reach Greybull by night." We planned to meet the second evening in Cody.

After washing our dishes, we went to the bar. I sat by Mary in the crowd, unsure how to act. What would tomorrow be like? Would I be okay? I floated through the evening, my brain only half present. Some guys named Dave and John bought us Fat Tire Ales, in honor of our trip. I wondered if they'd be disappointed that we weren't going to hook up with them, or if they were just nice guys.

We had a dance floor with good music, and it was a holiday weekend. I wished I could just have fun and take advantage of it, but I wanted to be out by the tent. I made myself leave, ignoring the pangs that I was missing something.

Outside, cold air hit me. We were up high, I remembered. I looked overhead, feeling closer to the sky and hoping to see bright stars; but with the lodge's lights, I couldn't. Maybe tomorrow I'd be somewhere darker, in the basin west of the Bighorn Mountains. Dread filled me. Wherever I was, Mary wouldn't be there.

I brushed my teeth and crawled into the tent, snuggling deep into my sleeping bag. How long would it take me to reach the summit, thirteen miles away? Would the road be uphill all the way? When would I reach the Medicine Wheel? Should I take off my panniers to ride up to the Wheel, making my bike lighter—should I leave them unattended? Would the Medicine Wheel be anticlimactic, like so many other things? Would I find a safe place to camp—maybe in the Bighorn Recreation Area west of the mountains? Would I sleep outside, or wimp out and pay for a hotel? Would I explore towns, and enjoy being on my own?

I couldn't know; the answers didn't exist yet. I tried to stop thinking and hoped I'd be protected as I stepped off another cliff.

## The Medicine Wheel, at which nothing important happens . . . or so it seems

I AWOKE WITH MY NOSE ICY in the mountain air. I snuggled deeper in my warm sleeping bag; once I got up, the day would begin and I'd have to leave Mary. But now that I was awake, an anxious gnawing began in my chest.

I wanted to see the Medicine Wheel; it seemed important, like its spiritual significance would somehow help me in my quest for inner calm. If I didn't get up, I might not have the time I needed later. So I forced myself to sit up and quickly pulled on clothes, shivering in the seconds before my body warmed them.

An hour later, I could think of no reason to stay. Mary fiddled with her bags. I'd imagined us setting off together. Should I keep waiting? Maybe my hovering bothered her, and with the distance I had to go, the more time I had, the better. It was already nine-thirty. "Are you all set?" I said.

"Yep!" She continued packing.

My brain reviewed the details again: I had the tent and the stove. We'd meet in Cody tomorrow. If anything went wrong, we'd leave messages with Mary's sister Laura. "Well, I guess I can go . . ."

Mary stood abruptly and walked over to hug me. "Good luck." She returned to her bike. Now I *had* to leave. I wheeled my bike up the bumpy drive to the road. Lifting my leg over it, I took a few breaths and pushed off. After a few pedal strokes to gain speed and stability, I glanced back at Mary, still bent over her bike. Then she disappeared behind the trees.

The two-lane road stretched before me under a perfectly clear sky. Ahead rose rocky, forested hilltops, and around me spread sloping fields, with trees in neat lines and patches. The wind blew across the fields, and my continuous pedaling indicated I still rode uphill, although I couldn't see it. A fence lined the road, thirty or forty feet away.

I stopped to photograph some blue and white lupines. They weren't as shriveled as the ones I'd seen yesterday; maybe they'd bloomed later than those on the eastern side of the mountain range. Snapping my picture, I hurried on, knowing I should cover distance. But it seemed a pity not to stop when I could do it without holding up Mary.

Biking through a patch of evergreen forest, I noticed a few thin trees with white trunks and glimmering leaves—aspens. The forest broke for a meadow strewn with boulders. A ring of aspens stood far out in the meadow, leaves flashing silently in the breeze, and I remembered the fantastical pictures in a book about unicorns I'd had as a child. With the gentle but steady—almost eerie—wind blowing, I could be biking through a fairy story. I felt an urge to go stand in the middle of the ring and look up at the silver-sage leaves. But I'd have to scramble over boulders to reach the aspens, and wade through tall grass.

So I halted in the road and snapped a picture, and then continued biking.

But then I kept wishing I had stopped. What was the point of freedom if I didn't do things I wanted to do? So when I saw another ring of aspens, I pulled over without thinking. These aspens didn't give me the urge to stop, but I didn't want to miss another opportunity. Besides, I rationalized, there were no boulders in the field here, and the grass was shorter.

Once I'd parked, I noticed the absence of sound. The aspens waited silently across the wide field. "There might be cows," I thought. Maybe this was ranch land—would I be trespassing? What if the herd had a protective bull? Or perhaps a bear was poking around nearby . . . I stepped up and hefted myself over the fence.

This cluster wasn't as nice as the last one. It stood in the sun, not shaded in a fairy tale glade. The trees didn't form a perfect ring; they stood disjointedly, like family members who don't get along.

As I neared, I discerned a rock amid the trees; I'd sit cross-legged on that rock, placidly communing with nature in the dappled shade. The sloped back looked easier to climb.

As I came around the rock, my heart jumped: a giant white skull stared blankly up from the grass.

The empty sockets watched me. It was just a cow skull. Maybe the cow had gotten hurt and died back here, and no one had found it. *But where's the rest of its body?*

I turned away from the skull, trying not to think of the symbolism I might be ignoring. Death? Danger? A pig's head on a stick flashed into my mind from tenth-grade English class. I focused on climbing the rock, alert for snakes or spiders or anything else that might turn my excursion into a disaster. But not a single thing moved except for the slight fluttering of the leaves.

At the top, I crossed my legs and sat. Instantly, the silence grew ominous, pressing in on all sides. Lichens clung on the rock like parasites. My tiny bike stood by the road; beyond it rose a steep hillside covered with tall conifers, like a giant box of evergreen crayons. Sunlight came through the fluttering leaves, striking my face—it was hot, not really shady at all. I squirmed in the heat, trying to relax and enjoy the place. Closing my eyes, I took deep breaths, willing myself to slow down.

But as soon as my eyes closed, I imagined someone stealing my bike. Would I hear a truck stopping, way out there at the road? What would I do—run and try to stop the thieves, or hide? I had to check; I opened my eyes. My bike was still there.

Maybe I should not have left it in plain sight. It gave away my location; someone might see it and decide to come after me. What would I do then, run toward the road or run away? Would another car come along to help me?

"Stop," I told myself. "These thoughts are not helpful." Maybe my bike's visibility would help me. Maybe a poisonous snake would bite me, and I'd fall off the rock—my bike would help the authorities find my body. Ironically, this thought made me feel better.

By now I couldn't stop checking for my bike every ten seconds. Sitting among the trees wasn't working. So after another forced minute, I climbed down past the skull and returned to the road.

I pedaled without stopping for an hour, no longer eager to explore. With my morning energy, the miles passed quickly. I felt less winded, like I rode *over* the mountains, rather than *up* them. A stream meandered along the valley to my left, while ahead, sunlight glowed on the beige rock of a cliff topped with evergreens. The scene still didn't live up to the pictures in nature calendars, but maybe I'd had unreasonable expectations.

And then the fence ended! A sign warned that cattle might cross the road. Now no signs of humankind ruined the view, except for the gray road with its faded stripe. Far ahead, a dark blot moved out of the trees. Was it a cow? It was too large, and cows didn't walk alone, or with such purpose; it had to be a moose! I pedaled faster, but the shape continued downhill and disappeared into the woods.

Finally, I saw cars at a turnout with a green sign: "Observation Point, ELEV 9430." The Medicine Wheel would be in about ten miles. Behind the guardrail, a hill sloped down, a thin layer of green vegetation clinging to the hard dirt. White sky filled the gaps behind distant hills. As I ate lunch, sitting on the hillside, I realized the white spaces were windows to the basin west of the mountains, blocked by haze.

After lunch, the road skimmed the mountaintops. Patches of snow remained, tiny rivulets or crescent moons that betrayed the contours of the hillsides. Sometimes I glimpsed the basin to my left. Lofty thoughts like "I'm at the top of the world!" alternated with the refrain of "Where will I sleep?"

I passed a dirt road lined with evergreens, with a national forest sign for Bald Mountain Campground. Another dirt road passed on my right, heading uphill. I watched for the brown historic site sign, but all I saw ahead were yellow caution signs. As I got closer, I read, "Next 14 Miles, Steep Grade 10% Sharp Curves, Check Brakes." Between the tall rocks, I glimpsed open air. The Medicine Wheel had to be soon.

The road dropped, and I picked up speed. Fourteen miles of downhill . . . that seemed like the end of the mountains. But the Medicine Wheel was on top of the mountains, right?

I squeezed my brakes, screeching to a long stop. It couldn't be ahead, but I hadn't seen any sign of it.

"Well, I don't want to climb back up *that!*" I thought, looking down the hill. Maybe I could ask a ranger at the campground. I walked my bike in a U-turn, shuddering to think I might have coasted to the bottom without realizing my mistake. I rode back.

There was the other dirt road. Could that be the Medicine Wheel?

In the campground, I found only a kiosk. A few tents were scattered among the trees. In the middle of the loop stood a gigantic orange pump on a platform, like the mother of all the little pumps I'd used in midwestern parks that summer. Maybe a big pump was needed to draw water from the depths of the mountains. I scanned the bulletin boards: instructions on how to pay for a site, a flier about the Medicine Wheel, but no maps. That other road had to be it.

By now it was two o'clock. I could go to the Medicine Wheel and then descend the mountains and try to find a campsite. But there was a campground right here—I'd feel safe staying here. I could start early tomorrow and work hard to ride the eighty miles to Cody. The first fourteen would be downhill, so really I only had sixty-six to do.

"If I camp here," I thought, "I can pitch the tent and leave my panniers rather than lug them uphill to the Medicine Wheel. And I can stay at the Medicine Wheel as long as I like. I won't worry about getting back on the road, or about where I'll sleep; I'll relax and enjoy being there." I tried to consider other options, but when I returned to the idea of camping on the mountain, the whole world shifted into a state of rightness.

*Mary would want me to stay and not to worry.*

I picked a site among the trees, pitched the tent, and threw in my sleeping pad to inflate. Then I undid the latch on a pannier and yanked the bag up. The bike twisted as its weight shifted. When all the panniers were off, my bike looked slim and naked with only its handlebar bag—like a naked lady wearing a huge hat.

Now I just had to refill my water bottles. I climbed the steps to the pump and tugged the handle with both hands. I pushed it all the way up, but nothing came out, not even a gurgling. "The well must be dry," I thought. Maybe there'd be a ranger at the Medicine Wheel, to ask for water.

I pushed off on my bike, wobbling as I adjusted to its weight, and rode out. I flew over the gravel, my bike was so light. I crossed Route 14 ALT and ground my tires into the dirt as I began to climb the new road. But the road inclined sharply and my speed disappeared. I pushed, trying to reclaim enough speed to downshift. Gravel scattered as my tires slipped across the ground. "It's a good thing I left all those bags," I thought. For once, I was glad to be on my mountain bike, with its small wheels and low gears. I'd soon downshifted to my lowest.

The driveway leveled, giving me a break to look over the landscape. Far below ran the tiny Route 14 ALT, heading to the edge of the mountains. The climb resumed at the next turn. Soon I could see to the north, where evergreens filled a bowl-shaped valley.

At last the road widened into a parking lot. Past a ranger hut, a dirt track wound out of sight. I pulled up at the door of the hut. Inside, a young man with glasses slumped in a chair. When he looked up, I asked, "Are bikes allowed in?"

"Yeah, go ahead."

I smiled.

Other visitors straggled from cars, cameras hanging off their necks, and began the dusty trek, which swooped down and then continued steeply uphill. I rolled past them, careful not to lose momentum as I hit the bottom and started up again. On the packed dirt, I ground my tires in as I pushed, left, right, left. The road twisted along the ridge like the Great Wall of China.

I rode the mile and a half and arrived at a sidewalk leading up a grassy hill. Two rangers stood at the top.

"Hi," one called out. "Welcome to the Medicine Wheel!" He sounded like Captain America, the cartoon version. "I'm Brent." He held out his hand as I approached. I braced for his handshake. "This is Tim." Tim smiled like his superhero sidekick.

The sidewalk continued upward. A rope fence ran along the top—that must be the Medicine Wheel. Brent opened his lips to launch into a spiel. But as his words bubbled to the surface, he checked himself; I could almost see the first word lodge in his throat as no sound came out. Then he said, "This is one of the rare times when no one is here. Maybe you'd like to walk around and get the history lesson later." I let out my breath and nodded.

I walked up the hill and got my first look at the Medicine Wheel: rows of large rocks stood on the grass, with some rock piles among them. It was hard to make sense of the rock formation, which looked flatter and smaller than I'd expected. An aerial view on a plaque showed the round shape, with rock spokes extending from a center pile.

Did I feel something inside? I'd imagined being moved when I reached this place—perhaps I would have a vision, or all sorts of meaning would fall into place. But nothing happened. The wind continued to blow quietly across the mountains, and I stood there, disappointed not to feel anything monumental, but not surprised.

The plaque had a quote from someone called Old Mouse: "Eventually one gets to the Medicine Wheel to fulfill one's life." I didn't feel fulfilled. I read on, "The wheel remains a mystery." It was built between 1200 and 1700 AD. Native American beliefs and archaeological evidence suggest it was a spiritual site. "People still come for inspiration, solitude, meditation, and vision questing. Please respect the solitude of those visiting."

At the sweat lodge I'd attended in North Carolina, we'd always walked in a clockwise direction to enter the space around the lodge, so I headed left. Some sage leaves hung from the fence. The leaves were tied into a bundle around a tiny leather bag. Glancing around, I saw more items on the fence—colorful bits of ribbon, feathers, and bracelets of braided grass. These weren't a permanent part of the Medicine Wheel, I realized. Visitors had left them.

I reached for my camera, but when I lifted it to my eye, the view inside was black. An eerie feeling overcame me, as if I'd known this would happen. The shutter was stuck open. The bumpy ride up the mountain must have jarred it. I banged the side of the camera, but it didn't help, so I lowered it and continued walking.

I tried to look at the Wheel, but instead I kept noticing the offerings. The ribbons were mostly red, yellow, black, or white. I knew from the sweat lodge and from my book, *Mother Earth Spirituality,* that these were the four sacred colors, and corresponded to the four seasons and directions.

I wanted to leave something . . . but what? All I had was a plastic "Love" necklace I'd gotten from a quarter machine in Sheridan. It seemed trashy alongside the feathers and grasses; I didn't want to be rude. But wasn't love a universal message, even written in plastic? I was still alone; no one would see me leave it. I took it off and kneeled to fasten it to the rope. It swung in the sunlight, sparkling green and out of place.

As I neared one completion of the circle, tourists approached up the hill. They infiltrated the space, talking, pointing, and moving every which way. I walked back to Brent and Tim to learn about the Medicine Wheel.

Archaeological confusion about the site, Brent said, stems from the site being in continuous use since it was built. When the government first placed the Medicine Wheel on the National Historic Register in 1970, they erected a tall, chain-link fence with barbed wire on top. Since then, they'd worked with Native American tribes, replacing the original fence with the more welcoming rope fence. Tribes wanted twenty-four-hour access to the site, so it did not officially close; the rangers would leave at five o'clock, but visitors could stay.

I imagined young Native Americans spending the night there on their vision quests. I'd daydreamed about spending the night . . . and it was actually an option!

As I realized it, though, my spirits sank with dread. I thought of the campground: my snug tent, making dinner at the picnic table, hot tea. I imagined moving camp to the Medicine Wheel, but pitching a tent up here seemed silly. On a vision quest you were probably supposed to brave the elements and sleep outside. And while lying under the stars sounded romantic, in reality it would be freezing. I wouldn't sleep, and I had eighty miles to cover tomorrow. So I dismissed the idea.

Was I being smart, or just scared?

After Brent's lecture, I walked another clockwise loop around the circle. Just after I'd passed some forget-me-nots poking up along the path, my camera clicked: the shutter had dropped shut. I turned back for a picture but stopped myself—I didn't want to walk counterclockwise, even for a few yards. I'd have to go around a third time. I continued my stroll, photographing the offerings hanging in the clear air.

After taking a picture of the forget-me-nots, I completed the circle a third time. I decided to make a fourth trip, to fit with the four sacred directions and colors. It seemed right.

BACK AT THE PARKING LOT, I poked my head into the ranger hut. The guy with glasses still slumped inside. "Hey, I was wondering, do you have any water?" I asked. "I couldn't get the pump in the campground to work."

"Oh, yeah, uh . . ." He sat up.

"I wouldn't ask, it's just I'm on a bike and I'm almost out, and I don't know where there's going to be more."

"Oh, okay." He pulled a jug from under the desk, and I handed him an open bottle. "We have to carry it in, but I can get more at ranger camp . . . so you're traveling on a bike?"

"Yeah."

"Are you alone?" He didn't sound creepy, just surprised. He looked younger than I was, but taller.

"No, I'm with a friend, but we split up—I wanted to see the Medicine Wheel and she wanted to go through Shell Canyon. We're meeting in Cody tomorrow night."

His name was Justin; he was on summer break from university. On his days off, he hiked or drove to Yellowstone or the Teton Mountains. He'd thought of doing a bike trip, so he had lots of questions. I assumed he was an experienced hiker and camper; he probably knew all the right things to do in the backcountry. It seemed weird that I had done something—traveled by bike—that he hadn't.

Sunlight glowed around me as I stood in the doorway, telling him about camping in parks and being taken home by families and eating grilled cheese for lunch every day.[21] The colors shining on the ranger hut grew more vibrant as we talked, until at last I said, "I should probably get back and make dinner before sunset."

"Yeah," he said. "Well, safe travels."

Now that I'd accomplished my mission—I'd seen the Medicine Wheel and found a campsite—I could enjoy my location. The campground felt secure, my home for the night; the wilderness crept nearby, barred from the ring of civilization. And being in the mountains felt wonderful. The air felt clearer and better to breathe, and the empty campsites resonated peace.

Mary had let me carry the olive oil, and as I used it, I noticed that I didn't have to wonder if she *noticed* me using it. But I had no one to tell about my day. As I recalled it, I imagined describing it to Mary.

The temperature dropped as the sun sank. I didn't think I should wash the dishes, but then I saw a camper using the pump. I hurried over. "Hey," I called out, "could you show me how this works?"

"Sure," he said, lifting the handle high in the air. "You just do this." He pulled it down and then pushed it up again, as far as it would go. After a few times, the stream of water turned into a gush.

"Oh, I get it!" I said—he was actually pumping! Previously, water had gushed out of pumps without effort, but here you had to work.[22] Now I felt foolish, but at least I knew how to get water.

Regulating the flow from the pump was difficult, and the water was frigid. By the time I'd scrubbed my dishes, my hands were stiff. The sun shone between the trees. I shuddered involuntarily as I hurried back to my site and placed a pot on the stove, then fumbled to light the burner. A cup of tea was the only way to warm my fingers. I held them near the flames while I waited, and then wrapped them around the mug after I'd poured the tea.

I took my tea to the field behind my campsite to watch the sun set. The sky faded behind Medicine Mountain. Right before the sun disappeared, its light expanded, obliterating the driveway and the trees, glowing off the tallest wildflowers. Then the light dimmed, and tendrils of cold crept through the chill air. I didn't have long. My tea had already cooled.

The sunset turned fabulous: blue, pink, and orange with bands of cloud strung across the sky behind evergreen silhouettes. But I left for my tent in the midst of the beauty. I didn't want to become too cold to fall asleep.

I set my alarm for two AM. I wanted to see the stars up here on the mountains, away from city lights, and the moon would be down by then. Then I lay down, the long day replaying in my head. "In the morning," I thought, "it will be cold, so I'll make tea first, to warm my hands . . ."

Then my alarm was beeping, and I fumbled to shut it off. Cold air struck my arm; did I really want to get up? It was like getting up at three-thirty on a winter morning to work at the bakery, only worse. I forced myself upright in the darkness, feeling for my hoody and pulling it on. I crawled out of the tent, zipping in the warmth behind me, and hurried down the path to the field, guided by starlight.

I reached the field and looked up. All I saw were the usual specks of light. How disappointing! A bright orange planet hung in the east, so I tried to suck a feeling of awe out of that. Then I returned to my tent, hoping the warmth hadn't faded from my sleeping bag.

## Powell, Wyoming, in which the presence of a cute guy makes my irrational thinking go completely haywire

L ATE THE NEXT AFTERNOON, I rolled into Powell, Wyoming. I'd procrasti-
nated leaving camp that morning; it had felt like home. When I'd finally
coasted down the steep western side of the mountains, with my hands
clamped tightly on my brakes, a tugging sense of loss had lodged in my chest.
The elated feeling of the mountains had drained out as I'd descended. At the
bottom, I'd headed into a heat-filled basin, desolate with only scrubby sage
bushes and the wind in my face.

By five PM, I'd traveled fifty-six miles as I drew near Powell. I had twenty-four miles left to reach Cody, and I still felt full of energy.

At the edge of town, I stopped at a restroom. Behind the concrete building, picnic tables and evergreens dotted the grass. Each table had a roof, like a
miniature picnic shelter. As I pulled my bike onto the sidewalk, I noticed a sign:
"Welcome to Powell, Camping Allowed."

Free camping! I wouldn't have to ask permission!

But I had to reach Cody. I'd envisioned arriving tonight, accomplishing the
eighty miles.

"But it's not like I've never biked that far in one day," I thought. "I did 120 miles once. And camping's allowed! And Powell might have a movie theater, or a Mexican restaurant."

As I entered the restroom, I thought of Mary: I didn't want to leave her alone, without the tent and stove.

But when I exited, the heat hit me. Could I really do another twenty-four miles? I'd arrive late and worn out. What if Mary went to a movie? I'd find her bike outside the theater and have to sit and wait for her. What if I couldn't find her? What if I couldn't make it? The fifteen-mile stretch before Cody had no towns—I'd be in the middle of nowhere.

A phone booth stood at the edge of the park. I trudged over and picked up the heavy book that swung from a metal cord inside. I found the cinema list—there was a theater in Powell!

I stood in the phone booth and tried to think. There was a movie theater and a place to camp. I had not expected to stop, but Powell was good. But should I change the plan?

I decided to call Laura. When she answered, I assured her that we were fine. "Where are you?" she said.

"I'm in Powell, Wyoming. Mary and I split up yesterday, and we're supposed to meet in Cody tonight, but it's another twenty-four miles. I was thinking of stopping."

"You should stop."

"Do you think Mary will be alright? I have the tent and stove."

"She will be fine," Laura replied.

"Okay, thanks. I really want to stop. If Mary calls, can you tell her I'll be there by noon?"

I hung up, and suddenly I felt better than I had all day—I was free! I knew Mary might want to head on from Cody the next afternoon. Had I just traded the famous city of Cody for undistinguished Powell? "Oh well," I thought. "I just want to enjoy Powell."

I rode into the quiet town, stopping at the visitor center for a map. Everything I could possibly need was within a few blocks: a coffee shop, the movie theater, a library, a post office, a bakery, a Mexican restaurant, and a grocery store. If heaven were a bike trip, this would be the town at every crossroads.

No cars moved on the main street. I scanned the movie posters as I rolled past the theater and noted the showtimes. Options ran through my head: The restaurant would be closed later, but I wasn't hungry. Library? I could always call home and not bother with email. Bakery and post office in the morning. I wanted to sit in the coffee shop.

I turned onto 2nd Street and searched the sleepy storefronts until I found The Coffee House. Sunlight gleamed off the white brick wall behind white patio tables and chairs. I switched from my sunglasses to my normal glasses and dug out my Ziplock bag with my journal, postcards, and pen, and grabbed my wallet. Then, feeling like a dork with my complicated routine, I put it all down on a table so I could adjust my clothing. I wiped my brow with a dry shirtsleeve, picked up my things, and pulled open the door, clanging some bells on the other side.

Cool air rushed out as my eyes adjusted to the dark interior. Deserted tables stood to the left. Opposite me, behind a counter, a young guy looked up from his studying. He had fluffy blonde curls and the nicest face. He smiled at me. Thoughts flew at me: I'm grimy, odd looking, sweaty. I smiled back, but I looked down.

I'd waited to catch the door, and now it swung shut and knocked me harder than I'd expected. I tripped into the darkened room. The guy was still watching me. "Hi," I said to the counter.

"What can I get for you?"

"Something cold . . ." I hunted for the menu. The cute guy waited for my answer, so I hurried. I found the iced drinks, narrowed down the choices, and said, "A decaf iced soymilk latte." I resumed breathing, which apparently had stopped at some point.

He slid off his stool and turned to make my drink. "Where you from?" he asked without looking up.

"North Carolina. I'm biking."

"By yourself?" He sounded a little surprised, but not discouraging.

"No, with a friend. But we split up for a few days. I'm meeting her in Cody."

He continued to work, and I looked around so I wouldn't be standing there, watching him. I didn't want him to think he had to keep talking to me. I feigned an interest in the artwork—if he looked up now, he'd see me occupied, disinterested. He'd never guess that I thought he was cute. I only turned back as he finished my drink.

"It's on the house," he said, sliding it across the counter.

Tears pricked my eyes, my self-consciousness momentarily sideswiped. "Thank you," I said as I took the glass. I wanted to talk to him, but I thought he probably wanted to get back to studying, so I moved to a table.

Once I'd sat, thoughts about my awkward appearance grew more insistent. In my tired state, it didn't occur to me to assess if my thoughts were rational: *He'll be repulsed if he guesses that I think he's cute. I have to do something, not just sit here.* I risked a glance; he'd gone back to reading. Pushing the drink aside, I opened my journal. My pen stood on the paper, but no words came. Instead, my mind raced with all the miles I had covered that day, as the day's heat dissipated from my body into the cool room.

I focused on the pen. "7/7," I wrote. "The Coffee House, Powell." What did I want to remember? "The cute coffee shop boy gave me a decaf iced soy-milk latte on the house. I like Powell." I made a list of all the places in town, and the times they closed, and wrote "Call Mom!" in a box. Then I managed to write half a page about leaving the mountains and my decision to stop in Powell. I stopped writing.

My brain ached to shut down. Maybe writing a postcard would be easier. I glanced toward the counter again—he still read his book, not looking at me. I shut my journal, jammed it back into its Ziplock bag, and got out postcards.

*Can he tell that I think he's cute?* I *had* to ignore him.

The bells on the door clanged, and another guy walked in. "Hey man," he said to the barista. "What time you off?" *For sure this newcomer will think I'm a loser: an ugly, sweaty girl hanging around the coffee shop, hitting on this friend.* I stared at my postcard and labored to write a line: "Hi from Powell, Wyoming." I paused, then tried again: "I'm sitting in the coffee shop." I heard steps and looked up to see both guys heading my way. My heart leapt, but then I realized they were coming to straighten up the tables. I looked back at my card. "It's super hot out," I wrote. The guys started putting the chairs on the tables, and the one who'd made my drink looked over.

"We're closing up, but you can stay awhile longer."

I nodded, but my discomfort skyrocketed—I'd be in the way. I downed the rest of my drink, a cube of ice tumbling down the glass to bonk into my nose. I shoved my postcards into their bag. Standing, I called, "Could I sit outside?"

He turned. "Sure."

"Thanks." I took my glass to the dish tub and hurried for the exit.

The door clanged, and I found myself back in the bright heat. I took a deep breath and sighed it out into the empty street. I sat at one of the white tables and got out the postcard, but I no longer tried to write. I just sat there, dazed, and several minutes later the door clanged one last time as the guys came out. They walked up the sidewalk and turned a corner.

The thoughts about my appearance disappeared.

I had thirty minutes until the movie. I contemplated rushing to the library to send an email home, but I didn't want to. I didn't want to move.

A car pulled up to the curb and stopped, and I watched a woman get out. I smiled at her. Then she came toward me, pulling out a key, and I realized she was going into the coffeehouse. Would she mind me sitting there?

She looked over. "Do you need anything?"

"Oh, no, thank you," I said. "I had a latte."

She opened the door but hesitated to go in. "Where are you from?"

"North Carolina." It sounded like another planet.

"You're biking alone?"

"No, I'm with a friend, but we split up. I wanted to see the Medicine Wheel." The words kept coming out. "We're meeting in Cody, but when I saw 'Camping Allowed' in the park I just had to stop. And I wanted to go to the movies."

"Well, come in and cool off," she said.

The impulse came to refuse, but instead I said okay and followed her inside.

"I'm Helen." She turned on a light. "Can I get you a lemonade? On the house!"

It didn't seem right to have two free drinks, but I didn't want to get the cute guy in trouble. "Well . . . he already gave me the latte free."

"Oh, good!" she said. "He knows what to do."

Talking to Helen was so easy and comfortable. Why hadn't it been that way earlier? The barista had been nice, but I'd still become self-conscious. This always happened when I thought a guy was cute, making it impossible to "be myself" and talk to him. And it happened so quickly—instantly. A switch flipped and a different Emily existed, an awkward, blank-brained Emily who couldn't make eye contact or say anything interesting. And being so tired had made it all worse.

It was hard to realize that thoughts led to my self-consciousness because it resulted so quickly, and even harder to identify the thoughts and combat them. Now I could see them: I'd imagined that I annoyed the coffee guy, that my interest would bother him if he noticed, that he saw my actions and thought me awkward, and that his friend thought me awful. And this had all seemed completely rational.

Irrational thinking pervaded my life. In some ways I'd learned to adapt—for example, I became friends with people who offered me reassurance, so that thoughts like, "No one really likes me," were held at bay. But the "cute guy" situation was one in which I'd made no progress. Faced with it now, the tactic of identifying irrational thoughts and stopping them fast enough to remain calm and converse with a guy seemed impossible. It almost seemed like fighting the thoughts made them try harder.

I had wondered if the way to fight off such thoughts might be meditating: if I practiced "turning off" my brain by meditating, would it be easier to turn off the negative thoughts at other times? Again I remembered the chain superstores, and the strategy of having something good in place to thwart them from coming. If I repeated a thought, a mundane thought such as, "I am in Powell, Wyoming, I am in Powell, Wyoming," maybe that would take up the space in my brain and forestall the negative thoughts before they resulted in self-consciousness. I had to remember to try it.

# Cody, in which I have a major theological revelation, and we attend the rodeo

CODY FELT LIKE A CARNIVAL. Brick storefronts lined the main drag, with American flags flapping and tourists crawling everywhere. I'd stopped in the visitor center, where posters announced Rodeo! Movies! Attractions! Continuing on, I'd come to Sheridan Avenue, where my Route 14-ALT met up with Mary's Route 14.

As I turned onto Sheridan, the wind hit me in the face, blowing down off the brown hill that towered over the far end of the avenue. The wide street (four lanes of traffic, plus two for parking) seemed excessive for such a tiny city, and I suspected the whole place had been planned as a tourist trap from the start.

Biking slowly, I tried to take in all the shops and restaurants and watch for Mary's bike. At the main intersection stood the impressive Irma Hotel ("Buffalo Bill's Original Hotel"!) with elaborate brickwork and flags flying. Signs announced "Cowboy Shop" and "Saloon" and "Saddle Shop," and I could hear Donnie and Jerome snorting in Spotted Horse. Did real cowboys ever shop in places like these?

I passed a library sign. Stone pillars across the street marked the entrance to a large park full of people. Had Mary spent last night there? The road curved sharply left past the Buffalo Bill historical center, a sprawling complex of low buildings and parking lots, and then left the downtown.

I U-turned and went to the library. Mary sat at the computers. We'd made it! I wanted to tell her about my adventures, but I repressed my excitement; I didn't want to interrupt her. I waved when she looked up.

"Hey." She smiled and returned to her email.

I emailed my parents. Then I scanned my inbox: I had a message from a coworker at the bakery, telling me to hurry home so that he could take an extended vacation like mine; he needed me to cover for him.

Anger welled up inside me. Why should I cover for him? I always did his work when he left town, but he never recognized me for it.

I'd never felt angry before. I'd always wanted him to like me, so I'd backed down from conflict.

"Don't think about him," I told myself. "Focus on Cody."

Mary suggested lunch at a Mexican place called Zapata's ("a revolution in Mexican food"). As we walked there, I kept seeing signs in store windows for the "Cody Nite Rodeo," which supposedly happened every single night. In Zapata's, I asked our waitress, "Is there really a rodeo tonight?"

She nodded. "Every night at eight-thirty. And if you go," she added, lowering her voice and leaning closer, "sit on the back side—in the 'Buzzard's Roost.' That's where the cowboys get on the horses—you can watch it all happen. And it's cheaper."

Mary and I caught up over lunch: I told her about the Medicine Wheel and Powell. She had spent her first night in Greybull—she'd asked to sleep at a Catholic church, and the priest had instead paid for a motel room. Last night she'd slept under a picnic shelter in a park, in a neighborhood east of downtown. I asked if she wanted to leave that day, but she said we could stay another night. "Do you want to go to the rodeo?" I asked.

"Maybe . . . it probably costs a lot."

How could I visit Cody and not see a rodeo? But it would be hard to enjoy without Mary. So after lunch, when we split up to look at shops, I walked up the street to the Chamber of Commerce and bought two fifteen-dollar tickets for the Buzzard's Roost. Then I window-shopped. The sunny, windy day kept me outside; the lure of a museum had no effect. "The museum might feel staged," I thought. I suspected Cody had an agenda: to further the vision of the "Wild West" that Buffalo Bill had created with his traveling show. And the museum would be crowded with tourists.

A rack of "WANTED" posters caught my eye. I entered the shop and spotted what I'd hoped for:

# REWARD
## ($5,000.00)
Reward for the capture, dead or alive,
of one Wm. Bonney, better known as
### "BILLY THE KID"

It was printed on brown paper to look old and described Billy as "the leader of the worst band of desperadoes the Territory has ever had to deal with."[23] I thought back to Billy's letters that I'd read in Indiana. Billy had sounded pathetic and earnest, desperate to turn his life around, but no frontiersman seeing this poster would have given Billy a second chance. I bought the poster. The clerk, like our waitress earlier, greeted me enthusiastically.

At three o'clock, I walked to the Irma Hotel to meet Mary. I had this idea that we'd treat ourselves to an Old West drink, like what they'd drink in an old-timey western movie. But when we entered the Silver Saddle Saloon, I realized I had no idea what an "Old West drink" meant. All I could think of was mint juleps.

"I want something that *fits*," I said to the bartender. He stared at me. "What's an old-fashioned, western drink? I keep thinking 'mint julep,' but that's the Kentucky Derby." I pictured a saloon full of men in cowboy gear, with a kind-hearted prostitute draped across the battered upright piano. "I guess they probably drank shots of whiskey," I said, discouraged. I wasn't about to do that.

"How about the new Bacardi drink?" the bartender said, pointing at a shiny black and glow-light-green poster with "Bacardi O$^3$" blazed across it. "Women seem to like them."

While I stood trying to come up with an alternative, Mary ordered a Bacardi O$^3$. The bartender looked at me and raised his eyebrows. "Sure, fine," I said.

We took our O$^3$s to the porch and sat at a heavy log picnic table. Dried peppers hung in bunches from the ceiling, and a painted wooden "drugstore Indian" stood by the wall. Farther down, a shriveled "man" slumped on a bench against a Coke machine; we'd seen one of these scarecrow-like figures at the Corn Palace in South Dakota, and I'd gotten a picture of Mary sitting next to him. This one wore a purple and blue cowboy shirt, deflated and sagging.

"There's another one of those men," Mary said, jerking her head at him. "Want another photo?"

The man shifted. Mary jumped and then began to titter. "I thought he was a statue!" she whispered. Had he heard us?

The saloon door opened, and four men swaggered out and gathered around a bar table halfway down the porch. Three of them wore white cowboy hats and shiny oval belt buckles; I couldn't see if the buckles depicted rearing horses or majestic bucks on rocky ledges. Patterned button-down shirts were tucked neatly into their tight jeans. Immediately I thought of Donnie and Jerome's "drugstore cowboys," just as Mary muttered the phrase. The fourth man looked like he'd just come from a NASCAR race, in a white tee, beaded necklace, and Hulk Hogan mustache, with mirror shades and a baseball hat.

They stood laughing and drinking beers. "Mary," I whispered. "Will you go ask to take a picture with them?" She glared at me. "Please?!"

Mary closed her eyes briefly and then let out her breath and slid off the picnic bench. As I grabbed my camera, her glare rearranged into a fetching smile. She stepped across the porch as I hurried to open my camera and follow.

"Hi!" she said to the men in a perky, sweet voice. "Could I get a picture with y'all?"

The men grinned, surprised, and stood taller. "Sure," one said, but I imagined him saying, "Sure thing, little lady!" They straightened into a line, smiles across their faces (except for the NASCAR man, who maintained a tight-lipped smirk).

"I'm having fun," I realized. "Not worrying. Not trying to do everything, like see museums." But I was also drinking alcohol again, like in Spotted Horse. Maybe that was just a coincidence.

After our drinks, we returned to the library to look for information about Yellowstone. I took copies of the free brochures. Public rest areas dotted the road, and closer to the park were half a dozen government campgrounds. I checked email again, but I didn't want to think about things at home. I wanted to be here, in Cody. We'd made it this far, and I felt like from now on, we would coast effortlessly along.

LATER THAT AFTERNOON, WE ATE dinner at a cafe. The girl behind the counter greeted us—"Hi! Where y'all from?!"—and then continued talking. Between her stories I managed to order a veggie burger, and as she made it she shook her head. "It's so small," she said, and then reached for the sprouts and added some, and then some onions, and mushrooms, and olives, until its size satisfied her.

"You been to the rodeo?" she asked.

"We're going tonight!" I'd shown Mary the tickets and told her I wanted to treat.

"Sit on the back side," she said. "That's where the cowboys are."

Later, when I ordered an ice cream cone, she made it with three scoops instead of one.

By the time we left, the sun had gotten low, hiding behind clouds over the hill west of town. We rode past the Buffalo Bill historical center, leaving the cover of buildings, and a gusty wind hit me as a wide view of the hill opened ahead. We passed a tire place, a western gear warehouse, and a twenty-foot statue of a man with a maniacal grin, wearing a cowboy hat and holding a branding iron.[24]

A long white building came into view with "Stampede Park" painted on the wall. A few cars moved in the wide lot. We turned in and bumped across the gravel to the arena's fence. At the gate, the ticket taker pointed us right, along a curving fence that rounded the end of the arena to the bleachers at the back side.

All the fences and railings were painted red, white, or blue. Giant gates, chained shut, led to various pens and chutes, all with the same trampled dirt floor as the arena. We reached the middle of the bleachers and climbed up to the front row. Just below us, cowboys milled around a row of blue metal chutes. From the bleachers, I couldn't see their faces under their hats, just lots of handsome chins.

Some cowboys slowly rode their horses into the arena, warming them up in a wide circle. Soon they'd be pounding the dirt, I imagined, lassoes swirling overhead. After a few minutes, the arena cleared. A lone brown horse trotted out bearing a rider with a giant American flag. She rode to the center and stopped, and the whole stadium stood for the national anthem. I got teary-eyed as I sang along with the recording. I'd always liked this moment at high school ballgames, with everything stopping for a moment, but usually I felt embarrassed to be too "into" it. Suddenly, in Cody, Wyoming, I didn't have to hide my patriotic feelings, which juxtaposed oddly with my usual fear of being uncovered as a "tree hugger."

As "The Star-Spangled Banner" lingered away, a gate opened and a multicolored herd of horses thundered into the arena, bare backed with manes flowing. My heart soared at the energy of the brown and white bodies moving together, powerful legs pounding on the dirt. But a moment later, three cowboys rode out. The fluid movement faltered as horses turned into each other, trying to evade the cowboys, who herded them back to the gate.

Our attention shifted to the right, where more cowboys waited. The well-known rodeo events—like riding the bucking broncos—came at the end of the night. First we had to sit through the ominous-sounding "calf roping."

The gate cracked open and a tiny calf dashed out, fleeing for all it was worth. A cowboy raced after it, lasso flying. The lasso caught the calf's neck and went taut as the horse abruptly stopped, yanking the calf to a halt. The cowboy hopped down, bodily flipped the calf onto the dirt, and whipped a rope around three legs while the calf squirmed. Scores were based on speed so it happened within seconds. How many times did a calf go through this each week?[25]

I flashed back to a conversation with my friend Cari in the lab in grad school. "I've always wanted to go to a bullfight," she'd said. I'd guessed that she didn't know what happened at bullfights. I'd read *Ferdinand the Bull,* so I knew.

"Really?!" I'd replied. "But they're so awful!"

A look had crossed her face, uncomprehending. "What do you mean?"

"Well, they try to get the bull angry, so he's really violent when the matador comes out to kill him. So they have all these other people—the banderilleros and picadores—and they come out first and spear the bull to upset him."

Cari's face had fallen. "They kill the bull?" she'd whispered. I'd nodded. "I thought they just, you know,"—her hands had made a dancing motion off to the side—"flashed a red cape in its face."

Now I knew how Cari had felt. I'd imagined cowboys racing horses and showing off their lassoes. I hadn't thought beyond that, to the creatures being lassoed.

The gate released the next calf. It raced across the dirt.

"Go cow!" cheered a wobbly voice behind us. I twisted around to see a girl, five or six, sitting with her mom. She stared intently at the arena floor, tiny fists clenched. "Go cow!" she called again. Her mom gave me an apologetic look, so I smiled before turning away. A lasso found the calf's neck and dragged it to a halt in a cloud of dust. Once he'd tied it up, the cowboy released it, and it skittered the rest of the way across and out the gate. The cowboy mounted his horse and trotted out after it.

Snap! Out came the next calf. "Go cow!" I heard again.

"Go cow!" I called. The little calf ran, horses thundering down behind it. The cowboy let loose his lasso, and it sailed forward . . . and missed.

"Go cow!" we cheered. The cowboy reeled in his rope, but then he slowed his horse, and the calf raced on to the gate.

As the events continued, the sunlight faded, leaving a pale gleam over the giant hill. We saw the barrel race—the only rodeo event for women, in which riders raced to and fro, maneuvering their horses around barrels.[26] I imagined Coleen from Spotted Horse competing; she'd had a ribbon for the barrel race in her scrapbook.

When the time came for the bucking broncos, I appreciated our seats. Down below, men loaded antsy broncos into the blue chutes. Each horse seemed to have a strap tied around its belly, maybe to make it buck. A cowboy climbed over the chute and mounted the bronco while his friends held the reins. When the chute door snapped open, the horse leapt out sideways, thrashing about while the cowboy held on, an arm out for balance. Three seconds began to seem incredibly long, as the broncos dumped one cowboy after another in a split second.

As the sky behind the hill darkened, Mary wanted to go. I was tired of the rodeo, but I hated to leave without seeing the final event, bull riding. But we had more rounds of calf roping to sit through, so after a few more riders competed, we slid out of our seats and left.

I didn't think I'd go to a rodeo again. But on the way out, we passed a gift shop. Light spilled out the door. On the back wall hung posters full of spinning lassoes and bucking broncos—the fantasy rodeo I had expected. "Cody Nite Rodeo!" they proclaimed. Most cost ten dollars, but the prettiest one just had a cowboy on a bucking bronco and only cost five, so we each got one.

THE SUN WOKE ME AS it peeked over the trees in the neighborhood. We'd slept in the same park Mary had used her first night in Cody. Since she'd slept without the tent, we'd decided to forego it, laying our bags in the picnic shelter.

"It must be six AM," I thought, glancing around at the quiet streets and houses. Mary lay asleep in her bag. Wet concrete at the edges of the shelter remained as evidence of last night's assault of sprinklers.

I got up, pulled on my hoody, and got out *Mother Earth Spirituality*. I'd reached the last chapter, with only a narrow wad of pages left. If I could finish it this morning, I could mail it home from Cody along with the rodeo posters and other souvenirs.

As the sun rose, I sat reading at a picnic table. After a passage about all the different peoples of the world, I came to a line that stood out: "After the Great Spirit, *Wakan Tanka,* placed them in their respective areas, the *Wakan Tanka* appeared to each people in a different manner and taught them ways so that they might live in harmony and true beauty."[27]

I'd always thought myself Christian, but the past year I'd been learning about Native American spiritual beliefs. I'd felt unsettled with Christianity and didn't want to stick with it out of habit, but I didn't necessarily think Christians were wrong. Now I had an explanation for how all religions could coexist. God had given each person the religion he or she needed.

I applied this to Christianity and what I knew of Christian Americans, and it held true: The "American dream" is to make money, for buying things and for security. But Christianity tells people to let go of possessions, which they can't take into Heaven. It tells them to let go of security in order to have more faith. Christianity addressed the areas that many Americans needed to work on.

If religions were just different ways of looking at the same thing, it didn't seem important to pick one. According to the book, Chief Sitting Bull advised that people "take the best of the white man's ways and . . . the best of the old Indian ways." Maybe I could do that.[27]

## The road to Yellowstone, on which the inner workings of the Universe are revealed

A FEW MILES OUT OF CODY, Route 14-16-20 entered a cleft in a rocky hillside that led into a small gorge. Irregular columns rose to the sky alongside a small river that reflected brown, pierced with aqua tints. The road hugged the rock wall. After almost an hour, the road climbed up past a small dam, and a vast lake spread out before me, the blue tingling my brain after the past hour of browns. I'd seen the lake on the map but hadn't realized it would be so bright and airy.

The road headed out along the lake's edge. Fresh wind blew in my face, and the cerulean water brightened my day. Around the lake rose rocky hills, sloping up gently, then shooting up tall. As I rounded the lake, the brown hills transitioned to a green slope running to the base of a mountain range. The low mountains had patches of snow on top. I'd forgotten we were at five thousand feet.

I took a break at Buffalo Bill State Park, a rest area on the lake. At a picnic table, I pulled out the brochures I'd collected in Cody. On my state map, only one town lay ahead, Wapiti, just past the end of the lake. After Wapiti, it was eighty miles to Lake Village in Yellowstone National Park.

Now, I stared at a glossy Wyoming Scenic Byways brochure, holding down the edges against the wind while I tried to figure out my location. I found the lake and worked my way west. The road would follow the North Fork of the Shoshone River into Shoshone National Forest, into a band called the Wapiti Valley. On either side, a void hung over the road in a wide green block labeled "Wilderness." Far to the west was a historic site, Pahaska Teepee, and the gate of Yellowstone National Park. The town of Wapiti wasn't on the map, which made me think we wouldn't find much of a town.

The Shoshone National Forest map, printed like a newspaper, had more detail. Eight campgrounds dotted the river. Would they be full?

Then my eyes caught on a phrase: "Hard sided campers only." We couldn't camp in our tent!

The two campgrounds closest to Yellowstone had the restriction. This meant that tomorrow, in addition to climbing a pass at the edge of Yellowstone and then biking twenty miles across the park to Lake Village, we'd have to ride an extra fifteen miles first, to reach the park's gate.

We'd always been able to sleep wherever we ended up. But here, we probably shouldn't sleep by the road or behind a church, because of the grizzly bears. If we were still biking at dark, what would we do?

A few weeks before, someone had told us that the large RVs on the road in Yellowstone made biking in the park hazardous. Mary and I had talked about getting a ride; we'd fantasized about an elderly, RV-driving couple who would pick us up, feed us, and drive us to see the sights. The excess of RVs seemed antithetical to our mode of travel; we'd joked about how ironic it would be to ride in one.

But now, the option of a ride returned. Joking about the elderly, RV-driving couple was one thing, but actually hitchhiking? It had been drilled into my head as dangerous. And I wanted to bike the distance. We could make it if we got an early start.

I folded the maps and prepared to go. At least there were plenty of campsites. Surely one would be vacant.

The lake narrowed until it rounded out into a swampy area. Soon only a ten-foot-wide river remained, rushing flat across smooth stones. I could have walked across it easily. The rocky hillsides looked drab after the lake, but the river's blueness stood out as if all the blue of the lake had condensed into the narrow band. The brutal wind blew constantly, with no trees or shade. I passed a group of rocks that formed a giant gateway. I'd read about rock formations in the brochure: "The road to Yellowstone winds through ranch land, hay fields and weathered rock—formed into bizarre shapes known as 'hoodoos.'"

Eventually the fields tapered, and the road and river passed into a narrow valley. After a break to eat my lunch (bagel with cheese, avocado, cookies, and cherries), I passed the familiar shape of a national forest sign, "Shoshone National Forest." The wind blew as if the valley walls channeled it down from the mountains. I passed a big yellow sign: "CAUTION! Bears Are Dangerous! Do Not Approach! Up to $5000 Fine."

Furry evergreens grew on the hillsides, with jags of rock poking out from the trees. The jags grew bigger and more elaborate, reminding me of the drip castles we'd built with wet sand at the beach as kids. Some of the rock towers were so thin the wind should've blown them over. As the shadows of late afternoon stretched across the valley, the rocks took on a chocolate color. The river faded like a pair of stonewashed jeans until it was the lightest thing in sight. Ahead, at the end of the valley, I glimpsed mountains.

I pulled in at a ranger station and found Mary scanning a bulletin board. The station was closed. "I've got bad news," I said. "Tent camping isn't allowed at some of the campgrounds." I opened the brochure to show her.

"That sucks."

"I don't think we should break the rules, I think they're probably strict here, because of bears." She didn't reply.

I scoured the boards for any information about camping. A list caught my eye—it was a list of animal sightings, recorded by visitors. "July 6," someone had scrawled. "Bear, Wapiti ranger station, crossing the river." I glanced around. Weren't we *at* the Wapiti Ranger Station? When was July 6th? I counted off days in my head. Today was July 9th—three days since the sighting. I relaxed. Then I scanned the rest of the list:

> deer
> bear
> bear
> bear
> deer
> bear
> moose?
> bear

"Holy crap!" I thought. "There are a lot of bears."

"I guess we should just camp as close to Yellowstone as we can," Mary said. She didn't mention what we'd do the next day.

At dinner, Mary said she wanted to get a ride into Yellowstone. I didn't speak up and say I wanted to bike. Instead, I agreed to hitchhike.

With worries about hitchhiking playing in my head, I finished my dishes in the special, bear-proof washroom and stowed everything in the bear box, a brown metal box on a post with a latch that bears could not open. Signs instructed us to store our food and even our toothpaste, toothbrushes, and stove in the box, because bears could smell these items.

Darkness covered the campground; thankfully a bright moon hung overhead, lighting my way back to our site. Trees kept each campsite secluded from its neighbors. Normally I hoped for this privacy, but now the trees and quiet made it easy to imagine a giant bear ambling through.

Mary had gone to visit a man she'd struck up a conversation with earlier. I tried to sit at the picnic table, but the mosquitos quickly found me, so I crawled into the tent. After sleeping outside in Cody, I hated to be in the tent, but with the bears and mosquitos, I didn't have a choice.

I woke up nervous. We were going to hitchhike. Would we find a ride? If we didn't, we'd be in the same predicament tomorrow.

After visiting the restroom and bear box, I ate and packed. A gnawing sickness filled my stomach to my chest. "Everything will work out," I told myself. Mary moved around the campsite quietly, and then left to say bye to her new acquaintance.

I had nothing to do. I sat on the gravel drive and tried to feel better. My hand scraped up handfuls of gravel and dropped them, the repetitive motion doing little to calm my nerves. I squeezed some rocks in my hand, willing myself to be calm, and then I happened to look at the rocks: there were four, and each was a different color: red, yellow, black, and white. The rocks were the four sacred colors of the Native American faith.

My heart pounded. I stared at the rocks, then closed my fingers over them and stood. My legs shook. I walked to my bike and stowed the rocks in my bags.

"See? Things will work out," I told myself again. *But how? And should we wait for them to work out, or try to make them work out? How should we proceed?* I tried to block the worries from my mind. I tried to keep thinking, "Things will be okay," and not to leave any room for the worried thoughts. But it took a lot of effort not to revert back to them.

When we left, the road headed into the narrowing valley, with the cocoa-brown rocks towering like turrets. I knew the scenery was pretty, but I couldn't appreciate it, with my insides churning about the plan to hitchhike. Mary pulled over at a place with a wide shoulder, and I followed. She walked to the edge of the road and stuck out her thumb. It felt so weird. Along came a white truck, and to my surprise, he stopped. Could it be this easy?

An older man leaned out the window. "D'you need help?"

"We need a ride into Yellowstone," Mary said.

"I'm not going that far. You might try heading up to Pahaska Teepee. Lots of people stop there." Pahaska Teepee was just outside the park gate, so it made sense. We thanked him and got back on our bikes. I felt more hopeful after how quickly he'd stopped.

But as the seventeen miles to Pahaska Teepee passed, the sun rose higher and the day slipped past, along with every car that drove by us. My body began to ache with nerves; a lump lodged in my throat. I couldn't face asking strangers for a ride. By the time I saw the Pahaska Teepee sign, I wanted to cry.

A tall, triangular building housed a gift shop and restaurant, with a motel behind. There were plenty of cars and a few RVs but no people in sight. How should we try to get a ride? Most of the vehicles couldn't carry our bikes. If we couldn't get a ride, they might not let us camp; they'd want us to stay in the motel.

"I think we should eat," I said. Things always felt better after lunch. It was already after noon; what was another hour?

Mary agreed. When we paid our bill, Mary asked the host if anyone there might give us a ride into the park. He disappeared in back and returned with a sketchy-looking guy from the kitchen who eyed us and said he might be able to take us after his shift. The idea made me nervous—would Mary say I overreacted? He didn't seem committed, and I hoped that that would be the end of it.

Lunch had calmed me, but my anxiety returned as we went back outside. We wheeled our bikes to the road and stood with our thumbs out. I felt stupid as cars and trucks whizzed past, the drivers intent on ignoring us. The RVs no longer seemed driven by nice elderly couples; instead I imagined suburban parents, terrified of strangers.

"What if no one stops?" I said to Mary.

"Stop worrying! You keep being so negative about everything."

I clamped my mouth shut. She said it as if my attitude were ruining our chances of getting a ride. Was she right? Did my lack of faith bar us from getting the divine help we needed? Hadn't I resented my parents' worrying all spring, when I was trying to be brave about going on this trip, as if their worrying would ruin my good karma? And what about that quote about faith, about stepping off a cliff and knowing you'll be taught to fly? How would I ever learn to fly if I didn't stop worrying, and stop trying to be in control all the time?

"But this is *hitchhiking!*" I silently defended myself. "It's dangerous; I can't help being nervous." Besides, I could see that our situation wasn't hopeful: the afternoon was passing and fewer cars were heading into Yellowstone. Most of them couldn't carry bikes. Mary's faith seemed foolish; maybe we weren't going to get a ride, and we should accept it. Wasn't there a difference between having faith and ordering God to send what we needed? Shouldn't we take care of ourselves as much as possible?

"Maybe a sign would help," I said. Mary nodded. Glad to escape the road-side, I crossed the lot and entered the gift shop.

"Do you have any scrap cardboard?" I asked the woman behind the counter. "I need to make a sign."

"Let me check." She went in back. Looking around, I spotted a rack of old photographs. I walked over and found the one I wanted immediately: Billy the Kid. It was the photo from his WANTED poster, but now I could see it clearly. He had a funny, lopsided face: an uneven mouth and ears that stuck out. He'd gotten dressed up for his portrait, in a jacket and vest with watch chains and a silk scarf. He may have been an outlaw, but he was also a teenager.

The clerk returned with a sheet of cardboard. As she rang me up, I asked for a marker. After considering, I wrote, "Ride PLEASE."

Outside, Mary sat on the grass. She leaned the sign against her knees. I imagined drivers laughing as they sped by, laughing at how stupid we were to think we'd get a ride.

As the sun headed down the sky, I began to lose all hope. I had to do something. "Why don't I ride up to the gate," I said, "and see if there's maybe a ranger who can drive us to the campground?" Mary nodded so I set off. What would I say when I got there? Maybe I could ask for the rangers' advice. Maybe they'd think we had ridden all day and gotten too tired to go any farther; they might not realize we'd been standing around.

The road widened, with a broad shoulder. I watched for the gate. A 1980s Oldsmobile slowly passed me. It drifted into the shoulder ahead and stopped. "The driver probably wants directions," I thought, pulling up to the open window. Inside sat a young man, smiling at me.

"How do I know him?" I wondered for a split second.

It was Justin, the ranger from the Medicine Wheel.

"Hi!" I said. It was Justin!

He grinned. "I thought that was you."

"We need a ride," I said. He didn't respond. I didn't want to inconvenience him, but I was desperate. "Did you see Mary? That was her with the sign. Come meet Mary." Mary would convince him.

Justin U-turned, and I followed him back to the Pahaska Teepee. Mary watched me returning and noticed his car. She was talking to Justin by the time I arrived.

Justin hesitated when we asked for a ride. "I don't want to get the seat greasy."

"We can put my raincoat over the seat," I said.

We removed our bags and stuffed them into the car. My bike rode in the open trunk, and Mary's fit in the back seat, along with Mary. I rode in front with gear piled under my legs.

"I'm off for the weekend so I'm heading down to the Tetons," Justin said as we pulled out, after cramming the cardboard sign into a trash bin. The anxiety-ridden Pahaska Teepee diminished in the rearview mirror.

A minute later, the brown gate to Yellowstone blocked the road. "Do you want money?" I said.

"I have a pass." We'd get in free!

He flashed the pass at the ranger and pulled through the gate, past the sign that read, "Welcome to Yellowstone National Park." The road narrowed, wound into evergreens, and began the five-mile climb up Sylvan Pass. In places, the trees broke for a meadow, but otherwise forest limited our view.

I worried about coercing Justin into driving us, but he acted glad of our company. The Medicine Wheel ranger camp was a lonely place, it seemed, and Brent and Tim, the other rangers, were romantically involved.

"Really?!"

Justin rolled his eyes. "It totally sucks, stuck there with them. Always kissing or arguing."

The road began to climb in earnest. We crested the hill at the top of the pass. Over treetops below us, Yellowstone Lake twinkled in the afternoon sun. The road dropped into the evergreens, leveling out at its new altitude.

We slowed for a glut of cars. A dark blot by the roadside materialized into a bison. I squealed in excitement. "It's an animal jam!" Justin sang as we drove, stop and go, into the cars. They'd pulled off willy-nilly for several hundred feet before and after the animal, who stood unmoving, staring out of a glassy eye and occasionally chewing as tourists clambered around him with cameras. I couldn't reach my camera, but Mary got hers. Justin slowed so she could snap a picture.

When we passed a sign for West Thumb Geyser Basin, Justin asked, "Want to stop?"

"Yes!" He turned in.

We extracted ourselves from the car, and I stretched my cramped legs. A cool breeze blew, competing with the sunlight, and I breathed in thin air. Walking toward a wooden fence, I looked over a weird steaming landscape of pools and rocky fissures. The cold blue lake sat beyond, coexisting with the hot pockets of earth.

We headed onto a raised boardwalk. Brown, algae-coated stream beds meandered underneath. Some pools were murky with vegetation, whereas others were clear and blue like a fresh batch of Miracle-Gro. In one pool, a craggy-edged opening led to pitch blackness. The clear water made it hard to gauge the depth of the streams and pools.

The ground looked stable, the steaming pools toasty, but signs warned of paper-thin ground and scalding temperatures. Some signs showed a distraught cartoon mother whose child had fallen into a boiling pool. Each time I felt tempted to reach a hand in, we passed another warning sign with the macabre cartoon figures.

At the lake edge, we passed Fishing Cone, a volcano-shaped geyser poking above the lake surface. At the turn of the century, visitors could fish from the cone and dip their catch into the geyser, cooking it on the line. They dressed in chef hats and had their photos taken. The geysers, I read in my brochure, were unpredictable. One called Twin Geysers had been dormant for twenty-three years until erupting in 1998; Abyss Pool had unexpectedly erupted in 1987, quieted for several years, and then erupted several times per day for a whole year.

I glanced at Justin, who leaned on a fence with Mary, entranced by the pools. He seemed to be enjoying himself, even if we'd coerced him into coming.

"So we were meant to waste our day, and be rescued by Justin," I thought. *Or were we?* If we'd biked into the park, Justin still would have passed us; maybe he'd have helped us reach the campground by dark. Or maybe Justin would have passed by, and a different ranger would have helped us. Maybe the Universe worked like a massive GPS, constantly "recalculating" to keep people on track as they bumble through life, making decisions. There might be "right" decisions that lead to a shorter or easier path, but the wrong decisions still get you where you're going. Both decisions are valid.

Maybe the decision between waiting for help and taking action was independent of faith. The important thing was to be open to whatever came along, whether you decide to hitchhike or attempt to bike the distance.

And in spite of the drastic imagery of the quote about faith—stepping off a cliff and trusting you'll be taught how to fly—maybe trusting was a state achieved with practice.[28]

# PART 5: Montana, Where All Traces of Shade Disappear and the Sun Beats Down

## Montana river valleys, in which the wind defies my impulse to escape the present moment

WALL OF EVERGREEN MOUNTAINS LOOMED ahead. Patches of snow lingered on the rocky tops under a cloudless sky. From a distance, the fields around me waved softly, but close up the grasses looked prickly. Sage scrub and yellow-flowered weeds choked the bottom of the roadside fence.

Yesterday, we'd crossed into Montana and camped in a national forest west of Yellowstone. I'd left camp at six-forty-five that morning, already behind Mary. I rode steadily, crossing the small Madison River and then following the shore of placid Hebgen Lake. Cows grazed; wildflowers waved in the breeze. Nothing made a sound except the mild wind, my tires rolling on the pavement, and my breathing. But in spite of the quiet, the air seemed loud, pressing down, almost humming as if the blue sky were too much for it. The lake dwindled back to a river and entered a canyon. By the time I came out into the next valley, it was lunchtime.

I headed into the broad valley, diverging from the river but catching glimpses of it off to my left. Grass filled the valley between rows of forested hills, with an occasional house. It wasn't beautiful, but it was prettier than the basins of Wyoming, those hard-packed deserts with constant haze. The clear sky of Montana made it feel more open, even with the mountain walls.

A cry from behind pulled my thoughts back to the road. A man on a recumbent bike whizzed past, waving. I called out hello. He had only a small gear bag. As he rode off, I heard, "On your left!" and a sour-faced woman biked past, not glancing up.

A few minutes later I heard more cries; this time, a couple rode up beside me. They beamed at me. "GoBike?" the man asked.

"Excuse me?"

"Are you on the GoBike route?"

I remembered the name—GoBike was the company that published maps of bike routes, listing campgrounds, hotels, bike shops, and restaurants. Mary and I had decided not to spend the money on their maps, and after our first week on the road, when we'd slept in the cemetery, at Joe's house, and in the Seven Valleys park, we'd concluded that an important part of our journey was seeing where each day led, without a set destination.

"Oh, no, we're not," I told the couple, who kept pace alongside me. "Are we on the route?"

"Yes," they said, grinning and pulling ahead. "See you on down the road!"

An hour later, I stopped for lunch at a general store. The day had grown hotter, so I was glad to see a shady porch. Inside, the clerk pointed me to the restroom and turned away. "She must get bikers all the time because of the GoBike route," I speculated, feeling disappointed. "There's nothing exciting about me."

After a rest on the porch, I returned to the blinding sun. Within a minute, my skin felt overheated. The wind was picking up.

By dinnertime I reached Ennis, where Mary and I found a riverside campground with a reduced rate for locals. As sunset neared, fishing boats came off the river, coolers popped open, and revelry began under the trees. I fell asleep regardless.

Sunday morning, the campground lay still, the parties over. I nestled in my sleeping bag, mulling over something Mary had said.

Over dinner, I'd mentioned my inability to relax, and how it frustrated me, and Mary had suggested I try accepting myself, instead of trying to improve. Even while my brain reacted against her words ("Isn't it selfish and arrogant to think I'm fine the way I am?"), the words rang with the authenticity of a good idea. Of course I'm supposed to accept myself, with my faults! Like when I had an inexplicable bad mood . . . what if I thought, "Oh well, I'm in a bad mood this morning, but I'll move on," instead of hating myself and trying to resist it? Would it go away sooner?

But what about my depression? I'd spent years feeling depressed during and after college and had always seen it as something to fight and defeat. What if I had accepted depression as "just how I am"? Would I still be crying every day, forcing myself out of bed, passing entire days with no joy as I had then? Surely it was better to change.

So which course of action was right: improving myself or accepting myself?

Mary rustled in her bag. We'd planned to be up early, to race the sun. Soon we rode through quiet downtown Ennis, where new morning sunlight illuminated the shops. Even the fast food places looked pretty in the morning light.

On the map was an ominous brown smudge followed by four ghost towns. The smudge turned out to be hills, but morning energy carried me up. A fog persisted, shading us, as the sun crept over the distant mountains. Soon I reached the top and rolled down the other side. Grasses raced past my legs, and then a few gnarled, leafless trees flew by. The road steepened. A weathered clapboard building appeared with metal gas pumps rusting out front. More buildings appeared ahead—this must be the first ghost town, Virginia City.

I braked as I rolled into the buildings, a solid row on each side. It looked like Frontierland in Disney World: signs read "Boots and Shoes," "Wells Fargo & Co. Overland Mail," "Fairweather Inn," and "Blacksmith & Wagon Shop, Ox Shoeing." The road squeezed between the raised sidewalks, and parallel-parked cars added to the congestion, but only a few people dallied outside. I spotted Mary and pulled over.

We leaned our bikes on a storefront. Old cans of food lined the shelves in the window, perfectly arranged like a museum display. The door was locked, but across the street, a bell jangled as a few tourists exited "City Bakery." In the bakery, we learned that Virginia City was a "revitalized" ghost town, abandoned after a gold rush and later revived to attract tourists. Several buildings housed artisans at work, whereas others were only for display. I wondered if the town might need an old-fashioned sourdough bread baker (i.e., me).

Mary and I got a slice of each breakfast item (banana bread and cardamom coffeecake) and cups of coffee. I also got a brownie for later and a brochure. Then we crossed the street to the porch of the Wells Fargo building and sat on the stone steps between its white columns. "Virginia City, Montana!" read the front of the brochure. "People say we're old-fashioned. We hope so!" Inside began with, "A vacation spot of the 90s. The 1890s." Sepia photos showed the street where we sat.

While we ate, the door behind us opened and a woman came out with a tray of perfect little Bundt cakes on paper doilies, headed for the bakery. "Hi," she said, smiling as she descended the steps. Then she turned and leaned forward, taking a cake off the tray. "Here, try one!" It was ginger cake, still warm.

As the minutes ticked past, more tourists arrived. With the steep incline and the buildings, cool shadows still stretched across the street. We wandered down the hill, peering into old-timey buildings. The "Montana Post" had ornate trim; everything was more beautiful in the old days, even a post office in remote Montana. Behind the buildings spread a valley dotted with rundown homes and old pickups. The ghost town looked in better repair than the places where people actually lived.

I left Mary to visit the quilt shop and the blacksmith's, where I bought a tin star made from a salvaged Montana roof. When Mary rode on, I stayed. Virginia City was so interesting; I wanted to see every inch of it, even if it meant biking in the heat later. We planned to meet in the next big town, Dillon, more than forty miles away.

I continued down the hill. At the bottom, red, white, and blue bunting decorated the railings of a train station that doubled as the visitor center and museum. Tourists milled on the porch. Then a whistle sounded and the crowd drew back as a old-fashioned engine chugged around the building, creaking to a halt where the track ended by the porch. The engine gleamed black and silver as steam puffed from its chimney. The tourists filed onto cars emblazoned with "Alder Gulch." In the station, I learned that the train only traveled three miles to the next ghost town, Nevada City. I wished I had the time to ride it through the gulch, the ravine with the river where prospectors had searched for gold.

I trudged back uphill to my bike. Now cars swarmed into town, and people crowded the sidewalks. I checked the map once more. Then I coasted down the hill, past the blacksmith's and the train station, and left the town behind.

The road headed into the rocky ravine, filled with a jumble of tall grasses and scrubby trees. Somewhere nearby ran the river, with the old train chugging along it, but all I saw and heard were trees shifting in the breeze. Blue wildflowers fluttered along the roadside.

Fifteen minutes later, I reached a handful of buildings: Nevada City. I pulled into the shade by the colorful Star Bakery. Clay pots with hot pink and purple petunias lined the blue windowsill. I couldn't see in through the glare on the thick, old panes of glass. A woman came out dressed in old-fashioned clothes and asked if I needed help. "Is this the whole ghost town?" I asked.

"Most of Nevada City's back there." She waved her hand. "It's an open-air museum."

"Do visitors pay to go in?" She nodded.

I didn't want to pay, and I didn't have time to explore a whole museum, plus I'd already seen Virginia City. Relieved to make an easy decision, I kept going.

I now had seven miles before the remaining ghost towns. The road stayed flat and sunny in the ravine. Without a view, the scenery struck me as dismal. I didn't feel compelled to stop for pictures; if I could focus on biking, I could catch up with Mary. Besides, I'd had enough fun in Virginia City to last all day.

But as I came over a short hill, I heard a noise ahead, like a low-pitched car horn but continuous, and then I saw animals. I stopped. They were on the road. Should I be worried? The animals were moving toward me, walking slowly but intently. They were all different shades of brown.

Cows! A herd of them, walking down the road.

It was a cattle drive!

A car overtook me and halted; the herd parted and ambled past it. A small RV passed and braked behind the car. Far at the back of the herd, half a dozen people rambled toward me on horses. As the cattle drew nearer, I decided to get off the road. I didn't think cattle were dangerous, but my bike might startle them.

I got my camera and hefted myself up the rocks by the roadside. I crouched on top, focusing my camera on the cows and snapping pictures. As they neared, I heard them more clearly, mooing in a cacophony of pitches: browns and blacks and several calves, all with yellow ear tags. As the front cow neared my bike, she moved to the opposite side of the road, eyeing it as she passed. One of the cowboys rode by, and we waved.

A plaintive moo carried above the clamor; a brown calf walked "upstream" through the herd. At the back, the trapped car broke free, followed by the RV. The cars following the herd inched along. The cows continued to avoid my bike until one mother approached, stretching her neck to sniff it, her calf hiding behind her legs. She had a jagged cross branded in her splotchy fur.

The bulk of the cattle headed away from me now, and the cars crept past. The rest of the cowboys rode up with the stragglers. Some of the riders were women; one girl looked about four years old, sitting upright and holding her reins like an adult. Again I waved.

"You're not scared of a couple a cows, are you?!" one of the men called.

I grinned and scrambled down the rocks. "No," I said, walking over, "I wasn't sure what they'd do . . . how far are you taking them?"

"Just about a hundred miles, to some new fields."

"Are you on the road all the way?" I imagined the herd passing through Virginia City.

"Oh, no! Usually we're on the fields—we just came up to cross the river." My timing had been perfect! If I'd left Virginia City any sooner, or not stopped for a picture of the Star Bakery, I'd have whizzed by the herd before they reached the road.

After the amusements of Virginia City and the cattle drive, I anticipated what excitement would come next. But the remaining ghost towns consisted of rundown houses where nothing stirred except the tall grass. Cars and drying laundry indicated the towns weren't entirely dead yet. Then the gulch widened, the land flattening, until I rode through a mustard-yellow valley between pickle-green mountains.

In Sheridan, I scanned the sidewalks for Mary's bike before finding a spot to eat on the porch of an ice cream shop. I had a cone before heading on. Mountains now rose ahead, and the wind blew insistently on my left. As I neared Twin Bridges, I again hoped for some excitement, but Twin Bridges offered none. There was no sign of Mary. I made the left turn toward Dillon.

When I reached the last building in town, the wind hit my face. I should have anticipated this: it had blown against me for hours. Now I rode into it. I hoped it would die down, but it kept blowing, and unwillingly I accepted that I was stuck with it.

I pushed and pushed, every pedal stroke a struggle as I crawled down the road. I watched for a dirt road on the left, five miles from town. It seemed like hours before I saw it. How slowly was I going? I reached a mile marker and checked my watch. Then I waited for the next marker. Five minutes passed. Then another five. Maybe a car had knocked it down. My eyes strained ahead but saw nothing. Another five minutes passed.

Finally, I saw the mile post ahead. I did the math: I was moving at three miles per hour. I had about twenty miles to go to Dillon. That would take me seven hours!

My heart sank when I realized I wouldn't be hanging out in Dillon at dinnertime, relaxing in a coffee shop or going to a movie. Where was Mary? Would she reach Dillon in time for a movie?

But then I thought back to Virginia City and the cattle drive—would I trade seeing them to reach Dillon in time for a movie? I wouldn't. And at least I would reach Dillon before dark if I kept up this pace. Usually I slowed later in the day, but it was hard to imagine I could go much slower than my three-mile-per-hour crawl.

I tried to resign myself to the dull afternoon, to the fact that no matter what I did, I'd be on my bike for a long time. But my brain kept trying to think of shortcuts, of ways to go faster or to escape the wind, even though there were none. I kept thinking of a Stephen King story I'd read years before, "Mrs. Todd's Shortcut," in which Mrs. Todd manages better and better shortcuts by "folding the map." My brain kept returning to the idea, wishing it were possible.

I tried to sing but the wind dried out my mouth in seconds. I tried to recount the plot of *Pride and Prejudice,* but the wind distracted my mind. I saw the next mile marker and checked my watch, recalculating my speed to see if I'd started to go faster. I hadn't.

More clouds appeared, puffy white with blue patches of sky between them. To my left, a yellow plain stretched to far-off mountains. To my right, cultivated fields filled the valley, bordered by faded blue hills. I appreciated the scenery for a while before becoming inured to the beauty.

My legs tired. I took drinks and breathed through my nose, but my mouth was perpetually dry. I turned my head to the side, to give my ears a break from the noise of rushing wind. It was fun to "turn on" the silence, but after a few times it lost its thrill.

I wasn't enjoying the tedious hard work, but at the same time, I noticed with surprise that I didn't feel depressed, just bored. I could find good things about the situation: my legs were holding out, the road was flat, there were no storms and no flat tires, and I'd had a good, filling lunch. I thought back on the day's special moments: Virginia City, the ginger Bundt cake, the tin star from the blacksmith and then finding the Star Bakery, the cattle drive, the giant ice cream cone for only two dollars, and how they let me eat on their porch . . .

But I wished I could enjoy the afternoon, not just remember the good parts of the morning, and not keep wishing to escape the wind into my imagination. Or, if I couldn't manage to enjoy the afternoon, was it still better to be present in it?

I didn't have much choice. I couldn't look forward to the wind ending like I could with an uphill or the rain. Just like the wind in the Badlands, it blew here with no end, and there was no escaping it while I rode. Accepting it was my only option.

After a few hours, I saw a barn beside the road. I stopped and moved to the downwind side. The wind died.

I stood panting, enjoying the heavenly feel of the still air on my face, and the quiet in my ears. Then I got out the brownie from Virginia City and a peach and sat, leaning on the barn wall with my legs out. *Will the barn's owner mind me sitting here?* I was too tired to care, and enjoying the shelter too much.

I ate the brownie first, one delicious chocolate bite after another. Then I ate the peach, leaning sideways so it would drip on the dirt. I licked the sticky spots off my fingers. Then I sat. "When I start again, I'll have energy from the food," I thought. "Maybe I'll move faster; maybe the wind will die down as the day ends, and I'll fly down the road and reach Dillon by seven PM instead of nine."

I pushed myself up, had one last drink, and wheeled my bike toward the road. As I came out from the building, a gust of wind hit me in the side. The gust didn't die down; it was the steady wind. I pushed off, resuming my slow pace as my dreams of flying along vanished. I had more than ten miles to go.

I started singing again—the Oscar Mayer bologna song was remarkably fun. As another mile passed, a massive rock formation appeared far across the fields. It had straight sides and a flat top. The sky was clearing, and a river crossed the valley. After another slow mile, I saw a historical marker.

I knew I shouldn't stop again, but I wanted to see if the marker mentioned the rock. It did: the rock was called Beaverhead Rock because it (supposedly) looked like the head of a mostly submerged beaver. When Lewis and Clark's party, called the "Corps of Discovery," had passed this way in 1805, Sacajawea had recognized the rock and known that they would find her Shoshone people nearby. The Shoshone chief had directed the party to the river that, as far as he knew, kept heading west.

Apparently, I stood where the road crossed paths with the Lewis and Clark Trail, the route that the Corps of Discovery took to the Pacific Ocean from 1804 to 1806. A silhouette of the famous explorers was the symbol of the trail. Mary and I were a year early: 2004 would be the expedition's two hundredth anniversary.

I walked my bike back to the road. A faint shout reached my ears. Back the way I'd come, Mary rode toward me, waving. She didn't wear her helmet, and the tent and sleeping gear were missing from her bike. I waved back and turned toward her. At last the wind pushed me forward.

"I stopped over there," she panted when I reached her, pointing to a log house on a grassy field a few hundred feet back. She'd asked permission to camp. She'd seen me pass and yelled, but the wind had carried her voice away. "I knew you'd stop at the historic marker," she said, grinning.

Two hours later, we sat in the dried-out yard as the sun moved down the sky. With no town to explore, I found myself with time. I didn't want to risk my journal or postcards with the wind gusting. I got out *Travels with Charley,* the slim book by John Steinbeck that I'd gotten in the thrift store in Worthington, Minnesota.

I opened to the first page and began to read. "When I was very young and the urge to be someplace else was upon me, I was assured by mature people that maturity would cure this itch. When years described me as mature, the remedy prescribed was middle age. . . ."[29] The words gripped me; the restlessness that had led me on this trip wasn't unique. Steinbeck made it seem universal.

As I read on, one passage after another reminded me of our trip. And the book traced out my childhood, with Steinbeck setting off across Long Island Sound to the coast of Connecticut, where I'd grown up, and then visiting the White Mountains of New Hampshire, where I'd vacationed as a child and seen the white pine that had collapsed on the first day of the trip, that Mary and I had heard about on NPR.

When I looked up from reading, the sun had reached the bottom of the sky. Shadows stretched across the front yard, growing longer as I watched. I closed the book and watched the shifting colors of the landscape—the blue sky turned golden to match the waving grasses, and the far-off mountains slipped from brown shapes to one long, blue silhouette. As the sun dipped lower, the tops of the grasses glowed in its final light, and then a shadow slipped across the lawn, not a sharp one created by an object, but a general shadow everywhere. A chilliness crept in. With a final fiery glare, the sun disappeared, extinguishing the glowing grasses, and then the colors everywhere began to fade.

## Southwestern Montana, in which I pretend
## at being able to talk to a guy,
## and it kind of works, and then I sit still

THE AFTERNOON REMAINED OPPRESSIVE AS I pedaled, on and on up the grassy slopes. A dull pain throbbed in my forehead. That morning, just outside of Dillon, I'd stopped to take a picture of a beehive, and a bee had flown up my helmet and stung me.

All day the bee sting had ached as I'd toiled up barren hills. There were no clouds in the huge sky and no trees or shade, just grassy slopes and hazy mountains in the distance. According to the map, the road climbed two mountain passes. Outside of Dillon we'd climbed Badger Pass, a climb of 1664 feet to a height of 6760 feet. Then the road had dropped into a valley, and after several miles along a river we'd started to climb all over again, up Big Hole Pass, 7630 feet high.

Now as I topped the second pass, I pulled up next to Mary and stared at the view: more brown hills, more far-off blue peaks. We'd covered most of the day's forty-one miles. The needle-pinch of the bee sting returned, reminding me to notice the dull pain. I scrubbed at my sweaty forehead with the bit of bandana that poked out from my helmet. After a minute of pretending to admire the scenery, I set off, doggedly heading for Jackson with Mary behind me.

We coasted down the pass and onto a flat road. Dirt powdered my legs; if I peeled back my socks, I'd have a line. I hadn't taken a picture since the beehives; nothing had seemed beautiful. As the sun descended, the scenery's colors changed: the brown fields showed hints of green, and blue mountains turned lavender. But even with the evening colors, the view looked hot and boring. "Maybe it would seem beautiful if I weren't so hot and tired," I thought. We had to be close to Jackson, but empty road kept coming at me.

I rounded a bend to find a crowd of orange construction signs clustered on the shoulder, turned every which way as if they were mingling at a party. Then buildings appeared. Mary rode up beside me as we neared the town.

A young man walked along the road, drinking a beer and watching us approach. He wore sunglasses and seemed kind of cute. Mary and I pulled over and introduced ourselves. He was Ryan.

"Are you on the GoBike route?" he asked.

"He must be used to bikers coming through Jackson," I thought. For some reason, I didn't want to seem ordinary.

"No," Mary said, "but we keep meeting them." After describing our trip, Mary asked if there was anywhere to camp.

"Not really," he said. "There's not much of anything here." He spoke without smiling.

"Is there a church? Or a school?"

"There's a school on the left after you go through town. Church is on the right."

"Do you live here?" I asked. I couldn't imagine why he would, in the middle of nowhere, especially because he spoke as if he didn't like it.

"Yeah, I work at the hot springs. It's the big building up ahead. I'm working tomorrow morning—if you come by, I'll let you in."

"Thanks! What time do you open?"

"Seven."

"I'll be there right at seven," I said as we pushed off.

We passed a log building labeled Jackson Hot Springs. The other buildings were unmarked, possibly deserted, with sheds and rundown equipment surrounding them. No traffic or people stirred. A convenience store was the only place open. Mary headed to the restroom, so I approached the woman behind the counter with my empty water bottles.

"There's a hose outside," she ejected, jerking her head at the door I'd just come in. Then she turned away.

"Thanks," I whispered and hurried out.

I AWOKE IN THE SCHOOLYARD the next morning, thinking about Ryan, the guy who worked at the hot springs. I'd been dreaming about him. As I lay in the tent, the dream came back to me: he'd kissed my forehead, right on the bee sting spot, and had told me, "I'll see you again someday." The dream made me feel attached to Ryan, even though it wasn't real. Then I remembered telling him I'd be at the hot springs at seven. I glanced at my watch: six-fifty. My insides lurched.

I wiggled out of my sleeping bag and stuffed it into its sack, trying to stay quiet because Mary still slept. I rolled my pad and crawled out of the tent with my things. At my bike, I donned clothes for swimming.

As I packed, Mary rustled. I didn't want to leave Mary to pack the tent, but waiting would make me late. "I'm gonna go," I called. Then I marched across the parking lot, leaving my bike. "I'm being assertive about what I want," I told myself, but I felt uncomfortable.

Just after seven, I arrived at the hot springs. Would Ryan be there? Had he meant he'd let us in for free, as I'd assumed? I pulled open the door and entered a massive entryway, dark with a high, beamed ceiling and heavy support posts. Light filtered in a doorway at the back. Far to the right, Ryan sat at a counter, illuminated by a lamp.

The same awkward feeling I'd had in Powell, Wyoming, in the face of the cute coffee shop guy, returned. I'd worn sunglasses yesterday when we met Ryan; he might be disappointed to learn I wore real glasses. But when I opened my mouth, confident-sounding words came out, calling hello. He looked up.

He waved and pointed toward the back. "You can go on in."

The open door led to a fenced-in patio where a rectangular concrete pool steamed. A few people floated in the water. I'd expected hot water gurgling out of rocks into a pond, with greenery and maybe some mud. I hadn't realized it would be a swimming pool. I moved away from the bathers to the far end, where I sat with my legs in the water. It was hot but not unbearable. I slid in.

Heat enveloped me as I sank up to my chin. Clouds of grime floated off my arms, so I moved to the nearest water intake, hoping it would remove the dirt from the pool quickly. After a few minutes of soaking, I scrubbed at my arm and layers of grunge and dead skin came off. I scrubbed surreptitiously all over. Mary arrived and came in; we didn't say much, but everything felt calmer now that I was in the steaming pool. Even after forty-five minutes, grime still came off me—I'd never remove it all.

I liked soaking but wanted to finish today's biking early, so I could beat the sun and relax in the next town: Wisdom, Montana. Mary and I had decided to stop in Wisdom, eighteen miles away, for a day of rest. The next morning, we'd climb Chief Joseph Pass. We'd heard that Wisdom allowed camping in its park.

Plus, I wanted to stay in a town called "Wisdom." I pulled myself out of the pool.

As I left, Ryan still sat behind the counter. Part of me wanted to call out "Thanks" and leave, but curiosity about him—about if there was any spark between us—drew me over to the counter.

"Thanks, that was really great," I said.

"So you're heading to Wisdom?"

"Yeah . . . do you live here all year?"

"Yeah. I think about moving back to Denver, but I wanted to get away from people." I nodded in understanding. "My cousin was supposed to be here with me," Ryan continued. "We got the job together, but then he met someone and went . . ." His voice trailed off as he shook his head. I detected a bitter edge to his final words, and suddenly his situation clicked: he'd come here with his friend, who now had other priorities, and Ryan was bored, or lonely. We kept talking, but I didn't feel anything—not like I had in my dream about him.

"If you come back this way," he said, "stay here and I'll take you hiking." A million thoughts flew through my head, like, "What exactly does he mean by 'hiking'?" and, "Oh, I'm no good at hiking—I'm not really athletic," and, "I'm managing to have this conversation with him, but I couldn't keep up a conversation for a whole day!"

But I knew I wouldn't come back; I wanted to see the West Coast or more national parks, not return to Jackson, Montana. So I didn't worry about the implications of his offer. "Want a postcard?" I said, a counter-offer within my comfort zone. He gave me his address.

As I returned to the schoolyard, I thought about the words Ryan and I had exchanged. Did Ryan just want someone to fill the space left by his missing friend? The thought of being that someone creeped me out. At one time I might have naively ended up in such a situation, flattered by his attention and not understanding the underlying dynamics, and then wondered what was wrong with me, that I didn't feel happier to have a boyfriend.

Our whole conversation had felt like we were trying to make something out of nothing—looking for a connection that wasn't there. I was glad I'd realized it.

LATER THAT AFTERNOON, A TOUR bus groaned to a halt before the Wisdom River Gallery, engine churning as tourists filed off. Bus fumes wafted onto the porch where I sat, hidden in the shade behind a screen of bushes and hanging plants. I wished the driver would kill the engine.

I'd asked to sit there awhile, and the restaurant host had said it was fine. Mary was inside buying lunch. I tried to ignore the bus and turned back to my journal. Tendrils of heat snaked into my space, but the shade held out, protecting me with its cool darkness. Two ladies rounded the corner, passing me in silence as they headed for the door. I ducked my head.

An hour passed, and at last the tourists drained out of the restaurant, drifting down the street to the Trading Post. Then they boarded the noisy bus, and its wheels creaked into motion, setting off a dust cloud in its wake. As it clambered out of town, a beautiful echoing silence remained.

I closed my eyes and appreciated the quiet shade. When I looked up, the two women were returning. This time they smiled. "Writing the great American novel?" one asked, patting my shoulder as they passed.

The blazing sun beyond the porch eliminated my desire to explore the town. When I'd caught up in my journal, I switched to reading *Travels with Charley*. Mary returned and pulled out her book. The afternoon wore on in peaceful silence. After a while, we went inside to have pie, leaving our things on the porch. I picked warm rhubarb crunch pie with ice cream. When we got in line to pay, a man in black leather asked about our bicycles. Then he paid for our pie. We followed him out to his Harley and waved bye as we headed back to our table on the porch.

"Do you want to play backgammon?" Mary asked. I had a travel backgammon board that someone had given me. I'd been carrying it all summer, and we hadn't yet played.

"Sure."

As the afternoon grew late, I wondered about the park. The women inside had said it was back in the direction we'd come. So when we finished our game, we packed up and rode back.

Clouds were moving into the sky. We passed the road to Jackson, crossed a stream crowded with bushes and trees, and arrived at the park: a corral fence marked out a rectangle in the grass, and a ranch sign on tall posts over the entrance read, "American Legion Memorial Park." Inside, the driveway petered out in the dry grass next to a screened hut. At the far end, where the grass grew tall, two outhouses stood by a derelict wooden picnic table. An RV and two pickup trucks were parked on the right. Behind them, flat fields stretched to the mountains. No one else was there.

While we pitched the tent, clouds covered the sun. Soon they obscured the whole sky, growing more threatening as evening came.

We took our supplies into the screened hut, a picnic shelter. While I boiled water for pasta, I heard the whine of a mosquito at the screen. Suddenly I understood the reason for the screened shelter—mosquitos lived near the river. Soon the whine grew to a drone, and clouds of insects hovered outside.

Some men tramped out of the bushes near the river, climbing over the fence into the park. They carried fishing gear. Two of them stopped outside the screen. After telling them about our trip, I asked, "Is this a good place to fish?"

"It's the best!" one said. "People come from everywhere to fish this river." I smiled to think that tiny Wisdom, Montana, had such a treasure. A low rumble of thunder sounded across the plains.

"Uh, oh," I said.

"Storms make good fishing!" one of the men said, grinning, and he smacked his friend in the chest. "Come on! We gotta get back out there!" They hurried off toward the trucks.

When I finished dinner, I started to think about the long list of pies at the restaurant. The clouds had lightened, the threat of rain receding. I checked my watch—it was past seven.

"I kind of want more pie."

"I know," Mary said. We both sat a moment. "Do you think they're still open?"

"I don't know." I checked my watch again: seven-twenty. If they closed at seven-thirty, we could just make it. "It's not like two desserts is bad, when we're biking so much."

"And we didn't have to pay for the first one." A minute ticked by.

"They might close at seven-thirty. Let's just go see if they're open."

We abandoned the stove and our dishes and hurried to our bikes. Suddenly my heart pounded—would we arrive in time? We pushed off toward town. As we neared the restaurant, I saw the neon "open" glowing in the window. I didn't relax until we were in the door.

We sat at a table in the middle of the room. This time I had chocolate peanut butter.

When we got back to the park, Mary went to bed. I took *Travels with Charley* into the shelter and made tea, periodically looking up from my reading at the sunset. The storms had gone, leaving behind a cloud-strewn sky. More fishermen trudged back to camp, and from somewhere across the fields came the plaintive low moans of cattle.

I tried to keep reading, but the book made me want to write instead. I didn't think I'd ever get down descriptions the way Steinbeck did. I paused to strain my senses, trying to notice everything I could: a thousand birds chirping in the trees along the river, the strange low sounds of the cattle, the smell of the rain that had not come. By now, the sun rested on the top of the mountain range's silhouette, a lemon yellow disc, lighting up the tips of the grasses across the plain. The grasses waved in random motion. I sipped my tea.

The sun slipped away, and the golden grasses faded to greenish brown. I expected the loveliness to end as darkness crept in, but instead the sky grew more glorious: the hidden sun illuminated the clouds into dark pinks and grays, with glowing cerulean bottoms and stark white, sunlit puffed tops. The mountains turned violently purple, as did the strings of cloud high overhead.

The book lay open on my lap. I pushed my bookmark into the open page and spotted writing on it. It was a quote from *Dune* that I'd copied out two months ago: "Deep in the human unconscious is a pervasive need for a logical universe that makes sense. But the real universe is always one step beyond logic."[30] Written in Ohio, the quote seemed to echo off the Montana mountains, as if I'd left the logical universe behind in the eastern states and reached the real universe out west.

I shut the book and got up, leaving the stove in the shelter for morning. I hated to go to bed—I wanted to watch the sky fade and the stars come out. But I had to be up early tomorrow, ready for another big climb.

## The Bitterroot Valley, in which the incredible feeling of awareness returns

B Y MORNING, THE CLOUDS AND the twilight colors had departed, leaving the usual boring yellow and pickle-green landscape under a blue sky. Biking away from Wisdom, we headed straight for the mountains, visible on the plain twenty miles away. Sage scent drifted in the thin air; scrubby plants lined the road. A waning moon hung in the sky, a brilliant white oval, and as the sun rose it seemed odd that the moon didn't fade.

I neared Big Hole National Battlefield, site of the largest battle of the Nez Perce War.[31] Facing the climb up the mountains made me too anxious to stop, even at a national park site. Already, the sun warmed the air. Passing the battlefield entrance, I looked up for the moon. It had disappeared.

The road remained flat, and as the tree-covered mountains loomed closer, I caught vague whiffs of pine. But the forest didn't register until suddenly I rode up to a wall of evergreens. I entered the trees, and cold shade enveloped me. The sunny barrenness of the plains disappeared in an instant, and I rode through a new world of pine scent and darkness, forest so thick that I could see only a hundred feet on either side. Shadows stretched wide across the road, and my eyes relaxed in relief now that the giant view had disappeared. I had forgotten about shade, as if I hadn't expected to see trees ever again, but I hadn't realized it until this moment, when they'd returned.

I kept looking at the trees, trying to soak them in. I stopped once, and trudged through dewy grass to sit on a log. Birds chirped as if I were in a museum display, a tableau of the American pine forest with recorded birdsong piped over loudspeakers. But after a minute or two, I stood and returned to my bike.

The road began to climb. I caught up with Mary, and she moved out, letting me pull up alongside her. I tried not to ruin the moment by worrying about cars coming behind us. The road grew steep, but climbing was easy in the morning. Besides, I never resented the hills I knew about, like this one, which was on the map. It was the unexpected ones that I had trouble accepting.

Soon the trees thinned and grew scraggly, and sunlight broke through, allowing daisies to grow along the road, bobbing their heads in the slightest breeze. The four-mile climb ended, and we came to a three-way intersection. A large sign mounted on a stone base read, "Chief Joseph Pass, Continental Divide." (We'd already crossed the Continental Divide twice, in Yellowstone, but we hadn't yet figured out what it was.)

We stopped for pictures. As I took my turn, I breathed in the cold thin air, smiling, waiting to hear the camera click. The road remained empty, quiet in the late morning.

Heading north, Route 93 dipped slightly, climbed over another pass, and began to descend. Trees closed in. Then the road plummeted, dropping three thousand feet in minutes. My hands clamped onto my brakes the whole time, until at last the whizzing forest slowed.

The trees didn't disappear at the bottom as they had on the eastern side; the forest continued with patches of shade crossing the roadway. The air felt too still. We passed another sign for the Lewis and Clark Trail, like the one I'd seen near the Beaverhead Rock east of Dillon; we'd joined this trail at the top of the pass and would now coincide with it for hundreds of miles. We stopped once to meet a biker headed east, who trilled with excitement over his ride to Yellowstone. I hated to tell him of the approaching climb, and the hot passes east of Jackson, and instead told him where he could camp in Wisdom.

The trees drew back from the road so that sunlight reached the pavement. People had exclaimed over the Bitterroot Mountains, so I expected something majestic and rocky, but all I saw so far were nondescript hills. When the road curved to run north, along the eastern side of the hills, I realized that those hills were the Bitterroots. The range had one evergreen-covered lump after another, with small rocky faces where trees didn't grow. Only one peak stood out, with two pokey triangles of rock and snow on top. On my right, thin trees covered a slope that hid the view. It looked unnatural, like a hill that you'd see in a landfill.

Gradually, the forest gave way to cleared fields and sometimes a house. Soon the only trees were the strips left between adjacent fields. The sun beat down, and now a hot wind blew across the open land. I stopped noticing the mountain backdrop. Mary had ridden out of sight.

Another hour passed. Finally I reached a sign—giant, brown, and Montana-shaped—hanging under a roof: "Welcome to Montana's BITTERROOT VALLEY and DARBY."

Houses clustered closer, and after a few blocks I reached a main street lined with storefronts. Banners hung from the light posts: "Darby, Montana's best-kept secret." The downtown was a relief after the hot roads. Mary's bike rested at a green surrounded by gingerbread trimmed buildings: the library, a museum, and a restaurant.

I figured we'd continue to Hamilton, but Mary wanted to camp in Darby to avoid the hot afternoon. I adjusted to the idea: I would rest on the green and write in my journal. Maybe the remaining stretch of Bitterroot Valley would look prettier in the morning.

In the library, I emailed a friend whose parents lived in Portland, now our final destination. I hoped to stay with them. I told her about Montana. I'd noticed myself feeling more attached to the towns—maybe I had been on the road too long and yearned for civilization. Work thoughts were popping into my head, too; I didn't want to go back yet. I finished my email just in time; the librarian booted us off the computers after thirty minutes, in spite of the fact that no one else was there.

The women in the museum greeted us enthusiastically. We glanced at the arrowheads and wagons and other generic "old West" artifacts. Then we asked about sleeping on the green.

"There's another park," one woman said, "Over on Tin Cup Road. That'll be quieter." She gave us directions. Then she said, "And you can go in the river—it's public."

"Oh great, a swim would be great," I said.

"The river's public. If anyone tells you you can't go in, don't listen. They don't own it." Was there something behind her statement, some small-town politics?

After lunch, Mary left to find the park. I stayed to poke around the shops and then settled on a bench on the green as I'd planned. Mary might resent me not setting up camp with her, but I tried not to think about it.

The green stayed quiet and shady as I wrote in my journal, as the sun moved across the sky. The museum docent exited, locking the door behind her. Some kids came through, playing a game, and then wandered off again. A mom with a toddler stopped to let him run through the sprinkler. Darby did seem like a wonderful secret.

Then Mary appeared. "I left the tent in the park. I'm going swimming."

"Is it easy to find?"

"Yeah, it's right on the side of the road where she said."

"Okay, thanks." She pedaled away. She didn't seem upset with me at all.

I looked up when a grade-school girl on a bike slowly passed. As soon as I smiled, she halted and started to talk. Then her mom exited the library and wheeled over her own bike. I always told myself I wanted to "meet the locals" but forty-five minutes later, when the mom finally stopped talking and they rode off, I realized my quiet place had been shattered. Low sunlight had crept under the trees, chasing away my shade.

Guilt pulled me toward the park; dinnertime neared, and Mary might need the stove. But I'd wanted to swim. *Well, why don't I drop off the cooking gear, and then go swim?* It was so obvious. Why didn't I always find solutions like this?

I followed the directions to Tin Cup Road and found a sloped green space bordered by unruly trees. Our little tent sat at the back by a picnic table. I unloaded the stove.

Even with the sun low in the sky, it beat on my back as I rode through a neighborhood in the general direction of the river. In spite of some rundown homes, I didn't feel scared or lost, just a pleasant wandering feeling. I didn't see a single person so I couldn't wave at anyone, but I felt welcomed in Darby.

I found the river at a mossy bridge. Below, the ten-foot-wide water tumbled across a rocky bed. Bushes and trees hung over. Paths to the water were worn in the grass on both sides.

As I rummaged in my bags, two grade-school boys rode up on dirt bikes, with inner tubes hanging across their bare shoulders. They dropped their bikes to the ground at a corner of the bridge. I smiled and said hi.

"Is that hard to bike with?" one asked, eyeing my load.

"Yeah, it's pretty heavy. I go really slow."

"Where are you going?"

The question struck me; most people asked, "Where are you from?"

"The Pacific Ocean. We started in New Jersey."

He didn't respond, so just to make conversation, I asked, "Am I allowed to go in the river here?"

"You can go in anywhere you want!"

"That's what we're doing! Don't listen if anyone tells you you can't!"

"Geez, these Darby people are determined to share their river," I thought.

The boys ambled down the path upstream of the bridge, so I took my towel and headed down the other side. I sat on the riverbank and took off my shoes, dipped my feet into the cold water, and listened to their voices drifting under the bridge. Within a minute, the heat of the whole day had disappeared through my ankles.

The boys' voices suddenly grew clearer, echoing under the bridge. They floated toward me on their inner tubes, talking nonstop. They drifted out from the bridge and passed me, talking and talking, and the stream carried them around a bend and out of sight. Their voices faded into the bubbling river noises, and then all was quiet except for the tumbling water.

I sat in the summer day, thinking about the boys floating down the river. How great would it be to be ten years old, to have a best friend, and to live in a town where you could leave your bike by the side of the road? And to drift off for the afternoon, with no plan, no worries—just letting go and seeing where you ended up . . . would they paddle back up the river, or would they pop out at a road downstream and walk back for their bikes? Sitting there, I realized the thoughts I usually had—worrying about what Mary thought, or what I should be doing, or if we'd get kicked out of the park—had quieted. Instead, I just felt a calm gladness for the people of Darby, Montana.

I wanted to get in the water. I moved to sit on the rocks in the stream. The chill water barely covered my legs. It tugged against me, and as I lay back, I started to float in places, pulled downstream, bumping into rocks. I hung onto a large one. Should I let go and drift downstream like the boys? It was only five; there was plenty of sunlight left.

I rolled onto my front, digging my elbows into sandy spots as anchors. "I need to get to camp" flashed into my head, but I made myself stay.

Eventually I stood, dripping, and climbed back up the slope. My bare feet padded across the pavement like a ten-year-old's. Dropping my shoes with a thunk, I got out shampoo and headed down the other side of the bridge, where larger rocks stood out in the water. The boys' shoes lay abandoned on the dirt.

Kneeling on a rock, I dunked my head. My hair swirled, then pulled toward downstream. I sat up and scrubbed in shampoo, and then dunked my head again, watching as the water carried off the suds. I had biodegradable camping shampoo, but here, that didn't seem good enough.

I scrubbed my hair clean and washed my face one last time. Suddenly I became aware of myself: *I'm kneeling on a rock, by a stream, in Montana! Washing my face in clear mountain water!* I felt overly alive. Conscious of my every move, I wrung out my hair and stood.

The feeling followed me to my bike, where I packed my things. I tried to dust off the bottoms of my damp feet before cramming them into my shoes. "I'll be barefoot again as soon as I reach the park," I promised myself. Then I rode back, noticing myself dripping on the hot road.

Where had the feeling come from? Was it from sitting still, like when it happened on that bridge in Minnesota? Or from having a restful afternoon, like in Madison, Wisconsin? Today I'd spent the afternoon at the green, and I'd lain still in the river. Maybe those rest periods had helped me reach this state.

I found Mary making dinner at the picnic table. She smiled hello as I parked. I tugged off my shoes, rubbing the dirt off my feet on the lush grass. I pulled off my wet soccer shorts and shirt, too, comfortable in only boxers and a sports bra. Once I'd hung the clothes to dry, I got out dinner things and joined Mary.

Other than our table and a trash can, the park didn't have amenities, but a small stream tumbled out of the woods, racing down a ditch toward the river, so we had water for washing dishes. The hot day had ended, and I'd rested and cooled off and washed, and everything felt calm. Mary and I acted like friends. But the aware feeling I'd had at the river had faded; I wished it had stayed.

I made corn tortillas with broccoli, spinach, tofu, rice, duck and soy sauces (from Chinese restaurant packets), fresh garlic, and water chestnuts from a can. A pickup cruised through the parking lot, and I had a feeling the driver was checking us out. Should I feel nervous? I didn't. The peacefulness of sitting in the late sun, river-washed, in my sun-dried boxer shorts and sports bra, permeated everything.

The sun fell down behind the trees, black silhouettes against the sunset, and I wrote in my journal until it grew too dark, and then I lay down to sleep.

What would tomorrow's small towns be like? We'd pass through several. Should I stop to explore, or push ahead to finish biking early? *Wait and see.*

## Lolo Pass, on which the truth about cattle (and some other things) becomes clear

EVEN IN THE MORNING LIGHT, our surroundings were ugly, with strip malls and buildings blocking the view of the Bitterroot Mountains. The towns north of Darby had been unidentifiable save for the green sign that marked each. We'd passed through them and spent a night in Missoula. Now we headed back to Lolo and the road up Lolo Pass.

When I finally came to an empty field, I read with dismay the sign posted by the road: "Proposed 70 lot subdivision on hay field to the south." Something about the inclusion of the word "hay" moved me. Letting Mary roll ahead, I stopped for a picture. Finally, I reached Lolo. There was no sign of the historic Lewis and Clark site or the river I saw on the map, only a gas station, a tavern, and a casino. Coasting to the light, I turned toward the pass.

As I left the busy road, the sounds of traffic dimmed, and after a mile, the ugliness had disappeared. Only fields, fences, and an occasional house indicated the presence of humans. The mountain range rose before me, appearing in and out of the trees as I traveled the flat road. Then the forest hedged in closer, down from the mountains, until I could no longer see the peaks.

I stopped twice to rest and ate a bagel with cheese and a piece of cake. In spite of the flat road, I felt myself fading.

A few hours had passed when yellow caught my eye: stopped bikers. As I neared, I recognized Mary with two older riders in bright jerseys with "Pedal de Ponds" logos. "Here she is!" someone said, and they all smiled. Mary introduced me to Roger and June from North Dakota, who were biking part of the Lewis and Clark Trail. We chatted about bike travel for a few minutes. Then Mary and I departed, and they followed. Soon the road started to climb; we spread out, and then we left them behind.

The first miles of the pass rose slowly. Then the road ascended more rapidly, with straight evergreens forming a wall of green needles on each side, with branches so thick I couldn't see the trunks. The sun by now was overhead, so that in spite of the tall trees, sunlight hit the road. I lost Mary.

How long would I climb? I feared it would be hours. When the road widened, I tried not to hope it was the top. The incline flattened, and the trees on my left broke to reveal a parking lot with buildings at the far side. An American flag flapped on a pole. Was it the top? All around, forested hills looked down. Then I read the bevy of approaching road signs: "Welcome to Idaho," "Entering Pacific Time Zone," "Visitor Center Main Entrance 500 Feet," and, finally, "Lolo Pass 5235 Feet."

I turned into the empty lot and rolled across the parking spaces. A few cars clustered near the visitor center. A ranger station stood next door. After parking in the shade, I got my lunch and sat on a bench, exhausted. If I sat quietly, maybe I'd feel better, like I had in Darby.

But as I ate, tourists kept asking about my bike and where I was from. So when Mary arrived, it surprised me to find myself feeling quiet inside, rested and ready to explore the visitor center. Maybe my intention of sitting quietly was the important part.

We passed a gift shop, full of forest maps and books about the Bitterroots. Near the register were chocolate bars in paper wrappers decorated with purple berries—they were huckleberry chocolate bars, made in Montana.

In the main room, I drifted toward a ranger who talked to a group of tourists. He was tall and lanky, with short blonde hair and an attempt at a goatee. His voice didn't falter as he answered questions about the Bitterroots, Lewis and Clark, and even other locations. A desire stirred in me to ask a good question. When the tourists left, the ranger turned to me. His nametag read, "Scott."

"What's a huckleberry?" I asked.

He stared at me. "I'm not really sure."

I hadn't expected to stump him. "I have another question," I said. "What is the Continental Divide? 'Cause we keep crossing it. I thought we'd just cross it once."

"That I can answer," he said. "The Continental Divide is an imaginary line, and on one side all the rivers flow out to the Atlantic Ocean, and on the other side they head for the Pacific. So it mostly follows the mountaintops, and sometimes it curves a lot, which is why you keep crossing it." I imagined all the rivers flowing across America, some curving around toward the Missouri River and the Atlantic, others heading west. Where did Darby's little river go? We'd crossed the Divide again before Darby, so it went to the Pacific.

Mary joined us, and Scott asked where we were from. He was in school at Washington State University, working as a ranger for the summer. Considering Justin at the Medicine Wheel, and now Scott, I wished I'd worked at a park or historic site when I'd been in school. I'd had no idea such jobs existed.

Hearing Scott speak about the area made him seem like a beacon of knowledge, and I found myself asking another question. "We met these cattle ranchers who were upset about the wolves at Yellowstone—how they're reintroducing them. They said the wolves kill cattle and they're not allowed to shoot them, and"—assuming a deep voice—"'they were killed off for a reason.' I felt kind of bad for the ranchers. How do you justify bringing the wolves back?"

"Wolves and grizzlies are national treasures," Scott said. "Cattle are not."

With his words, the issue shifted into focus; it made sense. I knew it wouldn't satisfy the folks in Spotted Horse, but it fit me. I guessed I was a tree hugger after all.

I liked the confident person who talked to Scott, even though my confidence didn't go deep. It felt self-conscious, like I'd have trouble maintaining it. But it was a start. My interactions with Scott were better than my extreme self-consciousness around the coffee shop guy back in Powell, Wyoming. I was glad I had taken the time to sit still before entering the visitor center—resting until the over-active buzz in my head diminished. Resting calmed the thoughts in my head, making it easier just to be somewhere.

Also, I noticed that, as with Ryan in Jackson, I didn't feel anything romantic for Scott. There was potential for confusion, though, because I felt good about myself for acting confident, and I interpreted that good feeling as coming from Scott. And also, I was in the habit of having a crush on every cute male I interacted with, so I expected to have a crush on him. When I wrote my name and address in the guest book, I fantasized that Scott would see it and write to me, telling me he'd remembered me because of my insightful questions. I imagined romantic feelings for him, concocting a plot line where his studies brought him to North Carolina, and I had to remind myself that I hadn't actually felt anything for him.

I remembered how, about two years earlier, I'd been hanging out almost every day with a friend. I'd thought I must be in love with him because I felt happy having his attention. I imagined romantic scenes between us, and he always said and did clever things that he never did in real life. But when he'd suddenly tried to kiss me, the whole world had seemed to shout "No!" I'd been confused, thinking something must be wrong with me, and had made myself kiss him anyway; it had felt awful. Now I could see that I'd never been attracted to him: I'd liked him as a friend, imagined a romantic connection, and become confused about what was real. Daydreaming made it hard to see clearly and to make smart decisions.

After exploring the visitor center, Mary and I returned to our bikes and walked to the road. We took pictures with the border sign, and of me changing my watch by the time zone sign, and then we rolled down the western side of the pass into Idaho.

Someone had told us that if we took this route, after Lolo Pass it would be "downhill all the way to the Pacific." So I imagined the end of the trip as a breeze, biking casually along the rivers that led down from the mountains until we reached the Columbia. My dad had said the Columbia River gorge was beautiful, and Dad didn't usually talk that way, so I figured it must be spectacular.

As we descended Lolo Pass, it all seemed true. First I passed a yellow caution sign with a wiggly arrow: "Winding Road, Next 77 Miles." Then the road began to wind between the beautiful straight evergreens, occasionally passing a pale, grassy hillside with bare tree trunks, perhaps left by a fire. The road briefly straightened to show a view ahead like a painting, a blue mountain with a snowy peak framed by evergreens. I passed a green sign listing the upcoming towns: Lowell, 77; Kooskia, 100; Lewiston, 170. The mileages, with all those 1s and lucky 7s, rang out fortuitously.

I STOPPED AT A HISTORICAL marker for "Devoto Grove." Pine scent filled the air, and after the empty grasslands of Montana, I couldn't breathe enough of it. A trail led into the trees. Leaving my bike, I walked in.

The trees were bigger than the usual evergreens, with trunks that flared out at the bottom. I thought they might be cedars. The road hadn't been busy, but the peace of the grove descended on me. Baby trees grew in patches of sunlight, green plants peeked out amid massive trunks, and ferns hung off dead logs. One fallen tree had new trees growing from its exposed roots. Near the back, a river slid past, silent and beer-colored in the sun, and a plaque on a boulder explained that the grove was a memorial to a conservationist and historian named Bernard Devoto, who had promoted the idea of preserving public land. Devoto had produced an abridged edition of the Lewis and Clark journals and had camped in this spot—a grove of old-growth red cedars—while doing his research.

On my way back to the road, I passed a sign on a tree that read, "Have you hugged a tree today?" I began watching for one I could hug without stepping off the path, so I wouldn't trod on any plants, and when I found one and hugged it, the comforting solidity of the trunk went straight to my spine.

I continued my downhill roll, and the road soon leveled and met the Lochsa River. There were several campgrounds, but I waited to turn in at number 17 (more 1s and 7s!). We'd met a woman named Joan, who'd been biking up the pass on a day trip, and she'd invited us to share her site. I'd assumed the campground was filled, but when I rolled in, it was empty. Maybe Joan just wanted company.

After dinner with Joan, I took my towel and went to swim. I walked along the driveway, glimpsing water through the trees, until I found a place where I could get through. Before me, the river stretched to the far bank, as wide as an interstate. A wall of trees rose up on the opposite side. Earlier, at the cedar grove, I'd seen the river narrower, flowing silently, but here, shallow and clear, it kept up a constant, rushing chatter as it tumbled over rocks. Even with the walls of evergreens, the river's width made the sky feel wide open.

I stepped carefully onto a grapefruit-size stone poking out from the water with weedy plants around it. With more cautious steps, the water got deeper, submerging the stones. Slowly, I made my way out from the bushes into the sunny river. Upstream and down, the river disappeared around a bend, leaving me in a section that looked like a grade school diorama.

The rushing water reached my ankles, but even with the cold on my pulse points, the hot air on my skin kept me from being chilled. Then the water stopped getting deeper. I kept going, wanting to reach the center anyway.

When I thought I'd reached the middle, I sat. With the sun beating down, the cold water didn't torture me, and for a while I just sat there, watching the river rush at me from upstream, smelling the pine forest all around. In a few places, rocks poked above the surface, creating small bursts of whitewater rapids. I kept looking at the evergreen wall on either side, and at the sky overhead, and suddenly I marveled at where I sat—in the middle of a river! In Idaho! And while the evergreens didn't look especially beautiful, the whole place *felt* beautiful.

I again wondered if sitting still brought on these new moments of awareness. It seemed, at least, that you had to stop moving to notice them.

Later that evening, I returned to the edge of the river. It was past eight PM and the sun was down, but the open sky by the river gave enough light to write by. I sat with my back against a sturdy tree that clung to the bank over the river behind me. The ground was smooth dirt, and in front of me, it dropped away and then rose, so I had a footrest.

The days were passing faster now, and darkness coming sooner; everything went faster as we neared the West Coast. The end of the trip with Mary approached. Instead of looking forward to the adventures I'd have afterward, traveling alone, I felt hopeless about my chances of having fun. I'd probably be scared and lonely.

I wrote until I began to notice the darkness. A little movement nearby startled me—I strained my eyes, scanning across the pine needles and branches until I found the offending squirrel. The distance back to camp suddenly seemed long, now that it passed through dark forest. Soon the light by the river would fade, forcing me to go. But I didn't want to leave yet; it was peaceful. The pine smell grew stronger with the darkness.

Another creature rustled on the forest floor—just another squirrel, but then the bark of the tree began to scratch at my back, nudging me to bed, and a chilliness permeated the woods. So I got up, stretching and taking one last look at the river. "I'll probably never see this spot again," I thought, and felt sad. The river kept rushing by. "The sun sets, and storms end, but the river never stops." Suddenly this seemed impossible. Where did so much water come from? Could it really be the sum of all those tiny trickles running through the forest at the top of the mountains, trickles of melting snow and collected rain? Shouldn't it all flow down at once, and then end?

I reached out and circled my arms around the tree I'd been leaning on, feeling how solid it stood, unmoving against me. "That's why trees are so good to hug," I thought. "It's comforting that *something* is so sturdy." The scratchy bark kissed my cheek. Then I turned into the mossy trees, leaving behind the remnants of daylight.

In the dark woods, the river sounds grew muted, and as the quiet surrounded me, I began to imagine myself into a horror movie, with a monster about to jump out . . . I cut off the thoughts so I wouldn't become more scared. Then a lost-in-the-woods type movie popped into my head, which wasn't much better. Then I imagined I was walking back in time, and that our tent would be gone and I'd find pioneers camping instead, and then I thought maybe I walked in a dream—a dream about going to bed—and nothing seemed real anymore.

# Part 6:
# The Northwest, Where Temperatures Soar to One Hundred and Ten

## Idaho, in which we coast effortlessly
## downhill toward the Pacific
## [insert sarcasm here]

I PAUSED AT THE TOP OF the driveway, standing over my bike and looking up at the blue morning sky. Beyond the points of the evergreens hung a half moon, higher and slimmer than three mornings ago when I'd seen it over Wisdom, Montana. I pushed off and rolled into the road, coasting at first and then pedaling to keep my speed. Even downhill, I had to pedal against the friction of my heavy bike on the road.

Today we'd follow the "wild and scenic" Lochsa River until it merged with the Selway in Lowell, Idaho, sixty-five miles away.[32] The only civilization on the map was a campground about halfway there; another campground waited just past Lowell. I passed a Route 12 sign and a Lewis and Clark Trail sign, with the silhouettes of the explorers pointing me ahead. Then I passed mile marker 162. I hoped the downstream road would keep running downhill.

Evergreens hid the river below me. In fact, all I could see were evergreens: up the slope at my right, down the slope on my left, covering the far hillside beyond the river, and blocking my view ahead, where the road disappeared. Then I rounded a bend and the trees dropped away, and I saw water shining below.

The river reflected the bright sky, a weird mix of mirror-whiteness and sapphire. Sunlight had reached the tops of the hills, but shadows covered the river. The road descended to run alongside the water, rushing clear over smooth stones. Together, road and river curved like a trigonometric function through the trees.

As the day brightened and the air grew hot, I found myself tiring, in spite of riding downhill. The wind picked up and blew in my face. Then I rounded a curve to find sunlight on the road. I pedaled on, stopping only to eat a few blackberries from the bushes at the roadside. The river and road wound on and on, one S curve after another.

After two hours of scenic but monotonous biking, I saw a suspension bridge spanning the river. Grateful for an excuse, I pulled over. Except for the river, all was silent. Only a handful of cars had passed me all morning. I took a granola bar and walked out on the bridge, which swung slightly. The river rushed under me, tumbling over rocks and reflecting the sun. I crossed my legs and sat, looking out through the railing; perfect spider webs hung between the beams.

After the rest stop, the river calmed, flowing deeper with a smooth surface. The incline was flatter, not rushing downhill, although the road still descended. In places, the evergreens gave way to grassy hillsides, or collapsed rocky ones.

About four hours after I'd left camp, sweaty and tired, I passed mile marker 122 and turned in at the Wilderness Gateway Campground. The driveway disappeared in trees ahead. A deserted shelter with picnic tables stood near the road. No person seemed to exist for miles.

I rolled onto the smooth floor of the shelter. Dark beams overhead glowed with reflected sunlight. I pulled off my shoes and peeled back my socks. My hot feet stretched on the cool concrete, a breeze between my toes, as I laid my socks on the floor to air out. Then I carried my lunch to a picnic table; the slapping of my feet on the floor made me feel carefree.

It was only ten AM. It felt later.

When I finished eating, I didn't want to leave the quiet, cool shelter. I lay down on the floor, flat on my back, and all the bones and muscles in my spine stretched as tiredness drained out. As I lay there, my mind wandered, and I found myself thinking of my college friends—the freshman dorm group. They'd been such good friends, staying up all night to listen, leaving presents at each others' doors. Why was I thinking about this now? I wished I could tell them how happy it made me to think of them. I kept lying there, minutes passing, until I noticed that my back had relaxed, and I felt rested. It was time to go.

Now the sun blazed straight down. A hot wind blew as I rolled back onto the road. Had Mary passed? The road resumed its endless curving. A few cars lumbered by, but mostly the road was quiet except for the rush of wind in my ears and the noise of the river. A few miles down, I saw Mary's bike leaning on a tree; she must have gone to swim.

The road kept snaking away, curving left, then right. The afternoon came; the sun beat at me. I began to imagine I was stuck in an M. C. Escher print, where the river dropped and dropped without ever progressing down. The heat blasted in my face as I pedaled. I knew I could stop for a swim, but I made myself keep going, one mile after another. I imagined myself as a potato, baked by the sun.

When I finally couldn't stand the heat, I watched for a place to pull over and spotted a shady area where a narrow path led into the bushes. I leaned my bike on a tree and headed down the path to a tiny beach. I pulled off my shoes and socks and stepped in. My ankles shuddered at the cold, and the heat emanating off my body immediately dissipated as the water cooled my blood. Out a few paces, I sat in the water in all of my clothes and lay back.

I cooled immediately, but I made myself stay to let it sink in.

By the time I'd walked back up the path, the heat was nipping at me. I had a drink and a granola bar and set off. The heat grasped me as soon as I hit the road. Hot wind blasted in my face, dry and breathless, as if I rode in a giant clothes drier. In minutes, no evidence remained of my swim except my damp seat.

I'd thought wind was my worst foe, but now that it had teamed up with scorching heat, it was ten times harder. And even rolling downhill, I had to pedal as the wind pushed at me. I'd thought I'd coast all the way to the Pacific! I had a hunch and U-turned to test it. Now I pedaled uphill, with the wind pushing at my back, and my wheels raced along effortlessly. It was easier to bike uphill, pushed by the wind!

"This just stinks," I thought, U-turning back. I didn't bother trying to day-dream my way out.

Finally, I passed mile marker 100. A few miles later, I reached a white building with red, white, and blue petunias nodding in planters out front. A brown sign stood in the parking area:

**Welcome to**
**LOWELL**
**Idaho**
POP. ~~24~~ 23     ELEV. 1280´

The "24" was actually crossed out, with "23" painted in above it. The long building looked like several buildings welded together. Signs posted by various doors advertised a gas station / grocery, a cafe/inn/bar, and a motel/cafe. I didn't see the motel rooms, or any mention of the campground.

Across the street, the wide Lochsa River merged with the Selway, dumping together a flood of water that churned slowly under a bridge as the new Clearwater River. I felt a sudden sadness that I'd reached the end of the shallow Lochsa and its wilderness.

Taking my journal, I headed to the grocery door. A thermometer on the building read 106 degrees Fahrenheit. An American flag flapped lazily on its pole; the wind seemed to die whenever I wasn't biking in it.

I got some postcards and then entered the restaurant. The chatter of the handful of customers poured over me. When a waitress greeted me with a smile, I pointed to the back room. "Could I sit back there?"

"Sure!" She led me to the dark room.

My eyes adjusted to the dimness as I scanned the menu. When I looked up, five deer heads stared from the walls. Across the room, a tiny bear stood on his hind legs, posed in a "fearsome" growling stance. A few traps hung on the walls, one clamped on a furry, spotted skin. I looked back at the menu, finding the grilled cheese. The prices were cheap, and the waitress had been friendly; I liked Lowell in spite of the dead animals.

While I waited to order, I read the list of pies in a plexiglass stand on the tabletop. Then I studied my placemat, which showed the United States presidents: Polk, Taylor, Fillmore . . . Hayes? Arthur? "I should memorize them while I wait," I thought.

The waitress returned and I ordered salad, grilled cheese, and marionberry pie with ice cream. Then I opened my journal to write about the day. I was glad to have time to write—I'd finally gotten somewhere first—but I hoped Mary was okay.

After I ate, I wrote all the presidents' names in my journal. When the waitress returned, I asked if I could stay to wait for my friend.

"That's fine," she said, taking my empty plate. "Let me know if you need anything else."

I began sketching one of the deer heads; he looked like he was smiling. Fur stuck out of his wide ears, which made me think of my grandpa. Near the deer's antlers, new antler stubs sprouted, frozen in their growth process.

I checked my watch: five-thirty. I copied down the list of pies: apple, cherry, marionberry, blueberry, lemon, chocolate, coconut, banana. Then I went to find the waitress and ordered blueberry pie (no ice cream) and decaf.

While I waited for the new pie, I walked around the room with my journal, cataloging the animals. In addition to the five deer heads, there were two mounted sets of antlers, the bear, a bearskin, a turkey, the spotted fur in the trap, and a mountain lion skin (with head).

"The lion is the worst for me," I noted, "because he looks like a house cat. His fur rolls like the sea, his open-mouthed head rising like a wave." I couldn't keep looking. I moved to the next deer head, which gazed back as I looked in his eyes. In the dim room, he seemed to move. I watched closely, trying to catch him, sure he'd move at any second. His neck extended out, as if he were trying to sniff me.

I continued on to the sad little bear, stuck in her attack pose in the back of the room. Behind her hung framed photos of a dead Kodiak bear. In one photo, a bloody hole oozed on the bear's side. A typed sheet, also framed, told the story of killing the bear. Then my pie came, and I returned to my seat.

At last Mary arrived, glancing around at the animals as she slid into a seat. "Oh my Lord, it's hot out there."

"I know, I'm glad you made it." I sipped my cold decaf while she had a grilled cheese.

We found the campground down the road. We entered under dark trees. Deserted sites greeted us. The first one perched over the river, so we took it. We pitched the tent, and then, since I'd already eaten, I found myself with the wonderful feeling of nothing to do.

THE SHALLOW, BUBBLING LOCHSA RIVER was gone. The land spread out and the trees disappeared as the curving of the road tapered off. The river ran wide and smooth, lined only with grass. But the river did nothing to quell the heat radiating from the ground. Yellow hills rose in all directions, like giant dunes with stark shadows on one side. Tall teasels grew along the road. The waning moon hung higher each morning.

I entered the Nez Perce Reservation without a second thought. The next sixty miles and seven towns were on the reservation, including Orofino, where we planned to sleep. I felt markedly different than when I'd been in South Dakota, anticipating the Pine Ridge Reservation and worrying about camping.

I stopped at a historic site called "Heart of the Monster." Under an open-sided shelter, I read the faded posters hanging behind scratched plexiglass: Heart of the Monster was in the Nez Perce creation story. A monster was terrorizing the animals on earth, so Coyote (their clever hero) killed it to protect them. He chopped the monster into pieces and cast them across the land, and a tribe of humans sprang up wherever a piece fell. The Nez Perce came from the monster's heart. Now, at this site, I could see the monster's heart where it had fallen.

It seemed too simple—the Nez Perce believed that their creation had happened at this one spot, in the middle of nowhere in *Idaho?* But why not? It made as much sense as anything else. It struck me as humble for humans to think that, instead of being created by God in His image, they were a watered-down version of a monster that had been killing the other creatures of Earth. Actually, as I thought about it, it was a pretty appropriate creation story for humans.

I started down the paved path. A short walk led to a fenced-off mound. It rose about thirty feet and looked like a pile of dirt left by a construction crew, covered with weeds, clumps of dried grass, and bald patches. I'd expected something grand and permanent, like a rocky edifice. This looked like a rubbish heap.

But maybe that was the point—it was monster-size, believable. And it looked ordinary only because I was used to human-made versions of such a mound; if the Nez Perce hadn't made it, but had found it in the wilderness before humans had altered the landscape, it *would* seem like a strange, mysterious place. With the green grass stopping at its base, and the dried grasses up its sides, it could be a giant, decaying heart.

I stood in a patch of shade, not wanting to trudge the rest of the sunny loop. But when I heard tourists approaching, their bright clothes bobbing down the pavement, I tore myself away and continued back to the shelter.

Now I counted off the miles to Orofino, waiting for the hot day to end. Another fork had joined the river, making it as wide as a football field. Deeper, it flowed slowly in smooth curves through the valley between the yellow hills. Patches of evergreens spotted the scenery. The blue sky glared down.

Occasionally the guardrail halted for a parking area. "I'll wait," I thought each time. "I'll cover more miles before stopping to swim." I kept hoping to find a place with no cars, where I could swim alone. But finally, I grew so hot and tired that I pulled into a clearing where a dozen cars were squeezed onto the turf. A family just arriving carried beach gear to a trail leading off into tall grass. The shrieks of kids came from below. Another man hurried from his car with sunscreen and called out when he saw me hesitating, "Come on down! The whole town's here."

I followed the path and came out on a sandy promontory covered with people. I felt them all stare as I emerged from the bushes, but when I actually looked, no one was looking back. Parents sat in chairs, some under umbrellas, with coolers and blankets spread as if they were at the ocean, while kids dug in the sand by the water. The yellow hills rose on all sides, channeling the river between them and out of sight. After I dipped myself in the water, a girl playing on the sand said hi. Then a family called me over, asking where I was from. My self-consciousness gave way to a shaky feeling of acceptance. When I gathered my shoes and socks and headed up the trail, I realized I felt happy.

LATER THAT EVENING, AS THE twilight faded, I sat on the wall of the picnic shelter in Orofino's park. My legs hurt as they hung down. "Please hold on," I willed them. "Just let me finish the trip."

We had only ten days left.

All summer, the days and miles ahead had been plentiful. Now the end was in sight. Mary had mapped out the miles we had to cover each day. Failing to reach the Pacific didn't seem possible.

But I did feel nervous about being on my own. Some young people walked by, glancing at us, and I contemplated how I'd feel if I were alone: I'd be scared to sleep, knowing that someone had noticed me. I allowed a tingle of fear to run through me, as if I were testing it out. I hadn't felt scared in so long, just a few times at the East Coast, and once in South Dakota when a man in a pickup truck had sat in a driveway, watching me ride past. I wanted to be excited about the end of my trip: after Mary left, I would spend more time in each place I camped. But instead I felt fear. Would I feel scared every night after Mary left?

Feeling scared made me want to spend weeks in Portland, in the safety of my friend's parents' house, rather than biking out alone. My thoughts tumbled around: I could rent a car to visit national parks. But I'd hate being in a park without my bike! Maybe I could ride alone for a week or two and then take the bus to visit friends.

What would happen when it came time to go home? When I thought of home, I didn't want to return. Out here, I felt freedom: no bills to pay, no possessions to lug around, to keep dusted and organized. Life was easier with my possessions in a storage unit! And I didn't feel ready to be around people, with their opinions and pressures affecting my life.

Where would I live when I got home? Would I have a roommate again?

The sky grew darker; someone shouted across the park. Suddenly, sitting on the wall felt too exposed. I looked at my sleeping bag spread on the floor under the cobwebby picnic tables and unhappily slid down to go to bed.

## Washington, in which we reach the Columbia River

MARY AND I RODE INTO the deserted parking lot of the Catholic church. We'd spotted it while investigating the parks in Clarkston, Washington, none of which were suitable for camping.

We'd escaped to Clarkston from Lewiston, Idaho, across the river. The calm Clearwater River, which we'd been following, a broad band channeled through a canyon by stark hillsides, had disappeared with the moon. After a morning of increasing heat, lanes, billboards, and traffic, Lewiston's maze of crowded streets had overwhelmed me. But Clarkston was perfect: only a few cars puttered down the wide main street, where afternoon sun cast quadrilateral shadows onto the pavement. We'd eaten in the diner and looked for parks on a town map at the library.

At the church, we discovered a patio by the backdoor, in an elbow made by the building. A short, grassy slope led up to the parking spots. Sleeping on the patio, we'd be hidden from the road.

We leaned our bikes on the church's stone and concrete wall. The glass doors (which were locked) had elaborate handles with crosses, Greek letters, and other symbols cut out of the rusty metal. The only trouble was the late-day heat radiating off the walls and ground.

"I don't think we're gonna need the tent," I said.

"Sounds good to me." Mary dropped it by her bike.

I tugged off my shoes and socks and rubbed my tired feet on the grass. When I started back to my bike, the concrete burned my soles. I leapt back to the grass, then sat. A minute later, Mary plopped down beside me. Soon we were both lying on the grass, motionless as we waited for the sun to set.

At the library earlier, I'd read with dismay that I couldn't stay with my friend's parents in Portland. I'd sent a quick email to another friend with connections there. "Wait and see," I now reminded myself, when I began to replay the situation in my mind. "It will work out."

At last the sun dipped below the trees, but the air didn't cool. I dragged myself up and returned to my bike, marching my feet to keep them off the scorching concrete. When would the ground cool? I laid my pad along the wall, where it slowly filled with air. Mary laid hers near the grass.

When I lay flat on my back, the heat of the patio radiated around me and permeated my pad. The air over me was hot, too, as if I lay in summer sun. At least my washcloth would dry by morning. I tried to focus on sleep, but the oppressive heat wouldn't let me go. I lay as if drugged, unable to fall asleep but too tired to do anything else.

A hint of impossibly cool air tickled my leg. Where had it come from? It happened again. It was air-conditioning, leaking out the bottom of the door. I pressed my leg closer; the door was cold! Mary lay quietly, and I wondered if I should disturb her. I could turn my body ninety degrees, and we could both press our feet against the door. But I couldn't move; sleep was drowning me.

I woke in darkness and reached to silence the alarm. A memory startled me: I'd talked to someone in the middle of the night. Two people had walked past and asked who we were. I didn't know what I'd said, but an explanation had come out. "Well, I'm glad they weren't dangerous," I thought.

We'd set the alarm for four AM. Soon, Mary and I sat on the front steps of the church, eating granola bars and bananas in the dark. Silent houses lined the street below. On the map, we traced Route 12 west out of the city, along the south side of the Snake River. About thirty miles away was a town called Pomeroy; after that came nothing for thirty-seven miles. We agreed to meet in Pomeroy at lunchtime.

As we headed across Clarkston, the eastern sky lightened. We met the river, wider than yesterday's, flat and still and reflecting the dark sky. Quiet breezes blew. Brown hills lined the opposite shore. The river held light; soon the whole sky had lightened to lavender.

A plant with sloping conveyor belts appeared on the far shore. Echoes rang across the river. As I drew nearer, I heard the rumble of trucks pulling in and out. Peach now tinted the lavender sky. The lines of the hills grew clearer; they were like giant floppy hounds, heads on their paws, ears spreading on the floor. I checked my watch: five AM.

Now in the east, the sky glowed a peachy-pink, the sun just below the horizon. A high bridge led over the river. I passed the back of a "Welcome to Clarkston" sign standing in tall grass. Then a rocky cliff rose up, and the road headed onto the narrow strip between the cliff and the water, curving along with the river. Looking back, I saw a few sparkling lights in Clarkston, and sunlight just beginning to strike the buildings.

As an hour passed, the sunlight crept down the hillsides until at last it gleamed on the road around me. The hill to my left turned a blotchy mustard-yellow as the sunlight came. Then the river bent north, and my road veered off to head west.

The road ambled through hilly grassland with hints of rock and creeks overgrown with brush. I began to climb, and as I pushed on my pedals, I noticed the heat of the sun, no longer a faint teasing warmth. Again I checked my watch: seven AM.

As the road climbed, the mustard hills rose on all sides, limiting my view. The road seemed lost in the irregular hills, with ups and downs in every direction, and bends ahead and behind. But the sky felt wide, and I sensed a vast space around me, as if openness lurked just beyond the hills. I'd seen a summit marked on the map—2785 feet—but that altitude had seemed so negligible that it hadn't registered as a climb until now. But I didn't grumble to myself as I rode. The slow uphill was just the next step.

A cry pierced the air. I scanned the empty sky. But the hawk perched on a fencepost, motionless and watching me, perhaps wondering if she could take me. I crept past.

The hills retreated as the pavement leveled. I rode out onto a plateau. As far as I could see spread beautiful, pale-gold wheat fields gently waving in the breeze, their color smooth and restful to my eyes. A clear sky soared overhead. Wind patterns raced across the fields, ruffling sections like seaweed on the ocean floor. I stared at the view, feeling like I'd arrived on the moon—it was so startling to find a plateau at the top. The lyrics about wheat fields waving popped into my head. "You can't know what that means until you see it," I thought.

A green sign read, "Alpowa Summit." I coasted past the fields, catching a sweet, earthy scent. "It must be the smell of wheat," I realized. I tried to catch more of it, to fill my lungs so I'd remember it later, but trying to catch the scent was like trying to see a star—the way it fades when you look directly at it, and its brightness returns when you look away. I'd catch a whiff, but if I breathed deeply, it would disappear.

I rolled off the plateau onto a long downhill. The wind rushed by. When I saw a sign for Pataha, I braked.

I rode into a handful of houses. Was this the town? The only sign of it was at an empty parking lot. A tattered American flag stuck out from a sign that read, "Visitor Center: Info * GIFTS * MUNCHIES." Two picnic tables stood underneath, on a patch of grass. A mural of Lewis and Clark decorated a tiny building in the lot. A sign announced "ESPRESSO."

It was a coffee hut! It was like the Pony Espresso I'd seen back in Montana—this one was called Holy Ground Coffee Co.

As I pedaled toward the hut, piano music wafted out—"Moonlight Sonata." Enchanted by the notes, I rolled my bike to lean on the wall. Then I noticed another sign: "Tour Pataha Flour Mills." It was a historic mill; I'd seen an ad for it in Clarkston yesterday.

I approached the takeout window. The chords of "Moonlight Sonata" halted mid-measure. After a pause, "Heart and Soul" clanged out. Someone was actually playing! Peeking in, I saw the end of an upright piano behind stacks of coffee cups and an espresso maker. Boxes blocked my view, but I could see the legs of the piano bench, and the small, bare feet of the pianist crossed underneath.

I stood at the window, not wanting to interrupt. After a minute, the music broke. I quickly called out, "Hello?"

The bench scraped, thudding into a wall as the piano player jumped up. "As if she'd been caught slacking," I thought. She hurried over to the window. She looked about twelve.

"I'm sorry," she said desperately.

"It's okay—I liked hearing the music." She looked even more traumatized at that. "Can I get a frozen mocha shake?"

She nodded and turned to make the drink. No cars passed; the emptiness echoed out, quiet and deserted, hot and sunny . . . but charmed. The unexpected magical music, and finding that a girl played it while she waited for customers—it was sweet. But did she like being there, or did she hate working all summer and practicing the piano? Did she daydream about being Rapunzel, locked in the coffee hut, waiting for a prince on a motorcycle to ride up and rescue her?

When she brought my shake, I asked about the mill. She pointed me down a side street. I thanked her and took my shake to a picnic table. While I drank it, Mary rolled up.

"Hi," I said. "I think I'm gonna go see the flour mill."

She nodded. "I think we should stop in Pomeroy."

A brief surge of jealousy pulsed through me; Mary would have all afternoon to lounge around Pomeroy. But I wanted to see the mill, I reminded myself. And I could relax as I toured it, knowing I didn't have far to go—Pomeroy was just three miles away. As Mary put her foot back to her pedal, I said, "Okay, I'll see you there."

It seemed crazy that she wasn't stopping at the coffee hut, that she could pass through Pataha without stopping, while to me it was an enchanted place. Did Mary see Pataha as just another dried-up town? Maybe she'd have her own adventure in Pomeroy. The difference between our trips struck me—two people on the same path having totally different experiences.

When I finished my drink, I set off down the side street, passing quiet homes. I rode under some trees, and then the mill towered before me: a massive, latte-colored building with a dozen windows and a green metal roof. "PATAHA FLOUR MILLS" ran across the top, painted in tall black letters. A white picket fence ran across the front with sunflowers bobbing, while nasturtiums and red-and-white-striped petunias waved lazily at the ground.

Inside, a middle-aged woman greeted me in a sunny room with tables and chairs—a cafe. A gentle bubbling came from a fountain hidden in a clump of potted plants. Wide wooden floorboards hinted of age. I glimpsed a kitchen through a doorway. Another doorway led into a darker room, with wooden walls and heavy beams.

"I wanted to see the flour mill?" I said.

"You can just go on back," the woman said, waving toward the dark doorway. "The lights are on."

I hesitated. Was there an entry fee? A docent? Why was there a cafe? Unable to think what to say, I headed back.

The mill was deserted. I climbed to the second and third floors, peeking into the office with its old-timey stapler and ledgers and edging past the milling equipment. The mill stood frozen in time; there was even a cone of white flour left under the chute of the bagger. Light poured in from a row of large windows near the ceiling; wooden beams ran up and across and sideways. There were giant belts that used to run the mill, pushed with water flowing down from an elevated pond nearby. Typed cards labeled the equipment. From a framed picture, I learned that the Pataha Flour Mill had produced XXX flour, the brand preferred by Bugs Bunny.

After walking through the mill, I returned to the cafe. I'd eat here, I decided, to support the mill. The menu didn't have prices, the young waitress explained, because they used a donation system. The bread was homemade, and the vegetarian sandwich was called "The Emma." The magic just kept coming.

IN SPITE OF A MIDNIGHT sprinkler assault, Pomeroy rated high. People had come to see us in the park's picnic shelter, including the girl from the coffee hut, who'd waved nervously and darted away. A mother had sat near us with two children and read aloud from *The Voyage of the Dawn Treader*.

Now we ate breakfast in the dark, sitting in the middle of the tennis courts where we'd fled from the sprinklers. We looked at the map. Route 12 followed the Pataha River for thirteen miles to a dot labeled Dodge and then nine miles to an intersection. Then it curved away from the river and ran fifteen miles south to Dayton. Gray smudges crossed the last stretch—were they mountains? Mary and I planned to meet in Dayton. Based on the previous day, that might be as far as we got.

By five-fifteen, with the eastern sky pink-orange, we rode out of Pomeroy on an empty road. Where the downtown ended, the wheat fields resumed. A few minutes later, when the sun peeked over the horizon behind us, the sky began its transition from morning lavender to blue. The remaining hints of green shadow in the wheat fields slipped away, leaving the uniform pale gold that I loved. There were no trees; the crests of wheat-covered hills met the blue sky on each side.

The sun rose higher. Already the day felt too hot. Mary pulled ahead and disappeared.

I found nothing in Dodge, so I stopped for a drink and then kept going.

The wind began, blasting in my face—it seemed to start at seven AM on the dot. The heat intensified as I chugged up a hill. Another hour slipped by as I daydreamed about the mill yesterday, and about arriving at the Pacific Ocean. (I'd feel exhilarated . . . I'd get tears in my eyes as I looked at the vast blue ocean . . . a cute surfer would ask where I was from . . .)

I reached the intersection where the road left the Pataha River, which I hadn't seen all morning, and began to climb a winding hill, slowly ascending as I tried to ignore the heat. Tiny plants grew in pavement cracks, and loose gravel spewed off the road onto the ground. A large black spider scuttled onto the road, and the hair on my neck stood up, but as I neared, I realized it was only a jet-black beetle with six jointed legs. Its almond-size body stopped on the hot pavement—didn't its little feet burn? Another beetle darted onto the road, and I swerved to avoid crushing it with my slow-moving tire.

As I kept climbing, the beetles kept coming. But I didn't see any beetles in the road farther ahead. They charged into the road as I neared, as if to attack me or ward me off. Their shiny bodies ended in bullet-pointed butts. As my tire rolled near one beetle, it stopped, turned 180 degrees, and thrust its butt into the air. Was it spraying some kind of toxin? No, the butt thrust itself was the "intimidating" defense mechanism.

At last I reached the top of the hill and rolled down the other side, enjoying the breeze until my speed evened out and I had to resume pedaling. The sun crept toward the top of the sky.

I'd been making good time, but now another hour slipped past. I pedaled more slowly. I needed another snack. Ahead, the guardrail ended, and the metal folded over on itself, casting a patch of shade on the ground just barely larger than the shade of the guardrail. It wasn't much, but any shade was valuable.

I stopped and eased a stiff leg over my bike. Once I'd stretched, I dug out a can of honey-roasted peanuts. The dirt at the edge of the pavement struck me as unsanitary; maybe cars had leaked pollutants onto the ground, or someone had spit out a car window. I tried to sit on the guardrail, but the sharp edge dug into my thigh and the hot metal burned, so I overrode my distaste and sat on the dirt in the tiny patch of shade.

More beetles entertained me as I rested, scuttling close, thrusting their butts at me, and scurrying away. When one beetle eyed me without turning tail, I dropped a peanut onto the ground. It rolled down the slope, stopping at a tuft of dry grass. The beetle scuttled over and wrapped its jointed legs around the peanut, jostling it loose. As the peanut rolled again, the beetle clamped on, turning over as they bumped together down the hill to bonk into another grassy clump. When I left, the beetle still held on to the peanut.

By the time I reached Dayton, my exhausted brain struggled to function. Was Mary at the library? Was there a library? *I'm too dirty to go in a library.* Sunlight beat down, and heat rose off the pavement. The noise of the few cars on the streets rang in my head, and I felt queasy. I saw a sign for a park and turned without thinking.

A green space opened with a sprawling lawn under thick-trunked trees. Walkways crisscrossed the grass. I rode into the park and stopped in a wide circle of shade. Painfully, I lifted a leg over my bike, then leaned the bike against a tree. I practically collapsed as I sat. Soft, cool grass soothed my legs, so clean compared with the roadside I'd sat on earlier. It didn't matter if ants crawled on me; I lay down and fell asleep.

When I woke, the queasiness had gone. I hoped Mary wasn't worried, but I was glad I had rested. I took the time to wash my face in the restroom and then pedaled back to the main road.

The first building in town was a former train station displaying an OPEN sign—the visitor center. Inside, I stopped at a display. My eyes glazed over as I scanned facts about Dayton: wheat-growing area, the state's first train depot, produces 37 percent of the world's canned asparagus . . . I couldn't focus. I approached the desk and asked about camping. She directed me to the fairgrounds.

I continued into town. Buildings lined the street; the blue front of a grain growers' association had wheat stalks carved into the door. A lawn spread out at a fancy courthouse. I found Mary at the library, but after emailing my parents, I returned outside.

I pulled out a new book, *Outlaws and Bandits of the Old West,* and flipped to the chapter on Billy the Kid. He committed his first robbery at the age of fifteen, I read, prompted by an older man who influenced him after his mother died. I was glad to read about the ambiguity of Billy's later crimes and the corruption of the New Mexico lawmen who charged him, because I wanted him to be not so bad.

Mary had also had a recommendation for the fairgrounds, from the folks at the city hall. So when she exited, we found their open gate. Inside, aluminum-walled sheds and barns lined the road. No one was in sight. We stopped on the grass under a tree by a white barn. As the sun moved across the sky, the barn would shade us.

A pump with a hose stood twenty feet away. Would anyone mind me using it? I knew I could fill my water bottles, but I wanted to wash up; with a hose, I could wash my hair. A wild, free feeling came to me, like when Mary and I had taken down the "No Fireworks" sign at the border of Wyoming. Who would care if I used the hose? The petty uptightness of life back east didn't matter out here. I dug out soap and shampoo and then dragged the end of the hose over to the pump and pulled up the pump's handle.

Cold water gushed out, and I leaned over and soaked my hair. The water trickled behind my hot, dirty ears. I scrubbed at my scalp with shampoo. Then I held my breath to dunk my whole head under. When the runoff began to clear of bubbles, I wiped my face with fresh water and breathed, fresh outdoor air, and suddenly, I again had that *alive* feeling that I'd had by the river in Darby, as if I were more present on the earth than usual. "I am washing my hair outside!" I thought. "With someone else's hose! In the fairgrounds in Dayton, Washington!"

This time, I knew better than to think the feeling would last. I just hoped it would keep returning.

THE NEXT EVENING, MARY AND I were still on the road at dinnertime. Even with clouds, the day had warmed with an oppressive brightness. The scenery en route to Walla Walla had dragged on, and I'd been led to take a seven-mile detour. (When I'd finally arrived in Walla Walla, I'd learned that Mary had ignored the detour signs and ridden through the work zone with no trouble.) The woman at the Walla Walla chamber of commerce, when we'd asked about a movie theater, had mentioned that the library had a free children's movie that afternoon. So at three o'clock, we'd sat in a room full of squirming kids to watch *Pirates of the Caribbean.*

Now we rode away from the city. The sun glowed low behind clouds, and the day had cooled. A few blocks from the library, the buildings gave way to dilapidated sheds and fields. After the city, it seemed like I rode into nothingness.

Riding was easy after escaping into the world of the pirates. *Pirates of the Caribbean* had been surprisingly amusing. While I rode, I daydreamed about Will Turner, the dashing hero. One scene kept coming to mind, when Will challenges pirate Jack Sparrow to a duel, giving the reason as "You threatened Miss Swann," the young woman he loves. It was the most precious, romantic moment, and it replayed over and over in my head as I pedaled.[33]

The road stayed flat, the hills distant. Wheat fields still surrounded me. Mary receded to a tiny dot ahead. After an hour, I found her sitting in the empty lot of a closed gas station at the deserted crossroads labeled Lowden, sipping a blue Gatorade—a gift from Liz who worked at the Dayton city hall. (She'd "heard we had visitors in the fairgrounds" and come to find us the previous night, bringing fruit and drinks.) We decided to ride the remaining miles to Touchet, hoping we might find something more.

The clouds in the west began breaking up, shining pink. A ridge rose up, far away on our left. Twig-like trees stood along the top—they were windmills! Each had one giant vane slowly rotating.

The wheat fields halted when we reached the next gas station. Rusty farm equipment lay in the tall grass next to falling-down sections of wire fence. At least the station was open. I picked up peanut butter cups and a bottle of Gatorade. Without much hope, I asked the clerk, "Does Touchet have a park or a church?"

"There's the school," he said.

"Where's that?" He directed me to take the crossroad one block north, and then to go left. The presence of a third road in Touchet surprised me.

Yesterday I'd stopped to eat lunch at a school, wondering if there'd be students. My disoriented brain had asked, "What day is it?" Thursday. But I hadn't seen anyone . . . because it was July. School was out for the summer. The usual patterns of my life that held such things in place—weather, holidays, the arrival of college students in Chapel Hill—were missing.

Now the yelling of a ballgame reached us as we neared the school. On a flat field, a crowd of boys ran, kicking a soccer ball. Two taller guys ran with the kids, blowing whistles. After the soccer field, we saw the brown school building with a green lawn under thick trees, and there was a picnic table. The table made me feel welcome.

By the time Mary and I had pitched the tent, brilliant pink-orange light gleamed in the western sky. The windmills lined the hillside to the south. Hundreds, maybe a thousand, stood in one long row as far as I could see. As the fiery sunset began to dim, Mary crawled into the tent.

I got out my book and journal and sat at the picnic table in the fading light. As darkness came, a white light bloomed atop each windmill. The lights blinked, brightening as the sky darkened, until they looked like diamonds flashing along the ridge, sparkling with a rhythm against the end of the sunset. I realized the noise of the soccer game had ended and looked up to see the two older guys walking up the road. They were both cute, and as I waved hello, I realized that I didn't feel like a dork the way I usually did around cute guys. But I didn't feel comfortable, either. I was maintaining a confident facade.

"We just wondered what you're doing," one of them said as they neared.

"We're biking across the country," I replied, and their eyes lit up.

One guy sat on the opposite end of the bench. "Where are you from?"

As I answered, I thought of asking if it was okay to camp. But as we talked, I realized our camping here was not a problem at all. Touchet was just a quiet, friendly place.

"Well, have a good trip!" the seated guy said, rising, and I smiled.

"Thanks!" I replied. I caught myself just before I blurted out, "You, too!"

As they walked back to their car, emptiness filled me. My confidence disappeared, leaving the usual Emily behind. Had I messed up somehow, I wondered, causing them to leave?

"Of course they left after visiting me," I told myself. "I didn't mess up. What did I expect, one of them to fall in love with me? At least I talked to them, without acting awkward." The negative thoughts seemed desperate to lure me in. I could see that my thoughts about "messing up" were irrational and tried to ignore the lingering feeling that I could have done better.

Only a little light remained. The white lights on the windmills had turned red—it struck me that red lights should feel menacing, but these didn't. I could no longer remember the things I had wanted to write about that morning, when we'd left the fairgrounds at Dayton, so I closed my journal and stood. With the final clouds clearing, the warm air, and the grass of the schoolyard, I wanted to sleep outside. It wasn't a big deal, the way it had been the first few times. I reached into the tent and dragged out my pad and sleeping bag.

I awoke when something landed on my chest in the dark—something small and fluttery, like a bird only more clackity. Inexplicably unpanicked, I extended a hand, prodding the critter onto it, and transported him to the nearby grass. His feet clung to me as I rolled my hand to deposit him. Then I found my travel alarm and pushed the button to light up the face: 3:45 shone out. I moved the light toward the critter. It was a giant praying mantis. His head tilted in the light, looking curiously back at me.

I liked praying mantises on principle, because they eat pest bugs in the garden. But also, they made me think of Zorak, the evil cartoon praying mantis on the TV show *Space Ghost Coast to Coast*. I imagined this green mantis opening his mouth and jeering at me in Zorak's gravelly voice. I rolled onto my side to face him. Now I could see him in the dark, sitting in the grass, looking back at me. After a little while, I closed my eyes, and when I reopened them, he was gone.

The alarm beeped. Mary and I had another early morning planned. Today we'd ride thirteen miles west to the Columbia River and then follow the river south to the Oregon border. After the border, it was another twenty miles to the first town, Umatilla. All our previous rivers (the Lochsa, the Clearwater, and the Snake) emptied into the Columbia upstream of where we'd meet it. I remembered sitting in the shallow Lochsa, just down from Lolo Pass; would I encounter the same water molecules, or had they long since made it to the Pacific Ocean?

While we ate, the sky lightened, and one by one the red windmill lights, high in the air, turned white. I packed my bike, and just as I began to wheel it toward the road, I spotted the praying mantis clinging to the wheel, bouncing slightly on his jointed legs and looking up at me.

"Oh, buddy," I said, halting. "You can't come."

Now that I was awake, I felt nervous about giving my finger to a praying mantis—did they bite? They usually seemed dangerously eager to grab at a finger. But this mantis drew back as I held out a finger, so I made a cage-like claw with my hand and lifted him off. His soft wings brushed my palm, like the inner husks on an ear of corn. I placed him on the grass and moved away, and he kept looking at me like he wanted to come, so that I felt sad leaving him.

As Mary and I rolled back to Route 12, the row of windmill lights twinkled softly in the pastel dawn. The tans and sage-greens of the ridge harmonized with the morning sky. The sun neared the horizon, and when it finally rose, we were several miles down the road under a blue sky dotted with white, gray, and golden clouds. As the twinkling lights on the windmills faded into the daylight, the windmills themselves emerged, stretching on in a never-ending line.

THAT AFTERNOON, I SAT ON hard, gravel-strewn dirt, sipping from a drink box of rice milk. Mary had placed her camera on the ground twenty feet away and now bent to peer through the viewfinder. She propped the camera on a piece of gravel to capture the giant brown sign behind me: "Welcome to Oregon." I reached for my granola bar, ripped the wrapper open, and took a bite. Mary hopped up and jogged to where I sat with my mouth full of granola bar. As

Mary turned to face the camera, I tried to smile while keeping my full mouth closed. After a series of flashes, the camera snapped.

We'd reached the Columbia River! And another state! In another week, we'd be at the Pacific. And two days after that, Mary would fly home.

As we rode on, the scenery disappointed me. I'd expected Oregon to be lush and green, especially near the river. I'd expected trees, or at least farmland. Instead, the land stayed barren with yellow fields. Far below on my right, the blue band of the river rested, darker than the sky. It was just so ordinary! Dull hills towered over the far shore, patchy and uneven like a badly frosted cake. Horizontal strips of rock showed where the cliff had eroded.

At least the space over the river was impressive, bigger than football stadium or concert arena. A steep slope descended from the road—I couldn't see the bottom, half a mile down. Wind gusted over me. A multicolored freight train appeared at the base of the opposite cliff. Now I saw the track, squeezed onto a ledge beside the water. I couldn't hear any sound from the train. As I rode, I counted the cars; I gave up at fifty.

The road meandered away from the river. I stopped at a porta-potty in a parking area. A campground spread out on a lower terrace, under a few scraggly trees. Small campers and pickup trucks were parked at the sites, where children ran around playing while beefy dads lounged near coolers. I didn't see access to the river so far below, and the view was desolate and there was no shade. The wind blew constantly.

When I opened the porta-potty door, the stench hit before my eyes adjusted to the interior darkness. Poop was smeared across the seat and filled the bowl. There were even smears on the walls. Somehow the mess made the campers seem threatening. But I didn't know when I'd find another restroom, and there was nowhere to be discreet by the side of the road, so I took a deep breath and went in. When I stumbled out, gasping for fresh air, I hurried to my bike and rode on without a snack.

I tried to forget the experience, but it stuck in my head as the miles stretched into the afternoon. I tried to think of something else. I replayed the romantic scenes from *Pirates of the Caribbean*. They were faded today, as if I had worn them out by replaying them so many times yesterday. My heart still twinged at Will Turner's words, "You threatened Miss Swann," but I knew that even that feeling would soon be gone.

The river finished a massive turn so that I headed west; all I saw ahead were more brown and yellow cliffs. The day felt hotter and hotter, but at least I had a wide shoulder. I pedaled along as the hours passed, sucking the remaining happiness out of the daydream of pirates.

## Route 14, on which I find my mantra

I SILENCED MY ALARM. QUIET FILLED Plymouth's park in the darkness. I lay on my sleeping pad and stared at the tree towering over me, trying to stall the day by not rising. What did I dread? The heat and exhaustion? Being on the move again? Leaving the park with its shade and showers? (Last night, I'd had my first shower in eight days—since Missoula, Montana.)[34]

Or was it the approaching Pacific that scared me?

I dragged myself up and plodded across the grass to the restroom. A sandwich board stood outside: Closed for Cleaning. Disinfectant drifted out the propped door, and the scratch of a broom on cement echoed inside. "It figures," I thought. "I'm in the middle of nowhere at four AM, and they're cleaning the ladies' room." Should I just use the men's room? I returned to camp.

I rolled up my sleeping pad and packed it. Then I sat, watching the restroom. Across the grass, Mary stirred. The park had felt wonderful last night; now it mocked me. Finally the custodian left.

Mary was up when I returned. I couldn't sit still, so we picked Roosevelt (forty-eight miles away) as a likely meeting spot. Then I climbed uphill through tiny Plymouth, Washington, and turned left.

We'd crossed to the Washington side of the Columba River because an interstate ran along the Oregon side. On the map, Washington's Route 14 followed the river, so I hoped there'd be places to swim. But as I left the town in the fading darkness, train tracks moved in between me and the river. There were no paths or sandy beaches, just bumpy grass and a rocky shoreline, or bushes hiding the water. White caps dotted the surface of the mile-wide river; on the far shore were low, brown hills.

When the sun rose, the familiar palette of yellow, brown, and blue returned. Already bored by the scenery, I pedaled on. Sometimes the road climbed a hillside. In a few places, someone had planted rows of crops.

After two hours, I reached the intersection of Route 221, where a town called Paterson sat above Route 14. I turned and pushed myself up the steep hill. Nothing moved in town; there were no cars and the restaurant was closed. It felt like a ghost town, but the buildings were in good repair. Near the top was a gas station with a porta-potty. There was no attendant, just a sign with directions to pay for gas.

I leaned my bike on a cinderblock wall that hemmed the parking lot and looked down on Route 14. Maybe I'd see Mary ride past. Would she stop to explore Paterson?

I didn't have high hopes for a porta-potty at a self-serve gas station, but I opened the door to find a clean stall. Fresh porta-potty fragrance drifted out; a service schedule posted on the door showed yesterday! A smidgen of joy entered my heart; a perfectly clean porta-potty!

When I exited the porta-potty, I checked my watch: seven AM. No wonder no one was around. I counted off the days of the week; today was Saturday. It was ten AM in Connecticut, in my hometown. The sailors would just be arriving at the boating club—at least the old sailors (like my dad) who wanted to putter around their boats before heading out to the races, which started at one. For the briefest moment, I felt the cool sea breeze and wished I were there.

I got out my journal and a granola bar and sat on the wall, concrete scraping against my thighs as I inched backward. My feet hung clear of the ground. I'd gone fourteen miles already; it was nice to rest with that accomplished.

After a few minutes, an engine noise pulled my attention. A truck trundled up through the town with two men in the cab. I closed my journal, immediately on guard. The truck turned in and sputtered to a stop along the wall where I sat, and the sixty-something driver got out. A younger man stayed in the cab, scowling. I stood to greet the driver, and he smiled.

"Where you from?" he called, lumbering over.

"We started in New Jersey."

He asked my name and held out a hand to shake. "I'm Ron . . . so, what d'you got in those bags?"

"Food, clothes, a stove. My friend has the tent."

"How far do you go each day?" He asked the usual questions; he seemed safe enough. Periodically, I glanced down at Route 14. Had Mary passed? Would she look up?

When Ron finally paused, I turned to my bike and packed my journal. He kept standing near me. "So you just look at the map," he said, "and pick a town to finish at, and just hope you'll find somewhere to sleep when you get there?"

"Yep."

His brow furrowed as if he was really trying to imagine this.

"Are you going to write about it? You keep a daily journal?" He nodded at the bag where I had just stashed it.

"Yeah."

"Just write about all the little things," he began, but then a noise sounded from over the hill and a semi barreled into sight, its brakes firing as it raced down the hill through town. As the noise receded, and the truck turned onto Route 14, Ron asked, "What do you do for a living?"

"I'm a bread baker," I replied, knowing it would surprise him. It always surprised people that there were still bread bakers.

His eyebrows shot up. "Really?! I never would of guessed that!"

The rumble of a truck sounded again and another semi crested the hill, riding its brakes continuously. Would trucks be passing me all day on Route 14? Ron yelled over the noise, "You're brave!"

I smiled awkwardly.

"Most people get so . . . *focused*," he said, putting his hands together in front of him and staring at them. His brow wrinkled again, and then he pushed his hands forward, driving a wedge through the air. "They get stuck in their jobs," he continued, as if struggling to find words, but suddenly I thought I understood what he wanted to say. I wondered that an older man who lived in the middle of nowhere would think about this—about how people enter the system of making money and buying things, and stop feeling alive, and never escape. I hadn't realized my thoughts were so universal. Ron started telling about his kids and their jobs, with long hours.

Ron had a "fiber farm" where he raised bunnies and a few alpacas, and he had just bought the blue and white building halfway down the hill, which he planned to turn into an ice cream parlor. He'd been working on the building for three years. I looked at it, wishing it were an ice cream parlor right now, and open early on Saturday mornings. An old school bus stood outside.

"Are you biking back east, too?" he asked.

"No, I'm taking the Green Tortoise. It's this adventure travel company out of San Francisco. They drive you across the country on these old buses.

You sleep at night, and go hiking during the day. The bus has bunks inside, not seats."

Ron listened, staring with wide eyes, and then a grin spread across his face. He pointed his thumb at the school bus by his building. "Someone abandoned that old bus in my lot," he said. "Maybe I'll put in bunks and give people tours!"

I smiled back. "Well, I'd better get going."

"It was good to meet you," he said, extending his hand again. In the cab, his companion stared out at the river.

I rolled down the hill, keeping my rear brake lever tightly clamped. Mary must have passed by now—I'd been stopped almost an hour. On Route 14, I saw no sign of her in either direction. As I rode, I kept hoping to see her ahead, or that she'd overtake me. I imagined myself falling farther and farther behind. "We're not competing," I reminded myself. But I couldn't shake my worries and irritation. Ever since we had left the wheat fields, the landscape had been dreary, with pasty yellow grass and no shade. The Columbia River had no access points and no greenery. And it was so hot! I just wanted to finish the day's miles, especially today when there was nothing interesting on the map.

A few miles passed, the sun beating down from the cloudless sky. I hadn't seen any traffic since leaving Paterson. My left knee twanged, so I reached down and rubbed it as I pedaled. Then I switched to the right knee, just to be safe. Even with my sunglasses, I squinted at the road ahead. I just had to keep biking and get it over with.

"On your left!" a voice shouted in my ear. My heart leapt. A biker pulled up beside me.

"He could have shouted a little sooner," I thought as he smiled behind his sunglasses and called out a hello. Under his helmet, sweat had beaded up all over his face. He wore black Spandex biking shorts and no shirt. His torso glistened.

"Hi," I replied, slowing, and he immediately slowed, too. We stopped in the road.

"Where you from?" he asked. He didn't have any bags, so I figured he was on a day ride.

"North Carolina." He nodded and started talking about the bike trips he'd been on. My mind wandered; without the breeze of movement, I was even hotter, and I hadn't slept well. My eyelids threatened to droop as he rambled on and on. I wanted to go! At last he wound down.

"Well, have a good trip!" he said, and I nodded and said thanks.

He pushed off quickly, and I lumbered after him. As he shot away from me, I saw a two-inch black spider clinging to his sweaty back.

"Wait!" I called. He wobbled and looked back, slowing. I pushed harder to catch up with him and reached out to brush off the spider, balancing as I coasted beside him. But when my hand made contact, the spider crumpled, legs folding in on its body, and fell off. It was already dead. The man's sweat lingered on my fingertips. He looked at me. "There was a spider."

"Oh, I thought I felt something!" he replied, his joviality returning. He must have swatted at it and killed it, and it had stuck to him. But where had it *come* from? Did giant black spiders leap off the grass onto passing bikers?

He kept biking beside me and didn't say thanks. "Well, bye again," I said, hitting my brakes so that he'd pull ahead. I watched him recede as I pedaled slowly along. Sunlight shimmered on his back until he disappeared around a bend.

The solitude settled back over me. This day was so weird! First my unusually long interaction with Ron, and now the sweaty-man-with-a-spider incident. I resolved to ride without stopping, to keep pedaling and keep up my speed. But just as I got some momentum, I saw an odd shape on the left side of the road, like a square stack of pale mud. It looked so out of place; I couldn't imagine how it had gotten there, so I kept staring as I approached. Then the wind blew and the shape ruffled into feathers, and I realized it was an owl.

I hit my brakes, stopping in the road. Now I saw a beak and eyes closed against the dazzling sunlight. I wheeled my bike off the pavement and lay it down. Then I crept across the road toward the owl. He stood facing the road and didn't move.

I stopped in the shoulder a few feet away. Other than his face, I couldn't tell what was what; he wore a shapeless coat of beige feathers that dragged on the ground, hiding his feet. I took a step closer, and his head swiveled toward me, his eyes opening to slits.

He shouldn't be out; something must be wrong. He shifted a little, and feathers slid across his body, revealing new feathers underneath. Then all the feathers lifted to reveal inch-thick stalks of legs coated with tiny white feathers like a child's craft project, and giant white, feathery feet with dark circles of claws curving out from white toes. "I'd better not get too close," I thought.

When he settled down, one wing did not fold back to his body. It lay on the roadside, jutting out at an odd angle. His slit eyes blinked and then closed. Down the highway, a truck roared. As it neared, the owl's eyes reopened. His head turned from me on his left, following the truck to his right. Then his head kept turning, all the way around until it faced me again, rotated 360 degrees.

I stood helpless. I couldn't take the owl; I had no way to carry him, and didn't know how to pick him up, and I doubted I would find an animal shelter out here anyway. But I couldn't just leave him there, standing by the side of the road. I could shoo him off the shoulder into the scrubby bushes. At least he'd be in the shade, and away from traffic. Could he survive without his wing? I tried to imagine him, trapped between the fence by the train tracks and the fence across the road, running after mice instead of flying. Maybe he could eat bugs.

I raised my hands and made a weak shooing motion. His eyes opened wide, yellow with giant black holes, and I backed off, scared of being bitten or clawed, and not wanting to scare him. His other wing stretched, flapping, and hope leapt up in my heart. Maybe he'd just been stunned from flying into a car; maybe his wing wasn't broken after all! But when the good wing lifted him, the bad wing dragged along the road so that his body circled around it, claws scraping the pavement, and he crashed back down. A pile of bird poop sat on the ground where he'd been. He settled into his new spot, facing west, and his eyes closed to slits.

After a minute, I walked back to my bike, thinking of all the dead birds I'd seen in the road that summer. I'd assumed they'd died instantly, not lain in the road suffering. I sat on the gravel and started to cry.

I cried and cried, my nose getting all gunky with dusty snot so that I had to stand and dig out a napkin I'd stashed in my bags. What should I do? I couldn't leave, but I couldn't just sit there! There wasn't any solution. And why did the Universe's master plan have to include this owl suffering by the roadside, anyway? It didn't make any sense.

A car approached and I stifled my sobs, embarrassed. I wiped my tears, anticipating the car slowing and someone calling out to ask if I were okay. But the car whizzed past. I resumed crying.

A few more cars passed, and each time I stiffened, hoping they wouldn't notice me. It seemed like hours, but probably it was only five minutes. Now a semi approached, and when I heard the grumble of his brakes, I knew he was stopping. I wiped my eyes, dreading the moment when he'd ask, "Do you have a flat tire?" or "Are you all right?" I'd have to admit I was stopped because of the owl, and he'd think I was silly. Twisting around, I looked at the open window in the cab as the truck rolled toward me. I scrambled to my feet.

The driver leaned out the window as the truck stopped. "Is that owl alive?"

Tears popped back into my eyes. I nodded and opened my mouth to say it had a broken wing, but he spoke first. "Do you want me to kill it?"

It wasn't my owl. I didn't have any right to order it killed. But what else could I do? Maybe I just wanted him dead so I could return to biking . . . *but the truck driver seems to know what he's doing.* And the owl was suffering. The light must've hurt his eyes.

I clutched my napkin and nodded. The driver said, "I'll kill it," and as I turned away, the truck started rolling forward. I listened as it picked up speed and drove on. I sat back down and started sobbing, and now I didn't care if anyone saw me.

When at last my tears subsided, I peeked across the highway. The owl wasn't as flat as I'd expected; a few feathers flapped in the wind. Carefully avoiding looking, I stood, wiped my eyes one last time, and blew my nose. I thought about saying a prayer over the body, but I couldn't think of any words, plus I didn't want to see it. Besides, when I thought about the owl, he no longer seemed to be in the pile of bones and guts and feathers on the road. Instead, I imagined him wheeling through the blue sky, a pale ghost in the bright daylight, and I didn't feel sad for him anymore.

A few residual sobs rose, shaking me as I pulled up my bike and got on. A new tear squeezed out onto my dry cheek, rolling down in a hot trail, and I wiped it away and pushed off.

As I picked up speed, hot wind rushed at my face. I again thought about the grand plan of the Universe and the owl. "Maybe he waited by the road because he was waiting to die," I thought. "Maybe that's why I stopped, and felt compelled to stay, so that the trucker would see me and then notice the owl. Maybe that's why the trucker came along right when I needed him; maybe that's why I got stuck talking to Ron for so long, so I wouldn't have to wait for the trucker."

Something I'd read in *Travels with Charley* came back to me: if you save someone's life, you become responsible for it. "What happens if you don't save it?" I wondered, and I twisted the words around, and in some abstract way it made sense: *maybe they become responsible for you.*

Drained from crying, I didn't want to go on; my body ached, and my legs had no energy. I watched for markers, counting down the miserable miles to Roosevelt. A state park, the only thing on the map for thirty-four miles, turned out to be an island in the river, accessible only by boat. I ate lunch in the shade under a dirty bridge, nervous to be away from my bike and out of sight.

As I headed on, I tried to recall my pirate movie daydream. It had been so vivid and romantic, but now it had faded, and as I thought over the worn out lines, I felt nothing. "You threatened Miss Swann." The phrase had no power left. I tried to think of a new scene filled with as much romance but couldn't come up with one. Instead I just had the dull reality of biking in the heat, made even less desirable by comparison.

Real life was never as good as my daydreams! Would I appreciate it more if I stopped daydreaming? Maybe real life was like an apple, and daydreams were like cotton candy, and if I'd just quit eating the sugary candy I'd appreciate the wholesome apple.

"You threatened Miss Swann," I thought again, just to see. The line didn't fill me with swooning love, but it took up the space in my brain. "You threatened Miss Swann. You threatened Miss Swann." It became a mantra that kept me pedaling, preventing me from fixating on the heat and discomfort, or from dwelling on the miles left to ride. And it stopped me from forming a new daydream. The words had no meaning left, but they filled the space.

LATE THAT AFTERNOON, THE FENCE separating me from the train tracks halted at a crossroad. Alongside the tracks stood a four-foot metal box that cast a tiny but solid parallelogram shadow on the ground.

"This is pathetic," I thought, but I wanted to sit in shade more than anything, so I rode across the tracks, under the red and white gate that loomed overhead. I leaned my bike on the box. It had an electrical warning sign; I almost expected it to spark when my bike touched it.

I got out peanuts, dried apricots, and my water bottle. As usual, my knees twinged in pain when they bent. Sitting, I stretched my legs, keeping my knees slightly bent so they hurt less, and leaned my sweaty back against the box. The tracks passed twenty feet in front of me.

I closed my eyes, feeling the ache in my legs and wrists. I'd never expected the Columbia River gorge to be so dry and treeless. The hills didn't even have scrubby sage bushes, just brown grass and rock. The heat and the landscape were wretched.

*Somewhere better than here? Or, nowhere better than here?*

The phrases popped into my head. I'd seen them during a high school field trip. Most of the museum's art had felt meaningless, like the film projector slowly rotating at the top of a stairwell to deposit a pile of film at the bottom (it was called "Waterfall") and the gallery hung with blank canvases. But one gallery contained an elaborate structure of corrugated cardboard, painted with child-like scenes and covered with small plastic toys. A viewfinder stuck out on each side: through one, I read, "Somewhere better than here." Through the other, "Nowhere better than here."

The two phrases had bounced in my head like Ping-Pong balls. "Somewhere better than here." It could be hopeful, like you are looking forward to the future; or it could just be a complaint about the present. "Nowhere better than here." It could express contentment with your current situation; or it could express hopelessness, the belief that things will never improve. The phrases presented four possibilities for viewing the world.

Through the years, the two phrases had periodically returned, and each time I would examine them, considering all four interpretations. Which would I pick now? Was there a hope-filled "Somewhere better than here," or a miserable, longing-filled "Somewhere better than here"? Or was there a happy, satisfied "Nowhere better than here," or a depressed and hopeless "Nowhere better than here"? Was I hopeful? Satisfied? Or miserable?

*I don't want to be on the bike trip anymore.*

Unbearable heat, relentless sun . . . my body ached, I could never keep up with Mary. I'd choose the unhappy "Somewhere better than here."

But as I thought it, I realized that it was the first time of the entire trip that I had not wanted to be there. In spite of all the disappointments—the slow pace of biking with a load, the tension with Mary, the unmet expectations about perfect scenery and "having fun"—and in spite of the discomfort of cold, rain, hills, storms, wind, heat, and sun, I had never wanted to be anywhere else all summer. All summer had been the satisfied "Nowhere better than here."

Admitting that I didn't want to be there tilted the scales, and I didn't feel as bad. So this day was going badly, but it was part of the bigger picture. "I'm probably learning some new life lesson," I reminded myself sarcastically: "I want to appreciate this moment, even if it stinks."

I reconsidered the options. Which paper *would* I choose? If I had to choose just one? I'd choose one of the positive interpretations, for sure. Somewhere better than here: looking forward to life and to the future, having plans and making things happen, constantly improving myself. Nowhere better than here: enjoying the moment, being present, not missing a thing, accepting myself as I was.

*I want both!* I wanted to do more with my life *and* to appreciate what happened every day. I wanted to improve myself and be happier *and* to accept myself with my faults and depressions.

Maybe I *could* have both. I could accept that I was sad sometimes but move on, instead of repeating it to myself, telling myself I was depressed and giving the sadness more power. I could acknowledge a bad mood without letting it frustrate me, which would only make it worse. The bad mood could evaporate in an instant, if I allowed it to. Maybe accepting myself was the way to overcoming faults, and being present was the proper way to get to the future.

Could I do it? Could I commit to living in the present moment, and waiting to see what the future brought, instead of spending my days protected in a daydream about a future I hoped for and would never reach? I spoke out loud. "I want to live in the present moment, even when it sucks." I still wanted to snort in derision, but saying it out loud added conviction to the idea. Maybe if I repeated it enough times, it would sink in.

The railroad gate dinged.

Was I sitting too close to the tracks? I was too tired to move. I settled back to watch. I had front row seats to a show: the train! A high whistle sounded to my left where the tracks disappeared around a rocky wall. "Ding! Ding! Ding!"

went the gate as it jerked into motion, tilting down to block the road. A low rumble began in the ground. Then the tip of the engine appeared, moving slower than I'd expected. As the engine neared, its rumble escalated to a racket and it seemed to accelerate.

The train reached me with a rush of wind and a clackity roar, and I listened for the whistle to drop, thinking of Dad explaining the Doppler shift to me as a kid. One car after another flew past, a periodic rhythm banging out as the wheels rolled along. They were flatcars hauling the backs of semis, two per car. The huge truck-backs looked minuscule on the train.

A hot gust of wind hit me as the cars rolled past. The engine moved out of sight and gave a low whistle. Then the end of the train rounded the bend. A dozen more cars clacked by, their noise easier to separate now that silence followed. The last car passed, leaving only the noise of the receding train. The gate cut off mid-ding and rose into the air, creaking slightly in the deeper silence, and then the last train car rolled out of sight and the silence was complete.

# PART 7:
# The End Draws Near

## Route 30 to Portland, in which I try to remember all the lessons I've learned

I STOOD ON THE ROCKY SHORE surrounded by bushes, with the river lapping at my feet. In the blue morning sky, Mount Hood radiated with the first light of the sunrise. Its white peak gleamed across the river over purple slopes. Rivulets of snow extended down; a child might have drawn it.

Shade still covered my gravel beach. I sat, clutching the bowl of blackberries I'd picked from the bushes around our campsite. The sky over the river lightened as I ate.

Mount Hood had appeared yesterday morning, dramatically framed in a cleft blasted in the rocky cliffs, through which the road passed. As soon as I saw the peak, I knew it—not from the map but because I had painted a mural of it in high school, a backdrop for our drama club's production of *One Flew Over the Cuckoo's Nest*. I'd always wanted to see the real thing, but I had forgotten.

Two nights ago, camped in the park in Roosevelt, Mary and I had met Angie, who was biking east. She'd insisted we cross the river back to Oregon, because the south side had a historic highway with several waterfalls. We'd passed the bridge at Biggs Junction because I'd wanted to see the Maryhill Museum, farther on. After the museum, we'd ended up at this strange, unmarked camping area: we'd stopped to use a roadside porta-potty and noticed the campsites. Paths led from each site through the bushes to the river. We'd made dinner on the river's edge, watching the sun set behind Mount Hood. This morning, we had only a few miles to the next bridge, at a city called The Dalles.

We finished breakfast and packed our bikes. As we turned out of the camp's driveway, sunny Mount Hood beamed at us across the water. Soon the sunlight reached us, and then the road veered away from the river and began to climb. I'd been looking forward to crossing the river, and here we were climbing again! I probably should have learned to expect it by now.

Tall forms clustered near the road ahead, but they didn't register in my brain until I topped the hill and found myself surrounded by evergreens. Cool shade enveloped me, and I breathed in the trees' sweet earthy smell. "When did I last see a tree?" I wondered. "A real, in-the-wild tree, not a landscaped one?" I'd reached a magic line, and trees could grow again.

I reached an intersection; to the left, Mary coasted down a long, beautiful hill toward the river. I turned after her, relaxing as gravity took over and pulled me down, like a cartoon character with a word bubble over my head proclaiming "Wheeee!" as I coasted on and on. The bridge came into sight, with huge, rusty beams overhead. Mary had stopped at its entrance, but I coasted past the Columbia River sign and onto the bridge. Ahead were buildings, and above them evergreens and houses on a hillside, and over that the yellow hills.

Mary rode up next to me, and we biked onto the sunny main street of The Dalles. Most of the stores were closed, but we stopped at the grocery. My food supply was low from our days in the boondocks, but as I shopped, I remembered that tomorrow we'd be with friends in Portland. Then we'd just have one more night of cooking before we reached the Pacific Ocean. I didn't have to stock up.

We headed west on Route 30, the road that Angie had recommended. A stack of signs greeted us: "Historic Columbia River Highway," "Oregon Scenic Byway," "Bicycles on Roadway" . . . The road approached a cliff and then began to climb, winding into an S curve that twisted its way up the hill. Low, arched stone walls at the turns protected travelers from sheer drops. The river glittered below, and occasionally a tall evergreen cast its shadow across the road. After several passes, I panted my way to the top of the third tier and pulled in at a turnout. Trees ran up the slopes around me, but across the river were brown hills and yellow fields. I was so glad we'd met Angie—otherwise we'd be over there.

After the turnout, the road coasted down into forest. It twisted along until, twenty miles west of The Dalles, it ended in a town called Mosier, where I found Mary. After one wrong turn, we found the trailhead for Route 30, now closed to cars. A historical marker told about the road, built from 1913 to 1922: Its designers had located beautiful spots and positioned the road to observe (and preserve) them; the road itself was the destination. But the construction of flat, straight Interstate 84 in 1950 caused the demise of the historic route. Crews destroyed sections of Route 30 to make way for the interstate. The rest fell into disrepair as traffic blazed past on the new highway.

The road began to roll down, and the cool breeze whipped at my face. It was fun, like riding a bike when you're a kid. And then I saw a tunnel! I whooshed into the dark. It felt like a ride at Disney World, like the "mining" roller coaster called the Thunder Mountain Railroad. The smooth wall gave way to jagged rock, prehistoric and wild. My skin soaked up the dampness and cold, and then I burst out into the sunlight even as another tunnel loomed ahead.

When the second tunnel ended, a roof continued over the road, creating a "tube" with large windows cut in the rock wall on the river side. I slowed when I saw Mary. We stopped in the deep shade and looked out a window. Evergreens covered the hillside below us.

While we rested, two guys on bikes chugged up the path from the opposite direction. They didn't carry bags or wear bike clothing, and their bikes were mountain bikes. They stopped when they reached us. Panting slightly, the bigger guy asked, "Where are you from?"

"New Jersey," I answered, not sure why I chose that instead of North Carolina. The men's eyes widened.

"When did you start?" the big man asked me.

"May 2nd."

He kept looking at me, half grinning. "Do you have a boyfriend?"

*What?* My brain reeled as it searched for a reply. Was he kidding, implying Mary and I were so interesting because of our trip that he immediately "liked" us? I struggled not to smile and look at the ground, my automatic response to flirty men. I felt uncomfortable not looking down. "No."

"I'm Donald," he continued right on. "This is Louis. We've got a boat—we could take you out on the river!"

The idea seemed preposterous, that I'd interrupt my trip three days from the Pacific to go on a boat with men I didn't know. "Would some women go for this?" I wondered. Did Mary want to go? Was I just scared to meet people?

"We've just got a few days left," I said, "to reach the Pacific."

"You could come back," Donald said. "At least give us your email addresses." It was the easiest way to get rid of him, so I pulled out a scrap of paper and wrote my address.

When Mary and I rode out of the tube, the air felt wetter, and the hillsides above and below us were thick with evergreens.[35] Mount Hood must have been passing to the south, but we could no longer see it. We rode for an hour, and the road flattened, taking us past a sunny orchard and more scenic overlooks. Finally we came to a parking lot at the end of the trail.

The next morning, Mary and I rode a short stretch of Interstate 84. I'd been on the interstate the night before as well, to travel from Hood River to our campground. I'd stayed in Hood River to lounge in the coffee shop and see a matinee, while Mary had gone ahead. Hood River was filled with shops, restaurants, and young people, some on bikes. After weeks of travel, I'd suddenly felt at home.

Now we coasted down the exit ramp toward Cascade Locks, and I looked out at the river with its mirrored morning surface. It had narrowed so that the trees on the far side, lit up with early sunlight, seemed just a few leaps away. The barren cliffs had vanished.

Route 30, again closed to cars, recommenced at a trailhead in a parking lot under a metal bridge—a sign called it the "Bridge of the Gods"—that spanned the Columbia River and disappeared into greenery on the opposite shore. Yesterday I'd been excited to see trees again. Today, as we started down the trail, I noticed how large the trunks were, too big to encircle with my arms. The trees shaded the entire roadway. A mossy stone balustrade lined the road as it passed over a creek.

Mary and I stopped once to carry our bikes up a tall staircase. As I rehung my bags, I noticed a bare spot on my front tire. I looked closer—I could see the threads of the tire's inner surface! Bare patches continued all the way around; I had worn it out. I remembered yesterday's descent into The Dalles, and then the steep descent into Hood River. Thank goodness the tire hadn't ripped open!

Should I use my spare? I'd carried it all the way from Fat Jimmy's Outfitters in Breezewood, Pennsylvania. Why had I bought it, if not for this moment?

But it would take so long to change a tire! In Portland, I could go to a shop and buy two new tires, and have the shop put them on. Today I wanted to see the waterfalls.

The trail ran straight with the forest rising on either side, and the air felt wonderfully damp and cool. I kept Mary in sight but stayed back, enjoying the silence. No wind rushed past. The only sounds were my breathing and the soft crunch of my tires on the trail. Ahead, a yellow leaf drifted down. I watched it come to rest at the center line, then scratch as a breath of wind moved it half an inch. I rolled past.

After another stint on Interstate 84, we returned to Route 30, now open to cars but still meandering through thick trees. A rushing noise sounded as I neared a bend, and I rounded the stone cliff to a white waterfall thundering down. It fell into a shallow pool, separated from the road by only a low stone wall. The road widened to give cars a place to stop, and a tiny patio squeezed in alongside the falls. I passed more arched stone walls. With the mossy rocks and overhanging branches, and with water tumbling down rocky hillsides, the place felt like fairyland.

I arrived at a parking lot. Far at the back, an arched bridge floated in the mist, high in the green trees. A waterfall tumbled off the cliff behind the bridge. The water reappeared under the arch, falling in a sheet to a bottom pool. The scene was so magnificent it seemed unreal, and I stopped at the edge of the road to stare.

Tiny figures moved on the high bridge, waving at friends on patios below. Greenery flourished on the wet, rocky cliffs. I passed a sign that read "Multnomah Falls" and found Mary near the visitor center. We followed the sidewalk to the bottom of the waterfall, where it slipped into a clear amber pool amid green ferns. A trailhead led into the greenery.

"If I walk up to the bridge, will you take my picture?" I asked Mary. She agreed.

I managed the steep climb and emerged by the bridge. The narrow falls to my right landed in a pool, then flowed under the bridge to dive off the second cliff. The sounds of the water rushed in the air as I breathed in dampness. Lush vegetation hung on dripping rock where the mist condensed. Mary looked tiny, sitting on a stone bench that lined the terrace below. I waved, and she lifted her camera. With the noise of the falls, I couldn't hear, so I pasted on a smile until she lowered her arms.

Snatches of sunny Interstate 84 showed through the treetops. The trail continued off the bridge—it led all the way to the top! But I couldn't leave Mary waiting.

"It's not that I want to go to the top," I thought on the way down. I hadn't even wanted to go to the bridge, really. I'd just wanted to feel something, to prolong our stay in the hope of magic happening. "But I should know by now not to expect feelings to happen on cue." I couldn't seem to learn that lesson once and for all.

Now patches of sun hit the road, and my eyes struggled to adjust when I reentered deep shade. I wanted to stop at each new waterfall but also to keep up with Mary. At Wahkeena Falls, water tumbled down rocks at the roadside. I did the short hike to see Bridal Veil Falls but skipped the last two waterfalls.

Then the road began an S curve. As it climbed, one curve after another, the trees diminished in size and sunlight filled the road. Wildflowers grew in the sun—masses of pink sweet pea. Through the dwindling trees, I saw the river.

Back east, the gorge now looked beautiful, lined with green hillsides that faded into a distant mist.

The road curved around the face of the cliff. Soon I looked across the river, and then I faced west. I pedaled in a complete circle, breathing hard, until at last I rolled into a sunny parking lot at the top. Carved stone railings lined the lot, and a curious building stood at the end: octagonal, with windows on every side, it perched like a sentinel over the river. A sign read, "Vista House, Crown Point."

I rolled across the sunny pavement to join Mary at the railing. From Crown Point, we could see up and down the massive Columbia River. With the distance in both directions, and the giant volume of air between us and the river and the opposite shore, I wished I could dive off and fly.

A group of tourists passed, two older and two younger. Mary began smiling. "Here you are!" the older woman exclaimed. "You made it!" Who were they?

It was Roger and June, the couple in the bright yellow jerseys that we'd met biking up Lolo Pass in Montana, eleven days ago.

"This is Jacob and Jenny," June was saying, introducing the young couple. "We finished our ride, and we've been visiting with them!" She explained to them how we'd met.

"We've just got two days left," Mary said when June finished. Everyone oohed dramatically. Mary continued, "We're staying with friends in Portland tonight."

"Well, let's get another picture!" Roger said. "Before and after!" When they heard we didn't have a map of Portland, they handed theirs to Mary.

Leaving Crown Point, the road headed more directly west, and after a few turns I didn't get any more views upriver. This was still Route 30, but it was wider and bordered by sunny fields. After an uneventful hour, the road began to drop, and I had a feeling that this was the last time.

MARY AND I MET IN Troutdale and set off for the final stretch of the day. The river looked so different, narrow and lined with buildings and roads and parking lots. It didn't seem like the mighty Columbia we'd traveled along for days.

The traffic increased on the road parallel to our bike path. We stopped to wait at a crosswalk as cars screeched past. The bike path turned away from the river and merged with a sidewalk. We reached another intersection. How did Mary know where to go? The "bike path" dumped us into one intersection after another. I stayed behind Mary, trying to check for cars before each crossing, my legs exhausted.

At last we turned onto a quiet street. Somehow Mary had found The Bike

Commune, a shop that friends had recommended. We wheeled our heavy bikes in the open doorway.

No one acknowledged us. Conversations buzzed as young people in grungy clothes worked on bikes. I had a feeling many were hanging out, fixing their own bikes. When someone finally approached, I told him I needed new tires.

"You just want the tires?"

"I'd like them put on," I said, feeling like a fool for not doing it myself.

"Hey Dave!" he called. "Can you get this woman tires?!"

I stood by my unwieldy bike as a young guy came over. After wordlessly eyeing my wheels, he trudged to a cabinet and dug out a pair of tires. They looked worn but cost as much as new tires, but I was too uncomfortable to question it. I couldn't find a different shop—I just wanted to get this over with.

"Take off your bags." Dave's monotone interrupted my thoughts. I struggled to position my heavy bike, leaning it on a workstand while Dave stood unmoving. I unclipped a bag. The bike's weight shifted, and I had to catch it and readjust it. Dave watched as the bags came off. I carried them to a corner where I hoped they'd be out of the way, while Dave lifted my bike into the workstand and removed a wheel.

Mary drifted over. Getting a bike boxed cost fifty dollars, plus the shipping fee, so she'd decided to do it herself. "There's another shop where they might give me the box," she said. I knew I would have paid the money, the same way I was paying them to change the tires, whereas Mary would have bought the tires and changed them herself.

"It's not that I can't change a tire," I reminded myself. "I'm tired, and it would take a long time." Did Dave think I didn't know how? Did he think I was a moron for going on a bike trip and not putting on my own tires? He didn't ask anything about me or show any interest in where I was from, and my confidence sagged onto the floor until I felt so stupid and self-conscious that I went outside to wait.

Early evening had come, bringing some shade at last, and I sank down onto the curb in front of the shop. Some punk-dressed girls were working on their bikes out front—giggling as they tried to figure out what to do. "They're not part of the inner circle," I imagined. "They don't go inside. But at least they're here, confident enough to try."

"I'm just tired," I told myself again. I wasn't "messing up." I was tired, and Dave was unfriendly, and I was anxious about the end of the trip. I stared across the street, glad to be doing nothing.

## Tillamook Forest, in which we spend our last night and I realize it was better just to have lived it

THE HOUSE IN PORTLAND WAS a rush of people: Mary's friend Kelly, her boyfriend Bruce, and several housemates. But with two days of biking left to reach the Pacific, it wasn't time to "stop" yet. I held my breath, keeping separate from their post-college lifestyle of late nights and drinking and band practice. The next day, Mary and I would head west. Then the cross-country trip would be over, and Kelly would meet us at the ocean and bring us back to Portland. Then would be the time to relax. Except that a few days later, Mary would fly back east, and I'd be on my own.

Online, I used a mapping site to plan a route out of Portland. I picked the shortest route; we'd cross one of the many bridges over the Willamette River that flowed through the middle of the city. Then, eight campgrounds dotted the road between Portland and Oceanside, Oregon. Mary and I had picked Oceanside as our final destination because it was the closest coastal town.

The next morning, we rode out on pared-down bikes—we'd left behind extra food, clothing, books, and maps. Following the Internet directions, we headed for the river. Soon we rode along a multilane corridor filled with morning traffic. More lanes joined our road, until it began to look disturbingly like an interstate. We had only one set of directions; it was too late to reroute ourselves. Dismayed, I watched the road grow to six lanes in each direction, and then the bridge came into view. As we rode onto it, cars shot past, shifting lanes left and right without signaling. Mary and I lumbered along. Giant highway signs rose over the crest of the bridge, and my heart thumped: "ROUTE 8, LEFT LANE." We had to cross six lanes of traffic! If we didn't, we'd end up on a highway heading north.

I chugged over the bridge, paying no attention to the river or the skyline view of Portland. Mary stayed behind me. When we were halfway across, I tried to pick up speed as the exit came into view. Then I glanced back and saw a break in the traffic. One last car flew past. A glut of new cars headed onto the bridge five hundred feet back. This would be our only chance.

"Let's go!" I yelled to Mary and veered left. I crossed one lane, then two, pedaling as hard as I could. I crossed a third lane and a fourth, not daring to check on the oncoming cars. We crossed the final two lanes and rode up along the left side of the highway, still pedaling hard to reach the safety of the exit. My heart pounded as a car whistled past, and then another passed and honked. I ignored it, focusing on the exit.

At last we rolled onto the exit ramp, and when it was clear, we angled back to the right side of the road. I tried to slow my breathing as we coasted down the curving ramp. My heart still pounded, but it wasn't fear—I felt excited. That had been a huge rush!

The new road had no shoulder, but the cars were less frantic. As miles passed, the city dwindled into housing developments and strip malls. I only knew we passed through towns because I saw them on the map. Mary pulled ahead and out of sight.

When I saw a sign for the library in Hillsboro, I stopped for the restroom. Then, because I was there, I checked my email and found a message from Dave, the man we'd met in the Badlands five weeks earlier. He'd emailed us the photo he'd taken: there Mary and I stood, in our jackets for protection from the wind, the jagged mud hills behind us under a cloudy sky. It seemed like years ago.

Then I saw a strange address in my inbox. I opened the message—it was from Donald, the man we'd met in the tunnel, who'd insisted on getting our email addresses. He didn't use capital letters or complete sentences. He wrote that I impressed him, and that he was active in the outdoors. He wanted to meet, and suggested we go boating on the ocean.

My stomach turned; I didn't even *know* him! I didn't want to hang out with him!

*I don't have to!* I didn't want Donald to interfere with the final moments of the trip. I'd leave the message unanswered until I returned to Portland.

I also got an email with contact info for friends-of-friends in Portland. But after yesterday, I didn't feel pulled to spend more time there.

Five miles after the library, I rode through Cornelius, another centerless town where gas stations clogged the road. A poster advertised the Berry Festival that weekend. If I came though again, on my own after Mary flew home, I'd be able to go.

A few miles later, I pulled over to rest in a strip mall. A faded sign at the end of the row read, "Simone's Diner." I hadn't planned to stop, but I walked over. The faded words illogically suggested that the food must be good, as if hordes of customers had worn out the sign.

Bustling greeted me as I stepped inside. A short woman behind a register pointed at the counter, and I moved over and slid onto a stool as if her waving hand controlled me. A young waitress strode by, handing me a menu as she passed. I glanced at it, verifying that they served grilled cheese and seeing which potato side dish I'd be eating that day. Then I looked around. The woman at the register moved faster than anyone I'd ever seen, and her voice barked orders at customers. "You have two fives!" she snapped at a man, snatching them from his outstretched hand. "I give three dollar back to you!"

The waitress stopped by me. "Ready?" Her eyebrows lifted. She had Asian features, like the woman at the register, but was younger and taller. Maybe they were mother and daughter.

"I'd like a grilled cheese, potato salad, and a chocolate malt, please."

She scribbled on her pad, snatched away the menu, and turned to the kitchen window to tack up the order. In the kitchen, a large man stared at the row of order slips, scratching his head. A chocolate malt slammed onto the counter in front of me. "That ought to cool you off!" the waitress said with almost a smile, dropping a straw next to the glass as she walked away.

I ripped open the straw wrapper and poked the straw into the malt. I sucked on the straw, but nothing happened. I sucked harder, watching the thick drink slowly move up the straw. At last it arrived, and I gratefully swallowed, chocolate filling my head. The heat of biking was dissipating into the cool restaurant, and I realized that the tension that had built while I rode was leaving, too. The fast-paced staff didn't stress me out—I liked them.

"I give you twenty-three cents!" I turned to watch the scene at the register. "I keep check!" She whipped it from the customer's hand and skewered it on a metal pike that held checks. The man looked blank, as if trying to figure out what had happened.

THE ROAD PASSED THROUGH TREES and came out into farmland. The change from suburbs to rural land was so abrupt, it didn't feel real, as if I'd just been transported by magic. I came to a stop, pulled out my water bottle, and drank at the side of the road. When I swallowed, I noticed the silence. I stood still, listening for birdsong or bugs, but all I heard was the click-click-click of a sprinkler across the cornfield. The air felt hot, and the sun beat down.

A truck passed, and a guy riding in the back stood up and mooned me. A chord of fear struck in my heart—I was alone, out on a back road. "But I've been riding alone all summer," I reminded myself. "He was just joking."

The day grew hotter as I pedaled; I didn't know how far I had gone.

At last, sweating in the sun, I passed a sign for Gales Creek. A building came into view, cluttered with newspaper dispensers, patio chairs, an empty produce rack, and cardboard boxes. It was a general store.

I rode into the shade of the awning that circled the building. Inside, I glanced over the candy bars. Then I noticed a giant watermelon on the counter by the register, with its end sliced off to reveal a deep pink interior. Was it for sale?

I drifted toward the melon. "Want me to fill that?" The man behind the counter nodded at the water bottle in my hands.

"Yes, please," I said, handing it over. "Do you sell watermelon?"

"Sure!" he replied, heading for the sink. After handing back my bottle, he got out a butcher knife and cut a round slice off the end of the melon. He cut it in half and put one half onto a paper plate.

"Could I . . . get *more?*" I asked. He added the second half-slice to the plate and looked for my approval. "How about two more?" I grinned sheepishly.

He cut another round slice off and cut it in half, piling the pieces on the plate, as a woman came in from the back room. She picked up the plate and placed it on a scale, and charged me a dollar and ten cents.

I took the plate outside, sat on a bench in the shade, and ate all four pieces. Then I threw the rinds in a trash bin and sat again. The quiet heat droned around the edge of the porch. How far ahead was Mary? Would she stop at the first campground? My head ached with a dull throbbing. The bench seemed to tug at my upper body. I couldn't help myself. I lay down behind my bike and fell asleep.

I woke when a giant truck roared into the parking spot next to me. A man slid out and entered the store. Sitting up, I blinked at the sunny surroundings outside the awning as my eyes adjusted to the brilliance. The ache had gone from my head. I checked my watch: two-thirty. I'd slept about an hour.

The truck's headlights stared at me like curious eyes. Another truck sat in the lot, away from the building; *that* truck hadn't woken me. But the driver of the giant truck had parked right where I lay, even though there were plenty of other spots. He returned and introduced himself as Lawrence and asked where I was from. As I answered "North Carolina," a woman came out.

"North Carolina!" she said. "This must be like an alien planet!"

"Relative to *Portland,* this is an alien planet!" I thought, but I just smiled.

"Well, watch out for the wackos!" Lawrence said, reaching for his door handle, and a chill crept down my spine.

But as his truck roared to life, the woman said, "If you have any trouble, I'm Kathy—just ask for me." She left in the other truck.

I wheeled my bike back into the sunlight.

A few miles past the Gales Creek store, I came to the T intersection at Route 6. Turning left, I rode through pine forest with shadows stretched across the road. I passed a restaurant at the intersection labeled Glenwood; if I came back this way, this was where I would turn to head north toward the Washington coast. "I'll stop and eat at the restaurant," I thought, planning my day; I'd start early, to be here by lunch. Then I remembered the Berry Festival and a dollar theater I'd seen. *Just wait and see.*

A few miles into Tillamook State Forest, I reached the Gales Creek Campground. A gravel driveway sloped down into quiet shade, with chirping in the shadowy trees like how I imagined a jungle would sound. Giant ferns hung over the drive as it descended. Mossy trees surrounded me. "This is beautiful," I thought, and then, "I hope Mary's here so I don't have to climb back up this hill."

A car crunched around the turn ahead, so I pulled over. As it neared, a ranger leaned out the window.

"Your friend's up ahead!" he said as his car crawled past.

I rolled the rest of the way down and stopped at a kiosk. A map showed cheaper tent sites, set back from the road. I wheeled my bike toward them, onto a carpet of pine needles. Shade filled the campground, with only patches of sunlight. Back in the trees, Mary's bike leaned on a picnic table, where Mary sat reading *Travels with Charley.*

It was the last evening of the trip, and I felt surrounded by free time. From deep in my bags, I got out a yellow, spiral-bound notebook that I'd carried all the way across the country. I'd imagined that I would write about the trip as it happened, that this would be the notebook where I composed a great literary work, with perfect descriptions of the places we saw. But I hadn't written anything. It had been all I could do to jot notes in my planner at the end of each day.

I took the notebook down to the creek, a narrow stream this late in the season, tumbling down the middle of a rocky bed. The splashing water faded out the other sounds: shrieks of children playing upstream, the rumble of an

RV pulling into a campsite. Small trees leaned over the water, and sunlight fell through. I washed my face and then sat on a clean log—moss free, as if spring floods had scoured it. I took off my shoes and socks, and my bare feet dangled above the ground. Across the creek, the forest wall rose steeply, making the trees even taller. Prehistoric ferns hung down.

I opened the notebook and started describing the campground. I wouldn't try to remember the start of the trip, I decided; I'd write about where I sat right now. At least this one memory would be vivid. But as descriptions flew from my pen, they struck me as flat, not capturing any feeling.

Mary called down from the campsite. "Did you bring the little fuel bottle?"

I turned. "No, just the big one!" She hovered at the top of the trail. She might want company, but I wanted to write. If I sat up there, she'd talk to me.

I kept writing. But I couldn't capture how I felt. Why wasn't it working?

A few minutes later, Mary called down again. I'd completed about a page. The writing was hyper, with thoughts jumping all over the place. Maybe it would have been like this all summer, if I had tried to write. Maybe it was better just to have lived it.

## Oceanside, Oregon, or the last day

MARY AND I PACKED AND ate quickly. Then we climbed up the gravel driveway. It wasn't difficult, maybe because we did it first thing in the day, or maybe because my tingling nerves added a touch of adrenaline. Leaving camp today felt like it had so many other days, except a thought kept popping into my head: today is our last day!

I felt disoriented by the sudden change from hot, sunny wastelands to the lush greenery of the coast, with chilly air and clouds overhead. I almost resented the change, because the new scenery differed from the pictures I'd formed of how our last day would be.

The trees parted at the road. Across the pavement stood a sign: thirty-five miles to Tillamook. After Tillamook, it was another ten to Oceanside. I was only forty-five miles away! The number was so small compared with the thousands we'd traveled.

I wore my lavender hoody, which had been packed since a chill morning in Yellowstone. I needed it, even when the road began to climb through the old forest. Between the hills drifted a haze with an unnatural bluish tint. I'd overheard news of forest fires—could this be a result? After several minutes we reached a sign: "Summit Coast Range Elev. 1586." I hadn't realized we'd be climbing a "mountain range" on our last day! It was ironic, given my inability to accept the never-ending hills. I didn't feel resentful today. The uphills would have to stop soon: we were almost out of land.

After the summit, the road rolled along, and I had to stop and don my raincoat for warmth. When Mary pulled ahead, my brain started circling through thoughts about where I would meet her. But we didn't have to find somewhere to sleep, I realized. I'd just meet her at the ocean. All I had to do was keep biking.

Mary receded until I rounded a bend and didn't see her ahead. Evergreens filled the view. Around each curve, I looked for the ocean, even though it was miles away.

I passed an orange "Construction Ahead" sign and braked as I neared a line of cars stopped at a man with a portable stop sign. Ahead, construction trucks pulled in and out of a parking area marked with more orange. Beyond, the road disappeared in the trees.

How far away was the end? I remembered a construction zone we'd traversed in South Dakota; I hadn't been able to keep up with the pilot truck, and I'd been on the road when traffic came through in the opposite direction. But in South Dakota I'd been able to see for a mile ahead and pull over safely; here, the road curved through trees.

What should I do? The pilot truck arrived and U-turned, and the idling cars followed it out. I pedaled toward the construction zone. Several workmen loitered near the road, so I stopped.

"Is it okay if I bike through?" I called.

The men gathered around. "It's dangerous in there," one said. "The road's all broken up."

"You don't wanna bike through there," another said.

"Do you know what happened to my friend?" I asked. "She's biking, too—did she go through?" They shook their heads, shrugging.

"That's because she wasn't stupid enough to ask," I thought. I didn't believe it was dangerous; they meant well, but I detected patronizing tones in their voices. I wished I hadn't stopped.

"I can get off and walk the bad parts," I said. The men kept shaking their heads. Could they stop me? Would it be rude to move on? Then a broad man with shades and stringy brown hair approached. He held out his hands like he was about to clap them, but instead he chopped them down through the air.

"Just wait a few minutes, and I'll take you through," he said in a gravelly voice.

"Oh, my God," I thought. "It's Macho Man Randy Savage!"

I reluctantly agreed.

"No problem." He jerked his head as if throwing off my thanks. He bustled across the construction site, his large sunglasses hiding his face, and the other men drifted away.

"He really could be Randy Savage," I thought. "Who knows what professional wrestlers do when they get older?"

A new group of cars waited, and the pilot truck returned for them a minute later; it couldn't be that far to the other side. The truck led the new group away, and I wished I could just go. It was the last day of the trip and here I was, waiting for a ride I didn't want! The cars disappeared, and quiet settled over the road; the man with the sign flipped it from "Slow" back to "Stop." Across the lot, the Macho Man[36] strode around, barking orders that no one seemed to heed.

The clouds were lifting, with blue patches showing through the treetops. More cars arrived and waited as a minute ticked past. Then the pilot truck returned again, and I wanted to scream. What if I just rode in? Would anyone notice? But I couldn't, after I'd stopped to ask.

Back and forth went the pilot truck as the morning passed. Maybe the Macho Man had forgotten me. But then he reappeared, heading my way. "Come on," he rasped. I followed him to a pickup hitched to a trailer.

I pulled off my handlebar bag to protect my camera as the Macho Man moved toward my bike. "It's really heavy—"

"No problem." He grasped the lightweight top tube and handlebar and, without bending his knees, lifted. My bike rose and then lurched forward as he realized how heavy it was and shoved it onto the trailer, barely clearing the edge. He let go, and it fell onto its side; I imagined the camp stove crunching under the impact. The rear wheel spun, hanging over the back of the trailer, with only the weight of the bags holding the bike on. I expected him to fix it, but he slapped his hands and moved toward the driver's door. I tried to push my bike farther on, but it didn't budge. The Macho Man's door slammed shut. I moved to the passenger door as he started the engine.

As soon as I shut my door he pulled out, bouncing onto the road as I hurried to buckle my seatbelt. I glanced back: my bike was still on the trailer.

"I'm happy to help you out!" he said, nodding and checking his mirrors as the truck swerved.

"Thanks." I forced a smile. We passed a crater-like circle where the road dropped about three inches—it was several feet wide. A few more craters passed. A five-year-old on a tricycle could have maneuvered around the craters. Why hadn't I just ridden through?

We reached the far side, where the pilot truck was preparing to lead more cars, and the Macho Man pulled over. I got out and hurried back as he strode toward my bike. "I can help!" I said, but he waved me off.

"I got it." He yanked my bike off the trailer by its handlebar. The heavy bag scraped across the trailer, and as soon as it cleared the edge, the whole bike dropped. I lunged forward to reduce the impact; the chain rings dug into my stomach, and I dropped to my knees to avoid being pierced. The tires thudded to the ground. I struggled out from under the bike. I hoped the drop hadn't caused a leak in one of the tires.

The Macho Man let go, and I reached to catch the handlebar as it twisted, the weight of the bags pulling the bike over. "Thanks," I forced out again.

"Happy to help!" the Macho Man replied, and then he got back into his truck and it roared to life, kicking up gravel as he U-turned and followed the cars back down the road.

I held my bike up in the quiet woods. Twenty feet back stood the man with the stop sign, staring at the ground as he waited to flip it. I leaned my bike on my hip, catching a pedal with my leg to hold it upright, and hung the handlebar bag. Then I straightened out my raincoat, which had twisted during the debacle of catching the falling bike. I'd invested in the coat that spring—my first expensive Gore-Tex raincoat. As I smoothed out the material, I saw a four-inch hole gaping in the side, smeared with grease where the chain rings had ripped it. A lump rose in my throat.

Wheeling the bike onto the pavement, I got on and pushed off.

The sun blinked out from the clouds, the sky brighter through the trees. A tear rolled down my cheek. My coat had a big hole! I wished I could cry on my mom and have her say, "I'll buy you a new one." I could buy myself a new one! But it was so much money. Maybe the hiking store sold patch kits.

But even as I reasoned through a solution, tears kept coming. The stupid Macho Man had been so careless with my bike, and arrogant to think he was helping me. Why had I stopped? I hadn't even ridden the whole way on the last day, and now I was probably way behind Mary. I wished I could redo the past hour.

I pulled into a rest area and rode to the deserted end of the lot, where I sat on the curb and cried. The day should have felt triumphant, and instead the Macho Man had ruined it.

After a while my tears subsided, and I took off the raincoat because the sun was finally shining. I rolled it up and packed it.

Two hours later, I passed a sign for Tillamook. I hadn't had lunch, and there might be an interesting cheese factory tour, but I didn't stop or look for the downtown. I crossed Route 101, the Pacific Coast Highway. I just wanted to keep going.

After a few more miles, I came to the split. I could take the right hand turn, heading northwest toward Tillamook Bay, then following the bay to the ocean and curving around to reach Oceanside from the north. Or I could turn left, heading directly west toward the coast and a town called Netarts, and then curving around to reach Oceanside from the south. The bay road might be prettier, but the road through Netarts was shorter, and since I was behind Mary, I turned left.

Now I rode past farmland. I hadn't imagined flat fields crammed between the Summit Coast Range and the Pacific. The air felt clearer and hotter. Which road had Mary taken? Would we have the same first view of the ocean? I kept biking, rolling up and down as another hour passed.

I reached Netarts. The ocean had to be close! Then I rounded a curve and saw blue through the trees, darker than the sky.

The trees thinned and the ocean spread out below me. A sandbar stretched along the coast. Behind it, blue water reached to a hazy horizon. I stared, trying to make myself realize that I had made it.

The road sloped down, bringing me closer to sea level. "Only a few miles to go!" I thought. I pedaled along in the cool shade, catching glimpses of the ocean on my left. Then the trees broke to frame a picture-window view: rippling water flowed in around the sandbar, which had ribbed patterns like a giant fish. Pools of cornflower blue and lavender filled the ribs, and white waves crashed on the far side. A clear sky rose overhead, except for hints of cloud far out over the ocean. To the south, haze covered a blue silhouette ridge that jutted out from the coast. Three evergreens stood in the foreground, stark against the ocean backdrop.

The road dropped more earnestly, clinging to the hillside, and a wide, sandy beach appeared on my left. I looked down on the tiny people walking on the beach—the white dots of their sneakers, the dark blots of their shadows on the sand. Whiffs of sea breeze reached me.

When the trees ahead cleared, I saw three sea stacks, massive rocks standing offshore, separated from the coast by erosion. They looked as tall as ten-story buildings. Dark ridges ran up their sides, and white coated their tops—bird poop, I guessed. Waves crashed at their bases.

As I neared water level, the trees cleared and houses lined the road and covered the hillside ahead. The road sloped into Oceanside. I rolled past the houses, looking for Mary's bike. People had parked along the road; the sound of the surf reached me. It was the perfect beach town: quiet, lazy, with so little traffic you could cross the street without checking. You could walk home from the beach barefoot, sandy feet padding on hot pavement.

At the cross streets, the wind off the ocean rushed over me, bringing with it the salty air. Bright flowers bobbed before weathered fences, and a handful of power lines crisscrossed overhead. A corner market had an old Pepsi sign. Faded red paint spelled out "Bayside Market and Deli." A cinderblock building with small windows was a restaurant. A building up the hill might be a cafe.

I turned toward the water. The wind whipped at me as I pedaled off the end of the road into a parking lot. Mary was not there. Could I have arrived first? She must have taken the northern road, but it wasn't that much longer.

I tried to clear Mary thoughts out of my head. I was at the ocean! A dozen cars sat in the sunny lot, and a fence bordered the beach. The sand spread wide and empty to the water.

Leaning my bike on the fence, I looked out at the water. "I'm here! I did it!" I told myself. But none of the thoughts pierced inside me; they floated on the surface as I made myself keep thinking them. I removed my helmet and bandana, abandoning my hair to the wind, and hitched myself up to sit on the fence, legs dangling.

Where was Mary? Was she okay?

"Just sit and appreciate the view," I told myself.

I thought back to Cape May, New Jersey, to our first day on the trip: a vague memory of being surrounded by light blue air at the Atlantic Ocean, encouraged by the calm sunny day. What color would stick in my memory of today? Everything looked darker, from the vibrant blue of the sky to the darker blue of the water, with long white waves rolling in and the strong salt breeze. The three sea stacks drew my eyes to where the tiny waves crashed at their massive bases.

I squinted up to check the sun; there was plenty of time for Mary to arrive. Three teenage girls carrying skimboards passed, headed for a sandy path through the beach grass toward the water. Seagulls flapped overhead. Far down the beach, people emerged from a tunnel in the rock wall. A family passed with blankets, beach toys, and an umbrella. I wished someone would talk to me, would ask where I was from.

*What if Mary never comes?*

All I could do was wait.

I felt too antsy to sit on the fence. I pushed myself off. I left my bike, so Mary would know I'd arrived, and headed back to the buildings.

The restaurant would probably have grilled cheese, but I wanted to check out the place up the hill. The wind quieted as I reentered the houses, and the heat of the sun returned. The town made me want to walk barefoot, but it seemed affected; it's not like I'd been on the beach.

I reached the hill and trudged up toward the cafe. Wide glass windows looked out at the ocean. A banner read "Espresso." Masses of colorful flowers grew in clumps: white daisies, wine-colored cosmos, lemony gladiolas, and low nasturtiums in all shades of orange. A band of mango-colored California poppies spilled onto the grass like a comical poppy war-party leaving the flower bed. At the far side of the flowers stood a bench.

I headed in. As the door closed on the wind, I realized how much a part of the outdoors I felt: hot, wind-whipped, browned tan, and like my skin was too tight over my bones. I fit in better out there. Inside, the silence oppressed me; the air was too still.

There was chili, but I assumed it had meat and ordered vegetable quiche and a pecan roll. Then I looked at the shop's bookshelf, noting the books about the Pacific Northwest, where I'd soon be biking. One oversize book documented the giant trees of the West Coast: redwood, sitka spruce, cedar, sequoia. I'd heard of redwoods but not the others. Some were thin but tall; others had massive trunks. "Largest" might refer to height, width, or "board feet"—the volume of the tree, or how many boards could be made from it. When I read "board feet," a sick feeling passed through me. It was like measuring the size of a human by how many buckets of compost she would generate.

While I ate my quiche, I tried to clear my head, to calm down. I wanted simply to be in the cafe, but instead I noticed where I was, sitting in a coffee shop, like a stereotype of myself. Here I had reached the Pacific Ocean, the climactic moment of the whole summer; I should be celebrating, enjoying the beach. Instead, what was I doing? Sitting in a coffee shop, same as always. But I hadn't had anyone to celebrate with. I hadn't known what to do, besides come here.

The sticky pecan roll was bigger than my fist. I didn't want it. At the adjacent table, the waitress took an order, and she told the patron that the chili was vegetarian. I took a bite of the roll, trying not to be upset.

Then the door opened and there was Mary, with tan cheeks and helmet imprints on her forehead, her bangs sticking every which way. I felt embarrassed to be found in the cafe but also relieved to see her. She hobbled over, her shoes clicking, and slowly slid into a seat. "How long have you been here?"

"Maybe an hour. Did you hit that construction?"

"Yeah. I biked through."

"I figured you would. I shouldn't have stopped—they made me wait and take a ride. It took forever . . . did you go through Netarts, or the other way?"

"Netarts. I stopped in Tillamook and met this guy who worked at the radio station, so I ended up going back to the station to be interviewed, and then I just hung out awhile."

Of course she'd been fine. She'd had a final adventure. Why had I taken the shorter route instead of the scenic bay road? Why hadn't I relaxed and enjoyed the beach, instead of wondering about her?

Because I didn't know how. She'd been right when she'd said it in the Badlands: it wasn't her fault I couldn't relax.

I licked the gooey residue of the pecan roll off my fingers. "You want anything?"

"Nah, not here."

Mary and I returned to the wind and sun. The day seemed even brighter. "What time is Kelly coming?" I asked.

"I dunno—midafternoon?" I followed her down the hill.

Mary decided to get lunch and a beer at the restaurant. I followed her inside, but became anxious. It was quiet and dark, and I couldn't stand the thought of sitting there. What did I want? Should I have a beer, too? Maybe it would help me relax. But I didn't want to be happy only because I was drunk.

Sitting outside would be better, I thought, so I told Mary I'd be by the flowers. As soon as I left, I felt uncomfortable. I had made the wrong decision; I should celebrate with Mary. But I kept walking.

I trudged back along the road and up the hill to the bench by the flowers. They were amazing. A hummingbird zoomed in, visiting one bloom, then darting to the next. He landed on a stalk, and I saw his tiny iridescent body. The bench boards were warm through the thin material of my skirt. The sun beat down and warmed my hoody. No one was around.

I pulled out a postcard and wrote it to Mom and Dad, noticing how it would sound when they read it, as if I had been happy:

> 7/31 Hello from Oceanside OR! We lucked out when we
> picked this town—the view is spectacular—but our ride
> hasn't shown up yet so we haven't taken pictures. The waves
> are rolling in and there are flowers. The weather matches our
> first day! Love, Emily

I lay down on my side on the bench, pulling my knees up. I didn't know what to do to stop feeling so "off," but lying still might be the one thing that would help. I breathed out, feeling my bones settling into the bench, and listened to the noise around me: the wind, the distant crashing of waves, the cry of a seagull, the lone rumble of a truck starting at the bottom of the hill . . .

When I woke up, time had passed. Without sitting up, I checked my watch: two-thirty. It was like yesterday in Gales Creek; I'd slept for an hour.

The day had gotten even brighter. Next to me, in my sideways view, the flowers endlessly bobbed, still colorful but the colors were dropping away as the sun crossed the sky. The wind still blew, but everything seemed quieter. I knew I was on the bench at the cafe, but when I tried to recall the bigger picture, I got confused. "I am in Oceanside," I remembered. "I have finished the bike trip." My brain was frying, or evaporating.

Why didn't I feel happy? I had done everything wrong. I had stopped at the construction zone. I had let the Macho Man mishandle my bike and rip my coat. I hadn't stopped in Tillamook. I hadn't taken the longer route along the bay. I'd sat on the fence by the beach, but I hadn't talked to anyone. I'd worried about Mary instead of enjoying being there. I hadn't asked about the chili being vegetarian. I had ordered the pecan roll, and eaten it, even though I hadn't wanted it. And I hadn't stayed with Mary to have a beer. Even if I hadn't gotten a beer, I could have stayed to sit with Mary.

I kept lying there. At least I felt better than I had before sleeping. Then Mary came up the hill. Kelly and Bruce had arrived.

FIRST WE STOOD AT THE fence at the edge of the parking lot, where Mary's bike now leaned behind mine. Kelly snapped a picture of us with our loaded bikes. Then we gathered around the hood of the car to make signs. Kelly had brought scraps of cardboard and a black marker. We made one that read, "Oceanside, Oregon 7/31" and another that read, "3291 miles, 5299 km." Mary had non-American friends, so we included the mileage in kilometers. I made a third sign, as a joke: "Pacific Ocean, Elevation 0." But no one laughed.

Then, in a mirror image of our first day, we took off our bags, stacking them along the fence. When our bikes were bare, we wheeled them to the beach. My helmet, hanging from the top tube, bumped against me as I carried the bike over the soft sand. Mom wasn't there to try to help. We reached the packed, wave-smoothed sand, and I lowered my bike and rolled it, leaving a faint track behind me.

Mary talked to Kelly, smiling. Did the beer make her bubbly, or was she just excited to be there? I didn't feel anything, except worry that I'd get sand in my tires. I almost felt like I wasn't even on the beach . . . like I watched my body go through the actions, like none of it was real.

At the water, Mary and I U-turned to face Kelly and held up our signs. I plastered on a smile, knowing I would want to be smiling in the pictures. Kelly snapped one after another, shooting the whole roll. Mary planned to develop the film today and send the photos as postcards from Portland.

Then we wheeled our bikes around and approached the crashing waves to dip our front tires into the Pacific, the symbolic completion of the rear-wheel dipping we had done in the Atlantic on May 2nd. We stopped below the wave line, held our signs, and looked at Kelly. She was poised, waiting for a wave to hit our tires. I listened to the crash, to the swoosh of the wave rolling in. It splashed against my front tire, which sank into the sand. I hoped no sand would get inside. I'd have to wash it off with fresh water, because salt water might corrode the metal.

A larger crash sounded, and I looked away from the camera to watch the wave roll in. Mary kept smiling at the camera as the wave swirled around her feet, soaking her shoes. She laughed. I felt only dismay as it reached my feet. Another wave came, and I tried to lift my bike. I lost my balance and fell, toppling with my bike into the wet sand. Mary kept laughing and getting soaked. I knew she wasn't laughing at me. I just wished I felt how she must feel.

I got up and we rolled our bikes out of the surf and lay them down. Then Kelly pulled out a green bottle of champagne and four crystal champagne flutes, and the crystal glasses made me want to cry because she had brought her good crystal to a beach for us. She and Bruce celebrated as if they'd been with us for every pedal stroke, as if today meant a lot to them. I held two glasses as Mary pulled out the cork. She stepped back in case the champagne overflowed, but it didn't.

Kelly snapped more pictures as Mary poured the two glasses, and then she and Bruce poured glasses, too, and we all toasted. I forced myself to drink the sour champagne.

We left our bikes and walked down the beach. Near the sea stacks, we took more pictures of Mary and me, with our arms around each other's shoulders. We must've looked like the best of friends, but we were separate. We walked the entire length of the beach and back. Our bikes lay on the sand as we approached, as if they were sleeping.

We returned to the car and loaded our bags into the trunk.

"Hey, I almost forgot!" Mary said. She held out her hand, and I saw the beach pebbles she'd picked up in Cape May, to throw into the Pacific. So Mary and I crossed the sand one last time. She gave me her camera. I took a picture of the rocks in her hand, and then she headed to the water's edge to throw them. Against the bright sky she became almost a silhouette, her shadow under her feet, and her watery reflection stretching back across the shallow waves, and as she threw each rock, I snapped a picture.

## Portland, in which the current saga ends

A N HOUR AFTER MARY THREW her rocks into the waves at the Pacific Ocean, we were back in Portland. The hot car ride, with sandy feet in the back seat, had made me nauseous. We arrived home, and I hurried out of the car, breathing the open air.

"Mary must be excited to be done, to be going home," I thought. She'd done it: she'd met her goal of crossing the country. If only my goals had been that simple.

We would spend a day in Portland, and her flight left the next morning. My heart convulsed unpleasantly when I thought about that morning, when I'd ride out of Portland alone. I planned to go to the same campground in Tillamook Forest for the first night, and then a state park for the second night, but after that, I head north up the coast with no idea what I'd find.

The next morning, the others slept in. I cooked myself my hot cereal, adding a few berries and pineapple wedges from the fridge. Then I organized my bags. All I had to do the next day, I told myself, was carry my bike down the steps of the porch, load on the bags, and ride out. I'd asked Kelly about the bridges across the Willamette River, and she'd written directions to a bridge with a bike lane, so I would not have to make the six-lanes-of-traffic left turn that Mary and I had managed when we left Portland the first time.

Later that day, Mary left with Kelly to get a box for packing her bike. I stayed to check email. When I turned off the computer, the silence of the house settled around me. I found a Gipsy Kings CD, one that we listened to at the bakery at home, and got out my journal.

Reaching the Pacific yesterday hadn't lived up to my daydreams. I hadn't felt triumphant; I hadn't talked to anyone interesting on the beach. Worse, I'd felt like a failure for having such a problematic day; I'd been depressed but pasted on a big smile for the photos.

Would the Pacific arrival have been less disappointing if I hadn't anticipated it so much? It was hard not to anticipate such a big moment. But now it seemed like I should have known that a moment so anticipated was sure to be disappointing, if not disastrous.

Life was never going to match my daydreams. Just because the Pacific Ocean had been the official end of the trip, it wasn't going to be climactic or happy. The elation didn't arrive just as you hit the mountain's peak or the spectacular view. Real life didn't have endings like movies did. Life just went on and on. Some other moment would be happy. And while the happy moment wouldn't last, there'd always be another one.

Could I have salvaged yesterday's moment, at the beach when I felt so depressed? I'd thought of so many tricks over the past few months: sitting still to calm my thoughts, repeating a mantra, accepting times of sadness as learning experiences, accepting depression as part of me while still seeking to let go of it. But I never thought to apply the tricks when a dire moment came.

I'd gone on the bike trip hoping for change. Had I succeeded? Based on yesterday, it didn't seem so. But I remembered back in college, in my intro art class, the first day we'd gone outside to draw after weeks of "learning how to see" in the classroom. Faced with a wide forest view, all the lessons about turning off my brain (to let my eyes connect with my hand) had flown away, and I'd produced a stiff, ugly drawing of an isolated tree that my classmates had mocked in the critique. I'd felt ashamed. But the next time outside, I'd taken a moment to settle and recall the lessons before beginning to draw. Failure didn't mean the lessons were obliterated; I just had to keep trying to use them.

Sometimes it even seemed like a hurdle to personal change ballooned up just as I started climbing over it, as if an outside force wanted to keep me as I was. Or maybe it was an inside force. The closer I got to my goal, the harder it tried. So maybe my "failure" at the beach was actually a good sign: the force was getting desperate, because it knew I was close to success.

When Kelly and Mary returned, we took the handlebar and wheels off Mary's bike and packed it all into the box. I didn't know what Mary thought of her trip: I assumed she felt success, but *had* she achieved her goals? Was she still processing? I was still in the thick of it, but Mary had switched gears, as if she was ready to go home.

We went out to ship her bike, and to pick up yesterday's photos. The bike took up the back seat, so I sat in front and Mary climbed onto my lap. I wanted to put my arms around her and hug, but instead I sat stiffly, minimizing the surface area of our contact. I had not overcome my barriers to talking with her. Instead, I'd settled into a mode of travel that worked, keeping the tension under wraps. Even now, I couldn't reach out to her. We were in different places, with Mary done riding and heading back east, while I continued to travel.

"We're leaving each other tomorrow," she said, "after three months." Her voice sounded so caring, as if it were simple. How could she care about me, while I felt a confused mix of tension?

All the words I could respond with clogged in my throat; I didn't know what to say. I leaned forward and rested my chin on Mary's shoulder. I hoped it would convey that I cared about her. It seemed like all I could do.

Maybe it was harder to change patterns with old friends. Maybe I'd learn to be more open with new friends, and get some practice, and then be able to do it with old friends, too.

After our errands, Kelly took us to a restaurant in her neighborhood, The Pied Cow. It was in a Victorian house with extra seating on a patio in the backyard, where we sat under strings of holiday lights. We got coffee drinks and hummus. On the way home, we passed a dollar theater showing a rerun of *The Two Towers,* the second part of *The Lord of the Rings* trilogy, which I'd seen five times when it was first in the theater.

At home, the crew set about chopping and mixing dinner in the airy kitchen. We made summer rolls, stretchy rice paper wrappers filled with shredded carrot and cucumber, avocado, rice noodles, bean spouts, and tofu; a peanut-soy-ginger-garlic dipping sauce; and Chinese barbecue broccoli with zucchini and mushrooms. We took our loaded plates to eat at a tiny table in the backyard. We belonged on the pages of *Martha Stewart Living,* I thought, with our beautiful meal in our picturesque urban backyard. I was so clean and cool, and couldn't help but feel relief when I thought back on the dusty, hot, shadeless, sweaty past few weeks.

At nine-fifteen, I rode to the theater and got a ticket for *The Two Towers.* Settling into my seat, I imagined that seeing this movie again would take me back to the clear winter sky in Chapel Hill, and pre-trip memories. And when the movie ended, I'd experience the confidence I always felt when I mounted my bike to ride home, like Eowyn riding her steed into battle.

The lights dimmed and the movie started with music that instantly came back to me. Familiar scenes flashed on the screen. But the movie seemed slower, as if the theater had slowed down the film coming off the reel. I could see *more* somehow—I could see every shot the camera took. The music swelled to indicate a time to feel emotion, but instead of feeling it, I noticed that the filmmakers were toying with me. The characters delivered lines on cue, machinations revealed behind the movie's facade.

I also noticed the scenery, fitting it to places we had been that summer: the boulder-strewn plains of Rohan could be Montana, and the dark, overgrown Fangorn Forest looked like Tillamook State Forest where we had just camped. On the screen it all looked beautiful, but biking through the real thing, I'd felt hot and tired and had not even noticed the beauty.

The movie ended, and I didn't feel my usual thrilled state. While the credits rolled, I reviewed the directions from the theater back to Kelly's house. Then I exited and rode off down the dark street, feeling more like a creeping Gollum than a galloping Eowyn.

I tried to project confidence as I rode through Portland's nightlife; looking confident would make me safer. But inside I felt wobbly. As I kept going, though, an awareness of myself rose and the wobbliness left. I *felt* myself biking down the street, sure of my ability. I felt at home; bikes were so common in Portland that I bet I looked like a native. I was glad I hadn't slipped into a movie-related daydream and left the theater feeling elated. Instead, I had stayed in the real world. It wasn't as exciting as the movie world, but I was glad to be in it.

# Epilogue

THE DAY I LEFT PORTLAND, I stopped at the Berry Festival in Cornelius, and later I stopped in Forest Grove and stood outside the dollar theater I'd spotted three days earlier, trying to convince myself to see a matinee. But I felt anxious to reach the campground, so I kept going. Later in the day, I breezed past the Gales Creek country store. It wouldn't be the same if I stopped, I thought; the watermelon wouldn't be a surprise, and if the storekeeper remembered me, I wouldn't know how to explain why I was back.

When I arrived at the Tillamook State Forest campground, the tent sites were all taken, and I had to pay ten dollars for a regular spot. I tried to ignore the extra expense and enjoy my woodsy campsite. I finally had my solitude, but it echoed strangely about me.

Instead of Oceanside, I headed for Seaside, Oregon, and spent the next three weeks biking north up the coast and then curving east through Olympic National Park. Those travels seem like a different adventure than my summer going cross-country with Mary. It was only August, but the coast's cool breezes and chilly nights reminded me of fall. I stopped at a thrift store and bought long black running pants.

On August 23rd, I took a ferry out of Port Townsend, Washington, on the north coast of the Olympic Peninsula. The ferry brought me to Whidbey Island, a strip of land stretching west to east across the northern end of Puget Sound. I thought the island would be nice for my last day. Exiting the ferry lot, I rode into forest, climbing up the ridge of the island. After a few hours, I glimpsed water through the trees. The road dropped suddenly and led into the parking lot at the eastern ferry landing.

I stopped at the gate for a ticket to Mukilteo, north of Seattle, a short hop across an unmarked bay, and then, alert for signs, I rode past the parked cars to the dock. I rolled to a stop and got off, leaning my bike on a railing, and walked to the wall where ferry schedules were posted, making sure I was in the right place. Once I found my ferry listing, I relaxed, and then I noticed my bike across the cement.

I had stopped biking! That had been the end.

A feeling came over me, the feeling I used to get when Mom took us to the beach after class on the first day of school. The summer people would be gone, and the empty sands warned that change was coming—fall was coming—and it always seemed I could feel the change in the air.

The ferry took me across the bay, where friends from college picked me up at the terminal. We removed the bags from my bike for the last time before loading it onto their car's rack. Before I left Seattle, we took my bike to a shop to be disassembled and shipped to my parents. I hated leaving it in the shop, hanging in a workstand amidst other bikes and bike parts. What if they forgot whose it was? But the mechanic who handled it was suitably tattooed and pierced like my mechanic friends at home, a fact in which I tried to take comfort. I glanced back at my bike, saying a silent goodbye, and then followed my friends out the door.

I also shipped the tent and stove. The next afternoon, carrying only one of my bike bags, a backpack from my friends, and my sleeping bag, I boarded a bus for Boulder, Colorado.

The bus headed south and eventually reached the Columbia River. The gorge looked a lot more beautiful now, with no hazy heat. I began to wonder if the bus windows were tinted, deepening the colors of the scenery outside. After we crossed the river and got on the interstate, I tried to glimpse historic Route 30 up in the hills but saw no sign of it. We stopped in Cascade Locks; it was more crowded than it had been at seven AM, five weeks ago.

As the sun set, the bus headed south across fields. I tried to rest, but the jerky movements of the bus kept me awake. At two AM, the bus pulled into the station in Boise, Idaho, and the driver shouted for everyone to get off. "Take all your bags!" he hollered. "This is our cleaning stop." I found my bags and dragged them off the bus.

From the sidewalk outside the bus station, I looked at the buildings, at the sleeping town . . . I felt land around me, a feeling that had been missing since I'd reached the West Coast. "Mary and I could be sleeping in this city," I thought. Was there a park? But I was an outsider now, the person seeing the loaded bikes, not riding them. Had Mary and I slept in parks, never knowing that people stood awake at the bus station a few blocks away?

Well before dawn, I gave up on sleep. As the sky lightened, I watched walls of rock flash past the bus, which was climbing.

Another morning passed, with the sunny landscape passing outside the bus windows. At our lunch stop, I sat on a curb in the sun, eating Chinese food. A young guy sat beside me and introduced himself as Jeremy. He was returning to Cheyenne, Wyoming, the city I had so wanted to visit. Now that the trip was over, missing Cheyenne didn't matter at all.

Jeremy had spent the summer collecting rocks. He was a chemistry major like me but wanted to work in geology. He seemed focused for a college kid, out gaining useful experience on his summer break. What could I have done in college, if I'd been confident?

"I always wanted to find a geode," I told him. "Do you know how to identify them?"

He dragged his backpack across the ground and unzipped it, digging through the clunking rocks inside. He removed two peach-size rocks and handed them to me. "You can have these. I think they're geodes." I stared speechless as he dug again, this time coming out with something the size of a gummy bear. I held out my hand, and he placed the object in my palm. Dusty white, it sparkled; one side was covered by a flat crystal the color of champagne. "That's a topaz," he said. "Take that, too."

Late that night, the bus dropped me at a gas station in Boulder. The station was closed, the lot deserted, but before I could spot a pay phone, my grad school friend Cari pulled in, grinning from behind the wheel.

I spent five days in Boulder. While Cari worked, I wandered the university campus, finding calm places to sit and write in my journal. But when I'd finish writing, I'd feel unsure what to do. I'd thought I would spend this time writing in the yellow notebook—the memoir of the trip—but now I didn't want to leave the beautiful clear air of Boulder to return to distant memories of the summer. The hours slipped past until I could meet Cari for dinner.

I kept noticing a funny feeling in my chest, a feeling that hadn't been there before. It got worse at night; I couldn't sleep in the closed-in, air-conditioned bedroom. My heart beat oddly, as if it might stop. What was wrong with me? Could it be the altitude? Was I about to have a heart attack? "Don't be ridiculous," I told myself. "You just biked three thousand miles; you biked over mountains higher than this and the altitude didn't bother you then."

*But maybe stopping biking is doing something to me.* The worries occupied my thoughts. My last night in Boulder, I felt so bad that I woke Cari. A midnight visit to the emergency room showed that I was fine. "I just biked across the country," I told the doctor, thinking it might explain something.

He looked at me like I was a nutcase. "You're probably just having a panic attack."

A panic attack? As in, "Don't have a panic attack!"—that phrase we'd used in grade school when someone got overexcited? That was a real thing? Besides, I wasn't panicking; this was the part of the trip where I relaxed. I no longer had to find food and shelter.

Why did the Universe throw this curveball, right when I thought life would get easy?

I left Cari to fly over the Rocky Mountains in a mail plane from the tiny Boulder airport. When the pilot asked who wanted to ride shotgun, I began to hesitate, to give the other six passengers a chance, and then changed my mind and raised my hand like a second grader who knows the answer. So I rode up front with the pilot, wearing big headphones snugly over my ears, as we soared over the snowy peaks of the central Rocky Mountains, four thousand feet taller than the Bighorn Mountains, over a wilderness devoid of people.

But in spite of the views, I didn't enjoy the ride. Exhausted from the visit to the emergency room, I struggled to stave off motion sickness. I couldn't stop thinking of our location. "We're in a little capsule," I thought, "miles up in the air." My ears ached; even my nose hurt in the unpressurized plane.

The mountains ended and the ground flattened into dirt flatlands with a solitary road stretching as far as I could see. "I'm glad I'm not biking that," I thought.

We landed to deliver mail to some sort of outpost. It was the most desolate place I had ever been. The descent had hurt my ears even more, and now we had to go up again. My stomach felt queasy even though I hadn't eaten break-fast. I traded seats to give someone else a turn in front.

We flew into clouds, and then finally we descended, and out of the clouds came the Grand Tetons of Wyoming, the green-gray hills familiar from my Green Tortoise trip five years earlier. We bumped down the runway to a stop, and I gratefully left the plane and entered the small Jackson Hole Airport. I found a spot in a corridor and slumped to the floor, willing myself to feel better before my ride, a college friend, came.

The odd feelings in my chest continued through my time in Jackson. During the day I hiked, trying to live the end-of-trip fantasy I'd imagined, but nothing felt enjoyable. I was just tired and going through the motions. I still couldn't sleep at night.

Then came a miserable bus ride to San Francisco that included leaving Jackson at three AM, a fight on the bus, and an unexpected layover in Salt Lake City when the bus broke down. But I made it. The sunny coast felt calmer than the damp mountains, or maybe it was just the magic of San Francisco. I bummed around the city, visiting the Arizmendi Bakery around the corner from my friend's place each morning. One evening, Melissa, a friend I'd made on the Green Tortoise, took me to a coffee shop out by the beaches where the city became slow. It was called the Sea Biscuit Cafe. Paintings of evil-looking mermaids covered the walls. A few days later, I got on the crowded downtown 51 bus and rode it all the way out there, just to sit in the Sea Biscuit again. In San Francisco, I had only one panic attack.

At last, on September 19th, Melissa drove me to the bus station downtown to meet the Green Tortoise tour that would take me back across the country. The familiar green bus waited with two dozen people clustered around it. Everyone had a friend, and I felt like a five-year-old on the first day of kindergarten as Melissa pushed me toward the bus. "Soon you'll all be the best of friends!" she reminded me, sounding wistful.

And she was right. The next night I was walking through Las Vegas with the others, and by the time we were making breakfast at the Grand Canyon, I had three new crushes and twenty new friends.

A week later, after crossing Arizona, New Mexico, Texas, Louisiana, Alabama, Florida, and Georgia, I awoke to find the bus churning its way north on Interstate 85. I'd slept on a table, so I lay in my sleeping bag level with the windows. Trees whipped by . . . familiar pine trees! No more giants of the Pacific Northwest, or Vegas palms or Arizona cacti. I gazed at the pine trees: boring.

All the places I'd seen that summer played through my head: the flooded Youghiogheny River in Pennsylvania, the flat fields of the Midwest, the wildflower-covered Glacial Drumlin Trail in Wisconsin, the spiritually moving Badlands and Black Hills, the Bighorn Mountain climb and the road to Yellowstone, the hot passes of the northernmost Rocky Mountains in Montana, the final climb up the Bitterroot Mountains, followed by the winding descent along mountain streams to the massive Columbia River. The hot sun of those last days stayed with me, even though it felt like a lifetime ago.

Now I was back where I'd started, with boring East Coast pine trees. Soon I'd be back to living in an apartment filled with belongings, going to work everyday, struggling to remain present in a life filled with clutter and activity.

"I'm not ready to be back!" I thought. "I don't want to go back!"

"I don't have to be the same person," I reassured myself. "I can go back to the same town but be a new person."

It was harder to be a new person in old, familiar surroundings, but not impossible. I could clear the clutter from my living space, and make time to sit still during the day, and remain focused on enjoying each day in spite of work. Even if I forgot, and had to relearn the lessons of the bike trip over and over for years, I had made a start.

But I didn't just want to be "the new Emily" indefinitely; I wanted to keep being a new person, day after day, never getting stuck in one form or set of circumstances no matter how much I liked it at the time, or how much I felt outside pressure to remain a certain way. I wanted to be open to constant change, embracing everything that came my way. Was I ready to commit to living in the present? Would I be able to give up my endless daydreams, to block the incessant barrage of thoughts that ruined my confidence, to overcome the worries that plagued me?

The bus rumbled along steadily, the trees a never-ending wall along the interstate. Then a bright blue sign whipped by, a familiar blue sign with a red cardinal and a white dogwood blossom. My eyes filled with tears as I read, "Welcome to North Carolina."

# Author Note and Disclaimer

I began to feel that myself plus the bicycle equaled myself plus the world, upon whose spinning wheel we must all learn to ride. He who succeeds, or, to be more exact in handing over my experience, she who succeeds in gaining the mastery of [a bicycle], will gain the mastery of life.

—Frances E. Willard, *How I Learned to Ride the Bicycle*, 1895[37]

This is the story of a cross-country bike trip. But it's also the story of everything I learned in the ten years following the trip. I've combined the two because it made a better story. I mention this because I want to be honest, and because I don't want any readers to feel disappointed when they go on their own trip and the answers they seek don't come crashing down while they ride. (Just wait ten years, get a good therapist, and write a book about your travels . . .)

Much of the change that started with the trip continued afterward, and many of the struggles, I'm afraid, will be lifelong ones. It's like in the *Silmarillion,* where the Men and Elves will never be able to defeat the forces of Morgoth, but they have to keep fighting regardless. Or like Angel says to Buffy in one of my favorite episodes, "Gingerbread":

B: Okay, so I battle evil, but I don't really win. The bad keeps coming back, and getting stronger.
A: I do know it's important to keep fighting.
B: But we never win, not completely.
A: We never will. That's not why we fight. We do it 'cause there's things worth fighting for.[38]

Everything that happens in the book really happened. I've noticed, however, that sometimes my memories are off. For example, I was sure that Kathy's truck was dark green, but in the photos it is silver. And I remember the store at Corn Creek as standing at the crossroads, but when I look at Googlemaps, it is located down the road a bit. So there may be mistakes because of the imperfect nature of memory. I changed most of the names and some details where it seemed necessary to protect people's privacy. I hope I have not caused any harm.

There are many scenes that I cut to make the book readable. So although I hope I still convey the feeling of biking across America, readers should realize that there are a lot more stretches of boring biking involved in such a trip. There were also a lot more ups and downs of mood, on a daily basis, but recording them all made me seem too crazy.

# Endnotes

1 Sources of epigraphs: Ralph Waldo Emerson, "The Young American," *Nature; Addresses, and Lectures* (Boston and Cambridge: James Munroe and Company, 1849), from a speech given February 7, 1844, at the Mercantile Library Association, Boston, Massachusetts. Virginia Heffeman, "Simple Lives," *Glamour,* September 1998, 304. Copyright 1998 by Condé Nast Publications. John Steinbeck, *Travels with Charley: In Search of America* (New York: Penguin Books, 1962), 4. Copyright 1961, 1962 by the Curtis Publishing Co., Inc. Copyright 1962 by John Steinbeck, renewed 1990 by Elaine Steinbeck, Thom Steinbeck, and John Steinbeck IV.

2 On waterproof gear: After seven years of biking daily, I still couldn't keep totally dry in a rainstorm. It was hard to invest money in gear when you didn't know if it would work. I had a good raincoat, but my lightweight rain pants were proving ineffective, and they channeled rainwater into my shoes, turning my socks into sopping sponges. I couldn't pedal in bulky rain boots; I'd invested in overpriced slip-on shoe covers and now saw they only worked for a few hours before the rain soaked through. I had my coat's hood up under my helmet, with the neck of the coat tugged uncomfortably though the helmet's chin strap; otherwise, the strap would funnel water inside my coat, soaking my shirt. My glasses always got wet, making biking treacherous as I peered through the smeary raindrops or tilted my head to look out above the glasses—blurry but sometimes better. Over the years I'd invested in numerous "waterproof" gloves; so far none had worked. I was testing a new pair.

3 Source of the ideas about the faith of the native Alaskans in *Tisha:* Robert Specht, *Tisha* (New York: Bantam Books, 1976), 197–98.

4 On Wreckage Site Number 3 in Ohio: I didn't think about the date on the wreckage site sign or notice the missile-like shape of the airship painted there. The *Shenandoah* was a zeppelin on a promotional flight to visit state fairs across the Midwest. Thunderstorms in Ohio on its first day tore it apart, and it crashed in three sections.

5 On thoughts about Frodo in Ohio: Perhaps I should have mentioned my minor obsession with *The Lord of the Rings*. I'd seen the movies a dozen times and found a lot of meaning in them, as well as in the books. Source of Frodo's quote: Fran Walsh, Philippa Boyens, and Peter Jackson, *The Lord of the Rings: The Fellowship of the Ring,* directed by Peter Jackson, produced by WingNut Films and The Saul Zaentz Company, distributed by New Line Cinema, 2001. Copyright 2001 by WingNut Films and The Saul Zaentz Company.

6 On the shape of the hills in Ohio: Gay Atha told us that the oddly shaped hills resulted because mining companies blasted off the hills' tops to expose

coal, and then scraped debris from the blasting into adjacent valleys, altering the shape of the land. While most coal mining sites must be "reclaimed" after mining and returned to their original shape, waivers allow the more destructive blasting technique by stipulating that the land be returned to "a level plateau or a gently rolling contour with no highwalls remaining" (Surface Mining Control and Reclamation Act of 1977). That day, we'd stopped at the Miner's Memorial, where we'd walked into a metal scooper bigger than a school bus. A poster showed the scooper in action, digging away at a cliff, a blurry dot supported by orange crane arms. The crane was the size of a shopping mall.

7 On Januarius MacGahan, whose statue stood in the park in Ohio: Born in New Lexington, Ohio, in 1844, Januarius MacGahan became a journalist and war correspondent. He described the massacre of Bulgarians by the Turkish. His coverage outraged the people of Britain and prevented the British government from giving support to Turkey, and Bulgaria was able to win its freedom. Many streets and squares in Bulgaria are named after him.

8 Source of the quotes from *Dune:* Frank Herbert, *Dune* (New York: Ace Books, 1965), 5, 8. Copyright 1965 by Frank Herbert.

9 On the concept of clean laundry: Mary and I hadn't been to a laundromat since one visit in Chambersburg, Pennsylvania. They didn't fit our routine—we'd have to find one, and then spend several hours unloading our bags, washing, and drying, and we'd have to pay. Instead, we rinsed our clothes in sinks and under pumps; I alternated outfits so one could dry while I rode in the other, and I often used my handlebar as a drying rack. Wearing totally clean clothes didn't matter when you were outside all day, riding a bike. But after washing up at camp, I liked to wear something relatively clean, so I kept one outfit for this purpose.

10 On the Chicago planetarium: The quoted material in the exhibits was created from memory to make the passage more interesting to read. The actual exhibit names and recordings were probably different.

11 Source of the quote "glazed with rain": William Carlos Williams, "The Red Wheelbarrow." First published without the title in Section XXII of *Spring and All* (Paris: Contact Publishing Co., 1923). Subsequently published in *The Collected Poems of William Carlos Williams, Volume I, 1909–1939,* edited by Christopher MacGowan and A. Walton Litz (New York: New Directions Publishing Corporation, 1986). Copyright 1962 by William Carlos Williams.

12 Source of the quote about praying in a garden: C. S. Lewis, *The Four Loves* (New York and London: Harcourt, Brace, Jovanovich, 1960), 39. Copyright 1960 by Helen Joy Lewis (this is printed in the book). Copyright 1960 by Clive Staples Lewis, renewed 1988 by Arthur Owen Barfield (this is from the Stanford copyright database).

13 On saunas: Only five years later, writing about it, did it occur to me that a sauna might have parallels with a sweat lodge.

14 Source of the quote about Cheyenne: Sam Cook, Tim Perry, and Greg Ward, *The Rough Guide to USA* (London: Rough Guides, 2002). I recycled the book before noting the page number. Copyright 2002 by The Rough Guides Limited.

15 On taking a ride in South Dakota: We'd taken a ride from Champaign to Milwaukee (via Chicago), but this ride took us north, so it didn't seem to me like cheating, because it didn't shorten our trip.

16 On the hog plant in South Dakota: Later, I searched "hog plant west of White River" online and read about the controversial plants, built on Rosebud Indian Reservation land by a white man who struck an economic development deal with tribal leaders, without the knowledge of most of the tribe. In addition to having environmental concerns, many people (both white and Native American) worried that the big-business enterprise wouldn't ultimately benefit the tribe, and the tribe voted out the leaders responsible for the hog plants in their next election. I don't know how accurate this account was and can no longer find it. A *New York Times* article describes controversy over the conditions of both animals and workers in the plants. The article explains that building on the reservation circumvented state laws that ban such a plant from the rest of the state. The tribe claimed it had not received the 25 percent of profits that were promised. Source: Melody Petersen, "Indians Now Disdain a Farm Once Hailed for Giving Tribe Jobs," *The New York Times,* November 15, 2003, http:// www.nytimes.com/2003/11/15/us/indians-now-disdain-a-farm-once-hailed-for-giving-tribe-jobs.html, accessed August 2016.

17 On Badlands geology: The ranger's description of the Badlands didn't match what I later read on the map, which involved an ocean that covered the Great Plains and then drained as the Rocky Mountains formed, leaving dead critters in mud.

18 On the history of the Black Hills: Later, I googled the quote about the Black Hills and found it repeated on many websites. But I looked up the actual, handwritten Treaty of Laramie, which is posted on the National Archives website; while it does give ownership of the land to the tribes, I did not find this quote or the president's signature, as the brochure claimed. I also read up on the history of the Black Hills: By 1872, the US government (now under President Ulysses Grant) had begun to want the timber of the Black Hills for building projects out west, plus it suspected the Black Hills held mineral wealth. A commission approached the Native American chiefs about signing away the Black Hills and returned to report it was, "the only portion [of their reservation] worth anything to them," and that "nothing short of their annihilation will

get it from them" (Colonel Smith to General Ord, June 27, 1873, Department of the Platte, Letters Received, National Archives). Nonetheless, in 1874 the US government sent the Custer Expedition to examine the region, resulting in reports of gold. Prospectors arrived, violating the treaty. At first, the US Army stopped the prospectors, but after a while they instead moved against Native Americans hunting in the region, even after the chiefs traveled to Washington, DC, to appeal for support of the treaty. From 1876 to 1877, the Black Hills War seethed, until the US government seized the Black Hills in 1877. In 1980, the Supreme Court ruled that the United States had to pay over a million dollars for the land, plus 103 years worth of interest, but the Sioux refused the money, instead asking that the treaty giving them ownership of the Black Hills be upheld.

19 Note on the quote about faith: The quote I remembered is similar to a longer quote by Edward Teller. Patrick Overton wrote a poem that is also similar.

20 On Ucross, Wyoming: I read the history of the Ucross Ranch in a brochure from the office. The ranch had originally been called Big Red, one of several belonging to the Pratt and Ferris Cattle Company in the late 1800s. (Before that, it had been Native American hunting grounds filled with buffalo.) The village around the ranch took the name Ucross after the shape of the company's brand. Later owners shifted the focus of the ranch to crops, added irrigation systems and tenant farms, and eventually sold the ranch in the 1940s. It changed ownership several times as the buildings fell into disrepair. In 1981, several people formed the nonprofit Ucross Foundation to raise money to restore the buildings and provide an artist-in-residence project. The corporation that currently owned the ranch donated 250 acres to the effort. Fourteen years later, the Ucross Foundation purchased the remaining 21,750 acres and continued to manage the cattle operation as a "developing model for ecologically sound, holistic ranching practices."

21 On grilled cheese for lunch every day: Mary and I were both vegetarians. We often ate lunch at a restaurant, and usually the only item we could eat was a grilled cheese. But we both loved grilled cheese.

22 On the large pump in the mountains: I later found out that what I'd considered pumps in parks and campgrounds were actually "hydrants" that were connected into a water system; somewhere, electricity was doing the pumping, which is why water gushed out in a steady stream, with no effort. This was my first real pump.

23 On the Billy the Kid "wanted" poster: I later read that no one has ever found an actual "wanted" poster for Billy, although Lew Wallace did put an ad offering $500 in the newspaper. Source: Lucky Bonner, "Wanted: Billy the Kid Wanted Poster," *True West: History of the American Frontier*, June 1, 2004, http://

www.truewestmagazine.com/wantedbilly-the-kid-wanted-poster/, accessed September 2016. There is no copyright information on the poster I bought.

24 On the statue of a maniacal-looking man in Cody, Wyoming: I later found out that the tall men statues are Muffler Men. Leftover from promotional campaigns in the 1960s, twenty-foot fiberglass Muffler Men dot the country, sometimes dolled up to look like cowboys, mechanics, or even Paul Bunyan. The hands used to hold mufflers: "right hand up, left hand down."

25 On calf roping: My memory of calf roping involved two cowboys roping the calf (one its neck and one its hind leg), the calf being dragged into the dirt by the ropes, and the leg-roping cowboy hopping down to tie three legs. I looked online to see if this accurately describes the event. In calf roping (according to 2016 *Wikipedia*), only one cowboy ropes the calf by the neck, and there is a penalty if the calf is dragged to the ground. The cowboy flips the calf over and ties three legs. There is also "team roping" that uses steers; one cowboy lassos the neck or horns, while the other lassos both rear legs while the steer is running. I seem to have mixed the two events in my head; I altered my description to be about calf roping, but it is likely we watched both.

26 On women in rodeos: According to 2008 *Wikipedia*, women participated in rodeos until the 1930s, when two women died and women were barred. Now they only compete in the barrel race; in professional rodeos, they might be allowed to compete in some lower-level roping. There are also, however, female-only rodeos.

27 Source of the quotes about the Great Spirit giving each person the religion he or she needs and about Sitting Bull: Ed McGaa, *Mother Earth Spirituality: Native American Paths to Healing Ourselves and Our World* (San Francisco: HarperSanFrancisco, 1990), 205, 206. Copyright 1990 by Ed McGaa.

28 On hitchhiking into Yellowstone: Part of the day's anxiety had resulted simply because I had agreed to follow Mary's plan when I hadn't wanted to. I might have felt better if I'd been honest about what I wanted to do, even if I'd ultimately agreed to her plan. Also, agreeing to her plan wouldn't mean that something was wrong with mine.

29 Source of the quote on the restlessness of youth from *Travels with Charley*: John Steinbeck, *Travels with Charley: In Search of America* (New York: Penguin Books, 1962), 3. Copyright 1961, 1962 by the Curtis Publishing Co., Inc. Copyright 1962 by John Steinbeck, renewed 1990 by Elaine Steinbeck, Thom Steinbeck, and John Steinbeck IV.

30 Source of the quote from *Dune* about the logic of the universe: Frank Herbert, *Dune* (New York: Ace Books, 1990), 373. Copyright 1965 by Frank Herbert.

31 On Big Hole National Battlefield, Montana: In 1855 and 1863, treaties

between the Nez Perce and the United States said that the Nez Perce could stay on their land. In 1873, Chief Joseph again negotiated with the government. But in 1877, General Oliver Howard threatened to attack if the Nez Perce did not go to a reservation that was a tiny portion of their territory. Chief Joseph reluctantly agreed, but when three Nez Perce massacred some United States soldiers, he feared retaliation against his people and fled. The Nez Perce under Chief Joseph and Looking Glass planned to go to Canada to join Sitting Bull and the Lakotas, but United States infantry caught up with them. In a predawn attack, the infantry killed men, women, and children at Big Hole. Then they followed the tribe for two months before Chief Joseph surrendered, agreeing to go to the reservation. At the surrender, Chief Joseph said, "I am tired. My heart is sick and sad. From where the sun now stands I will fight no more forever."

32 On the "wild and scenic" Lochsa River: That's how the state map labeled the river: "wild and scenic."

33 Source information for *Pirates of the Caribbean:* Ted Elliott and Terry Rossio, *Pirates of the Caribbean: The Curse of the Black Pearl,* directed by Gore Verbinski, produced by the Walt Disney Company, Walt Disney Pictures, Jerry Bruckheimer Films, and Second Mate Productions, distributed by Walt Disney Studios Motion Pictures, 2003. Copyright 2003 by the Walt Disney Company.

34 In Washington: I liked counting off the days from my last shower, but the truth was, eight days without a shower didn't feel much different than one or two, when you were biking in the sun all day.

35 In Oregon: I later read that the Twin Tunnels through which we'd ridden are located at the point where the climate of the Columbia River gorge changes from the dry, barren east to the humid west.

36 On the last day, a disclaimer: I'm not actually claiming that this was the Macho Man. He simply looked and sounded like him, and so I used that name for him in my head.

37 Source of the final epigraph: Frances E. Willard, *A Wheel Within a Wheel: How I Learned to Ride the Bicycle with Some Reflections by the Way* (New York, Chicago, Toronto: Fleming H. Revell Company, 1895).

38 Source of the quotes from *Buffy:* Jane Espenson, "Gingerbread," *Buffy the Vampire Slayer* (Season 3, Episode 11), directed by James Whitmore Jr., produced by Mutant Enemy Productions, Sandollar Television, Kuzui Entertainment, and 20th Century Fox Television, distributed by 20th Television, first aired January 12, 1999. Copyright 1999 by Mutant Enemy Productions.

# Photo Captions and Credits

9 Mary and me at two thousand miles in Wyoming, with a view of the Bighorn Mountains. Photo by Mary's camera with some help from Mary.

15 Mary and me dipping our rear wheels in the Atlantic Ocean in Cape May, New Jersey. Photo by one of our family members.

23 Mary and me with cotton candy at the Cinco de Mayo festival in Kennett Square, Pennsylvania. Photo by anonymous person on the street.

30 Me with the sculpture of a giant bike in the park in Seven Valleys, Pennsylvania. Photo by Mary.

36 Our lunch cooking at the base of an oak tree in West End, Pennsylvania. Photo by me.

43 Mary and me posed like ducks in the rain on the Great Allegheny Passage rail trail near Rockwood. Photo by Mary's camera with some help from Mary.

51 Me sitting among the appliances as we wait for Mary's bike to be fixed at Otto's. Photo by Mary.

58 The downtown of Sarahsville, Ohio. Photo by me or Mary.

63 Me holding hands with Januarius in the park in New Lexington, Ohio. Photo by Mary.

69 A topiary couple strolling in Old Deaf School Park, in Columbus, Ohio. Photo by me or Mary.

77 Me biking into Laura, Ohio. Photo by Mary.

85 The empty beach at Lake Michigan in Evanston, Illinois. Photo by me.

93 Brian, Meg, and Mary with the Forevertron in Sauk City, Wisconsin. Photos by me. Used with the permission of Dr. Evermor.

99 Our tent next to the farm with the cows. Photo by me.

108 Me at the Iowa border. Photo by Mary.

114 Me with the Green Giant in the Blue Earth, Minnesota, fairgrounds. Photo by Mary.

121 Mary gazing back at the Missouri River in South Dakota. Photo by me.

127 A Route 44 sign in South Dakota. Photo by me.

137 Me at the entrance to Badlands National Park, South Dakota. Photo by Mary.

144 Mary and me at Mount Rushmore, South Dakota. Photo by an anonymous park volunteer.

155 Mary and me at the Wyoming border. Photo by Mary's camera with some help from Mary.

160 The crew in Spotted Horse, Wyoming. Photo by me.

168 Mary opening our new bottle of olive oil at Shakespeare in the Park in Sheridan, Wyoming. Photo by me.

173 The view east from the top of the Bighorn Mountains, Wyoming. Photo by me.

179 Offerings tied on the fence at the Medicine Wheel in Wyoming, including my "Love" necklace. Photo by me.

188 My campsite in the park in Powell, Wyoming. Photo by me.

193 Mary and cowboys on the porch at the Irma Hotel in Cody, Wyoming. Photo by me.

201 Me with the bear box in our Wapiti Valley campground, east of Yellowstone National Park, Wyoming. Photo by Mary.

211 The cattle drive passing my bike outside of Nevada City, Montana. Photo by me.

220 A sign for Wisdom, Montana. Photo by me.

227 Me atop Chief Joseph Pass in western Montana. Photo by Mary.

233 Mary with Roger and June near Lolo Pass, Montana. Photo by me.

241 The wild and scenic Lochsa River in Idaho. Photo by me.

248 The Columbia River in eastern Washington. Photo by me.

260 Desolate scenery along the Columbia River near Paterson, Washington. (This was the only photo I had for this chapter!) Photo by me.

273 Me on the bridge at Multnomah Falls east of Portland in Oregon. Photo by Mary.

280 Our final campsite in Tillamook State Forest, Oregon. Photo by me.

286 The sign in Oceanside, Oregon. Photo by me.

296 Our bikes sleeping on the beach. Photo by me.

300 Mary and me holding our signs at the Pacific Ocean; Mary and me dipping our front tires into the ocean. Photos by Kelly or Bruce. Mary throwing her Cape May rocks into the Pacific. Photo by me.

301 Me at Hurricane Ridge in Olympic National Park, Washington. Photo by anonymous tourist.

# Acknowledgments

As always, I want to thank my family and friends for their continual support of me and my projects.

Mary deserves my eternal gratitude both for going on the bike trip with me, and for later telling me to go ahead and "write whatever you want" when I broached the subject of a memoir. Thank you for giving me the space to write it all out.

Thanks to Elizabeth M., whose discussions led to most of the revelations in these pages.

My former writing group, Mindy S., Kathy A., and Carol D., read the entire 1100-page first draft. Chris J. also read an early draft. Several friends volunteered to read the final draft and gave me the confidence to move forward with publishing: Mary, Sacha K., Elizabeth V., Brian C., Leah D., Janese T., and Kathleen S.

Thanks to Mary V., Linda F., and Sylwia S. for advising on the book's cover design. Thanks also to Sylwia S. for taking my author photo.

Thanks to Darcy for encouraging me to spend time writing, and for explaining the difference between a pump and a yard hydrant.

Thanks to Elsa P. for her help.

The bike I rode across America is a 1997 Specialized Hard Rock GX mountain bike. This, as you may know (or more likely not, because it's just my opinion), is the premium vintage of Specialized bikes. It rarely gets flat tires and it always… just *works*. Mine has been cared for over the years by more friends than I can name, and gifted with everything from a rack to a cushy seat to a giant bell that I will never put on it. When I finally returned to North Carolina, my friend Bill reassembled it. Did it need anything? Was anything worn out? "Nope." He chuckled. "Looks great!"

## About the Author

Emily Buehler is a writer and an independent editor, among other things. She still commutes on the bike that went across the country, and she's still friends with Mary, who also still rides her bike. She lives in North Carolina. Visit her online at emilybuehler.com.